BUREAUCRATIC ÉLITES IN
WESTERN EUROPEAN STATES

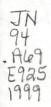

Bureaucratic Élites in Western European States

edited by

EDWARD C. PAGE

AND

VINCENT WRIGHT

OXFORD

UNIVERSITY PRESS

OXFORD
UNIVERSITY PRESS

Great Clarendon Street, Oxford OX2 6DP

Oxford University Press is a department of the University of Oxford.
It furthers the University's objective of excellence in research, scholarship,
and education by publishing worldwide in

Oxford New York

Athens Auckland Bangkok Bogotá Buenos Aires Calcutta
Cape Town Chennai Dar es Salaam Delhi Florence Hong Kong Istanbul
Karachi Kuala Lumpur Madrid Melbourne Mexico City Mumbai
Nairobi Paris São Paulo Singapore Taipei Tokyo Toronto Warsaw

and associated companies in Berlin Ibadan

Oxford is a registered trade mark of Oxford University Press
in the UK and certain other countries

Published in the United States
by Oxford University Press Inc., New York

© the several contributors 1999

The moral rights of the author have been asserted
Database right Oxford University Press (maker)

First published 1999

British Library Cataloguing in Publication Data

Data available

Library of Congress Cataloging-in-Publication Data

Bureaucratic elites in western European states : a comparative
analysis of top officials / edited by E. Page and V. Wright.
Includes bibliographical references and index.
1. Government executives—Europe, western. I. Page, Edward.
II. Wright, Vincent.
JN94.A69E925 1999 352.3'9'094—dc21 99-36966

ISBN 0-19-829447-6
ISBN 0-19-829446-8 (pbk.)

1 3 5 7 9 10 8 6 4 2

Typeset by BookMan Services
Printed in Great Britain
on acid-free paper by
Biddles Ltd
Guildford and King's Lynn

ACKNOWLEDGEMENTS

We are grateful to Professor R. A. W. Rhodes, University of Newcastle, for his strong encouragement of this project and to the Economic and Social Research Council for supporting the conference on which this book is based through its Whitehall Programme. We would especially like to thank Stephanie Wright of Nuffield College, Oxford, for organizing the conference as well as for coordinating the editorial task across two UK sites.

Editor's Note
Vincent Wright's death on 8 July 1999 was an enormous loss to us all. As well as making his own outstanding contributions to political science, he inspired, animated, and ran comparative projects such as this. He will be deeply missed.

Edward C. Page

August 1999

CONTENTS

LIST OF FIGURES

LIST OF TABLES

LIST OF CONTRIBUTORS

Marleen Brans	University of Leuven
Sabino Cassese	University of Rome
Charlotte Dargie	University of Cambridge
Peter Ehn	Parliamentary Committee of the Regions, Stockholm
Klaus Goetz	London School of Economics
Annie Hondeghem	University of Leuven
Hanne Nexø Jensen	University of Copenhagen
Tim Knudsen	University of Copenhagen
Barbara Liegl	Institute for Advanced Studies, Vienna
Rachel Locke	University of Sussex
Ignacio Molina Alvarez de Cienfuegos	Juan March Institute Madrid
Edward C. Page	University of Hull
Jon Pierre	University of Gothenburg
Jos Raadschelders	University of Oklahoma
Luc Rouban	Fondation Nationale des Sciences Politiques, Paris
Dimitri A. Sotiropoulos	University of Crete
Frits van der Meer	University of Leiden
Vincent Wright	University of Oxford

Introduction

EDWARD C. PAGE AND VINCENT WRIGHT

A Nineteenth-Century Institution?

Civil services give many outward appearances of being an institution stuck in the nineteenth century. Many senior French civil servants are educated in the École Polytechnique, a school set up during the Revolution, and on formal occasions wear early nineteenth-century military uniform, whilst others belong to *grands corps*, most of which owe their existence to Napoleon. The terminology of bureaucracy in Germany reflects ideas that would not be out of place in the work of Hegel; all civil servants have a *Dienstherr* ('service-master') and have to swear an oath, a *Diensteid*. Moreover, the legacy of the past extends beyond the symbolic to the essence of the civil service. Recruitment patterns to the upper echelons of the British civil service still reflect the principles of the Northcote–Trevelyan reforms of 1854 which specified the recruitment of the kind of candidate for senior office that Oxford and Cambridge have overwhelmingly supplied ever since. Modern civil services were, especially in continental Europe, shaped in their formative years by their position in the nation state, ruled by governments, and governed by the principles of the *Rechtsstaat*. They were created as part of a legal order that stands above the mix of particular social and economic interests that constitutes civil society. Many features of contemporary bureaucracies reflect this: the preponderance of legal professionals in the recruitment process, the security of tenure, as well as the endurance in many countries of the seniority principle for promotion.

The *Rechtsstaat* principle, although not necessarily its practice, gave enormous power to the senior civil service. Our understanding of this principle and the position of senior officials within it is dominated by German ideas of bureaucracy and the state as passed on to us through thinkers such as Hegel (1972) and Weber (1972). As a description of administrative reality such ideas have to be treated with caution inside and outside Germany. However, in an 'ideal type' of bureaucracy, the power of the senior official was likely to be exceptionally strong. He is at the apex of a hierarchically structured organization, with a clear line of command transmitting instructions through a chain of subordinates to its very base. While forced to share command of the administrative organization of the state with political leaders, elected or otherwise, the expertise, skill, and length of service of trained bureaucrats were generally likely to make them exceptionally powerful, if not dominant, in the relationship with their political masters. 'How is democracy . . . possible?' Weber (1972: 324) asks, in view of the rise of bureaucracy.

However, the *Rechtsstaat*, to the extent that it existed in practice, has given way to different forms of modern state. There is little real agreement about the characteristics of the modern state, still less about what it should be called. Strong candidates as successors to the *Rechtsstaat* go under labels as diverse as 'welfare state' or 'systems of governance' (Peters, 1996; Rhodes, 1997); but we must bear in mind that labels used to describe the character of whole political systems since 1945 have had relatively short half-lives—'mass society' (Kornhauser, 1960), 'corporate state' (Schmitter and Lehmbruch, 1979), and 'ungovernability' (Crozier *et al.*, 1975). Whatever term we settle on, we may look at literature describing the modern state and have good cause to believe that many of the bases of the traditional role of the senior civil servant no longer apply. Yet we may look in vain for any convincing discussion of how and why the position of this most crucial of groups has changed, and how the nineteenth-century institution has adapted to the modern state.

Existing theories and accounts of change in state bureaucracies are of little help in understanding how the civil service has developed in modern political systems. The most widespread account of what has changed since the early years of bureaucracy might be described by the title of Henry Jacoby's (1973) book: *The Bureaucratization of the World*. Taking cues from social and political theorists such as Max Weber and Alexis de Tocqueville—the nineteenth-century French political theorist, who saw 'administrative despotism' as the major danger to democracy in Europe— the bureaucratization-of-the-world thesis suggested that bureaucratic élites would become increasingly powerful.

Although the direction of the administration is controlled by parliamentary ministers, their functions are largely dependent on the ministerial bureaucracy. Each new minister confronts a smoothly running machine through which his political directives must pass. These are screened by the department of justice, the department of foreign affairs and various other sections. Any plans for the future which the politician might have hoped to see realized are strangled and pushed aside by official administrative business. (Jacoby, 1973: 162)

Such an argument is a common feature of much twentieth-century thought on bureaucracy, although the mechanisms for the growth in influence of bureaucracy differ quite substantially. For Max Weber (1972) bureaucratization came as part of an increase in formal rationality in all human affairs—the 'demystification of the world'—and thus was an unavoidable consequence of state modernization. For Robert Michels (1915) the collective psychological characteristics of both masses and élites lead to an 'iron law of oligarchy' in which the leaders of any organization become less concerned with representing the people they are supposed to represent and more concerned with remaining in office and strengthening their control over the organization. For Burnham (1945), it was the class struggle that was producing the managerial state. Marx's analysis of the class struggle was, Burnham claims, correct up to a point. However, it ignored the fact that once ownership of the means of production was wrested from the hands of the capitalists it would fall not to the workers but to the managers to run the economy and the political system.

Such theories, powerful though they are, are primarily about *bureaucracy* and *not state bureaucrats*. Bureaucracy, in this context, is a form of organization which shapes public and private organizations; business firms, parties, and interest groups, as well as state, para-state, and local government organizations become bureaucratized. Moreover, elected politicians are affected by the process of bureaucratization, since their ambitions and actions are increasingly limited by perceptions of what is administratively possible. In Max Weber's words, we are all trapped in the 'iron cage of bondage' (*Gehäuse der Hörigkeit*), and while the increasing role of the higher levels of the bureaucracy might be one feature of the demystification of the world, it is not its only one.

There is a second reason for avoiding the bureaucratization-of-the-world argument as a starting-point for understanding the changing position of the higher civil service in modern political systems: the available evidence to support it is exceedingly thin. It is by no means clear that the development of bureaucracy has seen an ineluctable progression towards increasing political power for senior bureaucrats. Doubts result from the fact that it is genuinely difficult to measure the power of a group like the senior civil service. For instance, Diamant (1968) argues that political instability in the French Fourth Republic made the bureaucracy *weak*, as it lacked any strong political leadership. Others, on the other hand, have suggested that political instability allowed senior bureaucrats to govern unchallenged by any strong political leaders. Recently, it has been argued that, far from following a trajectory of increasing power, the growth of government, and its increasing complexity, the role of the senior civil servant in developed nations appears to have diminished. Weller *et al.* (1997), for example, examine the popular thesis that the power of national governments, and this would include senior bureaucrats in national government, has been 'hollowed out'—transferred to non-state bodies such as privatized companies and to international bodies such as the European Union. In truth, if it is hard to assess the power of bureaucracy at any one time in any one country, then a longer-term assessment of its changing power over time across many countries is likely to be impossible.

A separate theory of change postulates changing role perceptions among senior officials. It was first set out by Robert Putnam (1973) and developed in the comparative study of western senior bureaucrats by Aberbach *et al.* (1981). This is an altogether more modest account of change than that of the bureaucratization of the world, and applies specifically to senior bureaucrats. Putnam postulates that two 'polar syndromes' might be used to classify bureaucrats in Europe; 'classical' and 'political' bureaucrats. The difference between the two is in attitudes towards politics. The classical bureaucrat sees himself acting as an agent of a 'monistic' public interest, the political bureaucrat sees himself participating in a pluralistic process of political decision-making. Politics is eschewed by the classical bureaucrat who, as the one who carries out orders, sees his function as completely separate from that of the politician who deals with conflicting interests found in the outside world. The political bureaucrat relishes his participation in the cut and thrust of policy-making alongside politicians and outside interests. The evidence from Germany, Italy, and Great Britain, Putnam suggests, points to a growing proportion of political bureaucrats in western Europe. A very similar theme is taken up by Aberbach *et al.* (1981: ch. 8), who point to a growing involvement of bureaucrats in what had traditionally been seen as 'political' roles. They set out four policy-making roles (implementation, formulation, brokering interests, and articulating ideals) and argue that a traditional image of this role is where implementation is a function of bureaucrats and the other three roles the sole preserve of politicians. They suggested, on the basis of a 'still nascent trend' they detected in their survey data, that formulation, brokering interests, and articulating ideals were becoming shared functions between bureaucrats and politicians. They went on to put forward a modern 'image' of the relationship between bureaucrats and politicians where there is a 'virtual merger . . . of roles'.

The central problem with this thesis of a growing 'political' role perception among senior bureaucrats, apart from the general lack of cross-time data on which it may be based, is that there is no evidence from studies of bureaucracies before 1945 to support it. Quite the contrary, in fact. The thrust of Max Weber's great polemic against the Imperial German bureaucracy was that Bismarck had created a system in which bureaucrats were willing and able to dabble in issues that should have been handled by elected political leaders. Lowell's (1896) discussion of the Prussian civil service similarly has few points in common with the 'classical' bureaucrat passed on to us through Weber's ideal type (or rather through the widespread understanding of the ideal type). Prussian bureaucracy was not very strictly hierarchical, since 'the administrative system [is not] in its actual working highly concentrated as compared with those of other continental nations, for the officials do not feel obliged to refer every important question to their superiors, but are willing to act on their own responsibility' (Lowell, 1896: 293). Nor could the Prussian bureaucracy be classified as a particularly cohesive group, since ministries 'were far more independent of each other than in most countries'. Moreover, while the bureaucracy was not pervaded by a system of political patronage and appointments, political loyalties played a part in appointments and promotion since 'the government does not give offices to its political enemies'.

Studies of the nineteenth-century French administration, which formally conformed to the Weberian ideal type, indicate the constant interconnection of politics and bureaucracy in bodies such as the Conseil d'État and the private offices of ministers (*cabinets ministériels*) and studies of individual top civil servants point to their policy-making discretion.

Lowell (1896: 166–7) points to the corruption of the Italian civil service where 'the host of officials who are . . . too numerous and too badly paid' to avoid 'a great mass of spoils, in the distribution of which the politicians take an active part'. Austria had a bureaucracy that appeared closer to the classical ideal since it 'seems to bring politics very little into its work' (Lowell, 1896: 78), although Lowell attributed this to Count Taaffe, prime minister of Austria 1879–93, who 'steadily refused to use [the bureaucracy] as a party tool and made few appointments or removals for party purposes'. Taafe's abstemiousness was all the more remarkable to Lowell given the pervasiveness of corruption and political favours at the time.

Moreover, even if Aberbach *et al.* were able to substantiate their argument that roles had changed over time by using cross-time survey data instead of data referring to one time point around the late 1960s and early 1970s, it is doubtful whether it would have meant anything other than that civil servants might have become more willing to describe their roles as 'political'. As Chapman (1959: 274) wrote, whether officials admit to being involved in politics is largely a question of semantics, since top officials are almost *ex officio* participants in the policy process. In the mind of officials, 'The word politics then [is] associated exclusively with the activities of political parties. Provided, therefore, public officials do not engage in party politics, they consider they do not engage in politics.' Similarly, Suleiman (1975) found that the objection among French civil servants to being described as dealing with interest groups was primarily a semantic one; the term invokes an undesired attribute of giving in to sectional interests, while receiving advice from 'professional associations' is an acceptable form of consultation. As Chapman (1959: 273) warns, 'the innuendoes and the discreet language used in this half-world are only imperfectly understood by the outsider'.

These broad theories seem to be of little use in understanding the changed position of the senior civil service in the modern state. Other theories of bureaucracy which are frequently applied in comparative contexts as well as in the context of individual nation-states, such as rational choice or policy networks do not directly address the question of describing or explaining the changing position of senior civil servants in the modern state.[1] While such theories might harbour assumptions about or implications for the changing position of the senior civil service, these are largely implicit. Considering the prominent role that civil servants have enjoyed, and appear to continue to enjoy, in national processes of decision-making, the implications of social and political change for the position of top officials have been substantially neglected. The purpose of this book is to redress this neglect and focus directly on the changing position of senior civil servants in the modern state. Before we can do so, we need to have a clear idea of what it is we might expect to have changed and why.

The Political Status of Senior Officials

We are interested in understanding the position of senior officials in the modern state, but from what perspective? Two main features of the bureaucracy interest us here: the *political status* and the *political roles* of top civil servants. By *political status* we mean the character of the bureaucratic élite and its position within the machinery of government. The *political roles* of the top civil service concern the functions that top administrators assume, such as coordinators of government policy or intermediaries with interest groups. If we consider the political roles of civil servants we can envisage a wide range of social, economic, and political changes that might have affected the top level of the bureaucracy. The growth in single-issue interest groups and lobby organizations, as well as the increasing professionalization of parties and the growth of related policy-advice organizations over the past three decades is likely to have eroded much of the claim by senior officials to a monopoly of specialist expertise. Moreover, there has been a decentralization of government in many countries. This decent-

---

[1] For a discussion of rational choice theories in bureaucracy see Dowding, 1995. The most imaginative and fruitful application of this approach to bureaucracy remains Downs (1967). For a discussion of policy networks see Rhodes and Marsh (1992).

ralization has taken many forms which include territorial decentralization through the creation of a federal system in Belgium, the increased provision of services through local government and other decentralised structures in Spain and Italy, and the 'hiving off' of administrative units from policy-planning ministries, as in Denmark and the United Kingdom. Again, one might expect such decentralization to reduce the role of senior bureaucrats in the policy process. Europeanization might also be expected to affect the political role of some top officials, since it further removes decision-making power from the national to international bureaucratic élites. Given the flow of power downwards, sideways, and upwards away from national bureaucratic élites, it is perfectly fair to raise the question of what role is left for them in the modern state?

However, before the task of understanding the changed role of senior officials can be attempted, there is a prior question that needs to be answered: what is the political *status* of the senior civil service? It is a prior question since any discussion of the role of the civil service requires description of what the senior civil service is and does within a political system. Such descriptions are simply not available for a large number of countries. In the English language it is remarkable that our understanding of the higher reaches of European bureaucracy is largely restricted to very few studies from a limited range of countries. Outside Britain, and leaving aside articles covering specific aspects of the subject, such as recruitment practices or structural reforms, rounded pictures of the character of the higher reaches of the bureaucracy are available only for France (Suleiman, 1975) and Germany (Mayntz and Scharpf, 1975). To find out about Italy, Sweden, the Netherlands, one has to consult book chapters and articles. Moreover, for some countries, such as Greece, Spain, Portugal, Belgium, and Austria, the nature of the senior civil service is a closed book, since virtually nothing devoted to its exposition has appeared in English. With some notable exceptions (such as Peters, 1995; Heady, 1979), British and American specialists of public administration have been notoriously shy about comparison. Paradoxically, probably the best comparative book on modern public administration was written by a Frenchman (Ziller, 1993), whose country is famed for its scholarly insularity.

The political status of the civil service refers to the internal characteristics of the senior civil service as a social and political group and the role of outsiders, in this case mainly politicians, in shaping this group. Existing evidence, patchy and often dated though it is, suggests enormous variation within western Europe in the political status of higher civil servants along a variety of dimensions. *Recruitment patterns* can involve the culture of top civil servants being shaped by a common or predominant education—typically law in much of continental Europe, a *grandes écoles* education in

France, or an Oxford or Cambridge degree in Britain. The *social status* of recruits to the senior civil service is much higher in France and Britain (where the civil service recruits from élite educational institutions) than in Italy, where lower status candidates from the South predominate. The *career structures* of the upper reaches of the bureaucracy also vary, such that in some countries, such as Britain and France, it is possible to regard part of the senior civil service as a government-wide élite, with bonds of common interests, if not solidarity, among officials from different ministries and organizations. In other countries, such as the Netherlands, Germany, and Italy, officials tend to make their careers in one department and interdepartmental bonds are weak. *Internal status differentiation* refers to the differences of status and power of different groups within the bureaucracy. The higher status given to members of the *grands corps* in France is well known, but there are other status differences, such as those that exist between officials of the Treasury and lower ranking ministries in Britain. The *politicization* of the senior civil service refers to the degree to which elected politicians are involved in making partisan appointments to senior administrative posts. Although Britain remains free of overt partisan appointments to civil service posts (top officials must be politically sensitive but free of party label), politicization appears to be endemic within most bureaucratic systems, and is especially marked in Belgium, Austria, and Italy, where party membership or at least personal connections to a party boss may be important preconditions for recruitment and promotion even in the lower levels in the bureaucracy. Or politicization might be limited, as in Germany, to the most senior positions, with the institution of the 'political official' (an official who is appointed by a minister and may be put into 'temporary retirement' by a minister). In this case, politicization is closely linked to an additional feature of the political status of top officials: the *political subordination* of the senior civil service. This refers to institutions by which ministers seek to exert control over the activities of the bureaucracy, including policy development within the executive. Perhaps the most famous, but not only, example of this is the institution of the *cabinet* within countries such as Italy, France, Spain, as well as the European Union.

Diversity and Change

It is possible to enumerate many social, economic, political, and cultural changes affecting modern systems of government, even since 1945, which might be expected to have profound effects on the political status of senior officials. Recruitment patterns within the senior civil service as well as the social status of senior bureaucrats are likely to be crucially affected by changes in the educational systems of European states. New disciplines, such as social policy, and the increased popularity of many longer estab-lished disciplines within the social sciences may have eroded the emphasis upon more traditional subjects, whether law or humanities. The expansion of public services, and the proportionate shift of priorities away from the 'defining' features of government (i.e. law and order and taxation) towards newer tasks of social welfare provision (Rose, 1976), might be expected to hasten this shift away from traditional academic subjects. Moreover, the massive expansion in post-secondary education throughout Europe, makes it more likely for lower status social groups to gain access to the higher reaches of the national ministerial bureaucracy than, for example, in the immediate postwar period when Chapman (1959: 315) concluded that the 'scanty material available suggests that the majority of officials in each class of the public service come from the corresponding social class, and that the remainder comes from the social class immediately below'.

The growth of managerial theory, especially the influence of theories of strategic management in the 1960s, might have been expected to pose a challenge to those systems with administrative structures in which careers are started, developed, and ended within the same organization and in which cross-sectoral mobility is an exception to the rule. Moreover, the growth of mechanisms of financial control, such as were developed with the 'rationalization' of budgetary procedures in many countries after the 1960s, might lead one to expect Finance Ministries to occupy an increas-ingly important role in offering coordination to the whole of government and civil servants in these ministries to become correspondingly more powerful. If we follow Katz and Mair's (1992) discussion of the develop-ment of the European party system we might also expect to find a growing politicization of the bureaucracy: as parties transform themselves from mass parties through catch-all to cartel parties we would expect politiciza-tion to increase (cf. also Koole, 1996).

There are other possible social, economic, political, and cultural changes that *might* have a direct bearing on the political status of higher civil ser-vants. The growth of government and the increasing complexity of its in-ternal structure might be expected to affect the homogeneity of the senior civil service as well as its ability to shape what goes on within it. Changes in technology might be expected to have a countervailing effect and in-crease the ability of senior officials to monitor and control what happens within their sphere of responsibility (Grémion, 1978). 'Silent revolutions' in culture may erode the deference paid by politicians as well as citizens to senior officials (see Inglehart, 1990; Listhaug and Wiberg, 1995).

However plausible such arguments may appear, we have no evidence to evaluate them. It is quite possible that many such changes do not have the expected impact on the senior civil service or are counteracted by other changes or by the ability of the senior civil service to adapt to its new environment. The purpose of this book is to provide evidence on which to base an assessment of the changing political status of senior civil servants in Europe. In order to offer a comparative evaluation of change we chose to invite contributors from a wider range of European countries than is generally included in comparative discussions of the civil service. Thus, in addition to the countries on which we already have substantial information (albeit, in some cases, dated in respect of material available in English) of France, Germany, Britain, and Italy, we have included countries in which past English-language coverage has generally been more patchy— the Netherlands and Sweden—as well as countries where coverage was very thin, even in some cases in the relevant original language—such as Spain, Greece, Denmark, Austria, and Belgium. The wide coverage in this book gives a mix of different types of administrative system which are generally assumed to be very different—'southern' and 'northern' systems; federal, unitary, and regionalized systems; systems with reputations for extensive patronage in public services and systems with reputations for excluding such patronage; *cabinet*-based systems and those without such forms of political supervision.

Contributors were asked to describe the position of senior officials in their countries using the characteristics of political status we set out above. The twelve chapters that follow present a picture of diversity at least as substantial as that observed, say, by Lowell in the late nineteenth century or Chapman in the middle of the twentieth. We did not seek to impose any particular theoretical perspective on our contributors. In our conclusion we pursue this theoretical discussion and seek to answer our central question of how the political status of senior civil servants in modern states is developing.

REFERENCES

Aberbach, J., R. D. Putnam, and B. A. Rockman (1981). *Bureaucrats and Politicians in Western Democracies* (Cambridge, Mass: Harvard University Press).

Burnham, J. D. (1945). *The Managerial Revolution* (Harmondsworth: Penguin).

Chapman, B. (1959). *The Profession of Government* (London: Allen and Unwin).

Crozier, M., *et al.* (1975). *The Crisis of Democracy: Report on the Governability of Democracies to the Trilateral Commission* (New York: New York University Press).

Diamant, A. (1968). 'Tradition and Innovation in French Administration'. *Comparative Political Studies*, 1(2): 251–74.

Dowding, K. M. (1995). *The Civil Service* (London: Routledge).

Downs, A. (1967). *Inside Bureaucracy* (Boston, Mass: Little Brown).

Grémion, P. (1978). *L'Ordinateur au pouvoir* (Paris: Éditions du seuil).

Heady, F. (1979). *Public Administration: A Comparative Perspective* (New York: Dekker).

Hegel, G. W. F. (1972). *Grundlinien der Philosophie des Rechts* (Frankfurt-on-Main: Ullstein).

Inglehart, R. (1990). *Culture Shift in Advanced Industrial Society* (Princeton: Princeton University Press).

Jacoby, H. (1973). *The Bureaucratization of the World* (Berkeley: University of California Press).

Katz, R. and P. Mair (1992). 'Changing Models of Party Organization: The Emergence of the Cartel Party', *Party Politics*, 1(1): 5–28.

Koole, R. (1996). 'Cadre, Catch-All or Cartel: A Comment on the Notion of the Cartel Party', *Party Politics*, 4(2): 507–24.

Kornhauser, W. (1960). *Politics of Mass Society* (London: Routledge and Kegan Paul).

Listhaug, O. and M. Wiberg (1995). *Citizens and the State* (Oxford: Oxford University Press).

Lowell, A. L. (1896). *Government and Parties in Continental Europe* (London: Longmans Green and Co.).

Mayntz, R. and F. W. Scharpf (1975). *Policy Making in the German Federal Bureaucracy* (Amsterdam: Elsevier).

Michels, R. (1915). *Political Parties* (Glencoe, Ill: Free Press of Glencoe).

Peters, B. G. (1995). *The Politics of Bureaucracy*, 4th edn. (London: Longman).

——(1996). *The Future of Governing. Four Emerging Models* (Lawrence, Kan.: University Press of Kansas).

Putnam, R. D. (1973). 'The Political Status of Senior Civil Servants in Western Europe: A Preliminary Analysis', *British Journal of Political Science*, 3(3): 257–90.

Rhodes, R. and D. Marsh (1992). 'Policy Networks in British Politics: A Critique of Existing Approaches', in R. Rhodes and D. Marsh (eds.), *Policy Networks in British Government* (Oxford: Clarendon Press).

Rhodes, R. A. W. (1997). *Understanding Governance: Policy Networks, Governance, Reflexivity and Accountability* (Milton Keynes: Open University Press).

Rose, R. (1976). 'On the Priorities of Government: A Developmental Analysis of Public Policies', *European Journal of Political Research*, 4(2): 247–89.

Schmitter, P. and G. Lehmbruch (1979). *Trends Towards Corporatist Intermediation* (London and Beverly Hills: Sage).

Suleiman, E. N. (1975). *Politics, Power and Bureaucracy in France* (Princeton: Princeton University Press).

Weber, M. (1972). *Wirtschaft und Gesellschaft*, 5th edn. (Tübingen: JCB Mohr).

——(1988). 'Parlament und Regierung im neugeordneten Deutschland', *Gesammelte Politische Schriften* (Tübingen: JCB Mohr, Paul Siebeck).

Weller, P., H. Bakvis, and R. A. W. Rhodes (eds.) (1997). *The Hollow Crown: Countervailing Trends in Core Executives* (Basingstoke: Macmillan).

Ziller, Jacques (1993) (in collaboration with Jean-Philippe Brouant) *Administrations comparées: Les Systèmes politico-administratifs de l'Europe des Douze* (Paris: Montchrestian).

1

A Description of the
Greek Higher Civil Service

DIMITRI A. SOTIROPOULOS

Introduction

It is a paradox that powerful people who occupy positions of authority often claim that they feel powerless in the face of circumstances and interests which they had been unaware of before they came to power. People not in positions of authority may listen to such complaints of powerlessness with disbelief. After all, authority is synonymous with legitimate power, even if the people who gain power do not have as much of it as they thought they would.

Formally, the higher civil service of Greece is a powerful group, with a legitimate claim to relative powerlessness. At best, the higher civil service is one among many state-dependent interest groups in Greece. At worst, it is a fragmented category of civil servants which lacks cohesion, organizational autonomy, and social status. It is telling that, in 1967, 1,093 different corps of civil servants represented 169 fields of specialization. This number was somewhat smaller in 1996, since there were approximately 850 to 890 corps.[1] But the extreme fragmentation in the Greek civil service remains evident.

As individuals and as members of informal cliques, Greek senior officials may enjoy some leverage with their political supervisors, the ministers, and, in fact, may succeed in obstructing the implementation of personnel policies which affect them adversely. Among the weapons higher civil servants may use to defend their interests are deliberate delay of action, disclosure of information which may be embarrassing to their political

---

[1] The first number is cited in Demetrios Argyriades (1970: 208). The second number is an estimation of top civil servants of the Ministry of Interior, Public Administration, and Decentralization in two anonymous interviews which I conducted in that ministry in December 1996 and February 1997. Additional information was provided by Ms Tina Minakaki, head of section in the same ministry, in March 1999.

supervisors, misinformation, distorting interpretation of regulations, and loss or destruction of documents. Despite the availability of such organizational weapons, it can be argued that higher civil servants have played a secondary, if not subservient, role in the organization of public administration and the formulation of public policies in Greece.

The subservient role of the higher civil service is correlated with the perennial and problematic features of the organizational structure of the Greek public administration, which, in certain respects, make it resemble a pre-modern political organization (see Langrod, 1965; Spanou, 1995; Wilson, 1966; while the current crisis of Greek administration is presented in Makrydemetris, 1995). The main features of the top management level of the Greek civil service are as follows.

1. There is a shifting and extensive overlap of jurisdictions among ministries and among divisions of the same ministry.

2. There is inadequate horizontal communication and coordination among ministries and among divisions of the same ministry.

3. Every ministry has an overabundance of political appointees who aid the minister and who supervise and, at times, supplant top civil servants.

4. Authority is centralized at the top political layers of each ministry, where policy-formulation and the execution of the most important policies take place. Below those layers, top administrators concentrate on the processing of less important policies and avoid (or are excluded from) long-run strategic planning and, formulation of policies (Spanou, 1996*a*; for a discussion of the perennial aspects of Greek public administration see Sotiropoulos, 1996*a*: 138–44).

5. A wide range of decisions are taken by the Prime Minister himself. Top civil servants are rarely, if ever, members of his immediate entourage. They are not regularly consulted by his staff nor are they instrumental in the preparation of the agenda for the sessions of the government's Cabinet. Given that the Prime Minister's staff and the Cabinet are at the peak of the executive branch of government, it is telling that top civil servants almost never come close to it.

In such a structural context, it comes as no surprise that higher civil servants in Greece play a minor role compared with their counterparts in other European countries; nor is it surprising that in each ministry the energy of higher civil servants is consumed in defending their small privileges *vis-à-vis* middle and lower ranking civil servants and protecting their sphere of formal competence against challenges from senior officials from other ministries. For this reason, among others, senior civil servants play a minor role in the shaping of policies of their ministry. While Greek higher civil servants may be at the top of the career ladder, this top is not really high.

On a higher level, planning, decision-making, and even executive policy-application functions are performed by a multitude of political officials.

A Brief Description of Ranks of Senior Civil Servants in Greece

Greek public administration is top-heavy and politicized. In every ministry there is a large number of political officials who are appointed by the ruling party at the beginning of its term in power. These political officials constitute a thick administrative layer inserted between the minister and the senior civil servants. Some of the political officials serve as advisors to the minister and to the alternate and junior ministers and have 'staff' organizational roles in ministerial *cabinets*, structured along French lines. Other political officials, standing below the level of minister, are in charge of large administrative sections into which every ministry is subdivided, and play 'line' organizational roles.[2]

Although political advisors were appointed by members of the Caramanlis governments between 1974 and 1981, political staffs in Greek ministries were expanded on a massive scale after the fall of Caramanlis's New Democracy from power in 1981 and the complete abolition of the posts of directors general by the government of PASOK in 1982. The enabling law was voted in February 1982 against the fierce opposition of the New Democracy and the liberal press. The political staffs were reorganized again by PASOK into political *cabinets* of ministers in 1985.

The largest administrative units which are managed by 'line' political officials are the general secretariats, while smaller units with particular missions bear the title of 'special secretariats'. In each general secretariat there are a number of general directorates headed by senior civil servants, the directors general.

So the highest ranking civil servants, the directors general, are already two or three levels below the level of minister, and this explains why they actually occupy middle-management positions. For example, in a ministry which has a minister, one or two alternate or junior ministers, and below them, one or more general secretaries, covering different jurisdictions, the directors general face two ranks of political officials separating them from the minister, excluding the personal *cabinets* of each minister, junior minister, and general secretary.

At the beginning of 1999, in the nineteen Greek ministries there were fifty-six general secretariats overseeing a total of approximately seventy

---

[2] The first piece of legislation which abolished the posts of directors was Law 1232/1982. The reorganization of political staffs was included in Law 1558/1985.

general directorates. There were also sixteen special secretariats, many of which were founded in the previous two years in the Ministry of Education.[3] Since 1994 special secretariats have been rapidly multiplying in ministries that have been most affected by the demands of European integration and the need to the implement European Union regulations. The special secretariats have felt the need to organize their units better under the management of experts hired as political appointees in the capacity of 'special secretaries'.

In 1999, the government of Constantine Simitis included forty-three ministers, alternate ministers, and junior ministers who supervised fifty-six politically appointed general secretaries. The number of general secretaries was only slightly smaller than the number of directors general. Obviously, these figures reveal symptoms of distrust of the higher civil service by the incoming governments, and of the concomitant need felt by political élites to superimpose layers of political authority almost symmetrically on existing layers of administrative authority.

None of the above is a peculiarity of the Simitis government. In fact, the current Prime Minister has cut down the number of ministers from the fifty-six reached in the mid-1980s, in the Socialist governments of Andreas Papandreou, while in 1990, in the conservative government of Constantine Mitsotakis, there were forty (Makrydemetris, 1992: 96 and 98–113; Sotiropoulos, 1996b: 278 and 281–5). The current Simitis government has also hastened the process of filling the posts of directors general, after the complete abolition of this rank by the PASOK government in 1982 and the reintroduction of the same rank by the New Democracy government in 1990.[4]

In a typical pyramidal fashion, in every ministry there is a hierarchy of functions: at the top there are a few general directorates. Each general directorate consists of several directorates and each directorate is made up of several sections. Currently in Greece, senior civil servants are career public employees who enjoy tenure and work at three distinct management levels below the two political levels of general secretariat and special secretariat: the management levels are the post of director general, the post of director, and the post of head of section. Whether heads of section can be classed as 'senior officials' is debatable.

The posts of head of section are too numerous and enjoy too little prestige and power to enable us to include their occupants in the higher civil service. The most important point here is that this hierarchy of functions,

---

[3] Ministry of the Presidency of Government (1996) and communication with an anonymous advisor to the Minister of the Interior, Public Administration, and Decentralization (February 1997).

[4] The corresponding laws were 1232/1982 and 1892/1990. For the complete abolition of the rank of directors general see Tsekos (1986: 165–206) and Sotiropoulos (1996a: 81–5).

which includes directors general, directors, and heads of section, is not matched exactly by a hierarchy of grades or a hierarchy of pay. The career ladder is made up of three distinct scales; the hierarchy of *posts*, the *grade* scale, and *pay*. These three scales are not closely linked to one another; the grade scale does not correspond exactly with the hierarchical post, and pay is not linked to the grade scale. The hierarchy of top posts is made up of three levels: general director, head of directorate, and head of section. The grade scale consists of seven levels: (1) general director, (2) director, (3) A, (4) B, (5) C, (6) D, (7) E (from highest to lowest, according to the new Civil Service Code of 1999).

Promotion in the hierarchy of posts depends on a heavily politicized process undertaken by a service council in each ministry. Promotion in the grade scale (up to A) depends on the number of years in service in combination with educational credentials (i.e. whether one holds a high school diploma or a university degree and has served in the same ministry for a specific period of time). Promotion in the payscale (up to grade A) depends on seniority (i.e. the number of years in service) and is quasi-automatic with the passage of time. Basically only civil servants of grade A may be promoted in the hierarchy of top posts, but there are many civil servants in grade A who receive a high salary but do not have great authority because they have not been promoted to the top posts.

In the past, advancement was not semi-automatic and the three scales were closely linked to one another. From the end of the Second World War until the mid-1980s there were links between grade and post as well as pay and grade (see Kapoulas, 1995). Given that a promotion and a corresponding pay rise were possible only when a directorial vacancy arose, there were bottlenecks created below the top management posts in each ministry, as many university graduates with senior grades had no access to the higher paying jobs of directors and directors general (see Spanou, 1996*b*). As a consequence, between 1963 and 1981 in the three-tier grade system that had been established by the Civil Service Code of 1951 (grades A, B, C), one in three civil servants were in the top grade A (Langrod, 1964: 195).

In the last twenty years there have been at least four major reforms of the grade scale, but the congestion in the top grade persists. To give an example, research in the Ministry of Finance, conducted in 1996–7, shows that among tax collectors, 44 per cent were at grade A in the then five-grade system.[5]

Top grades become overcrowded due to pressures from below. Since the

---

[5] According to Law 2190/1994 the grades were A, B, C, D, and E (from top to bottom). Statistical data on the *corps* of tax collectors was provided to me by the electronic data centre of the Ministry of Finance (KEPYO) through an anonymous top civil servant in November 1996 and in January 1997. I sought to confirm the more recent data in March 1999 by contacting the Ministry of the Interior again.

mid-1970s pressure from qualified civil servants has led to the creation of more top management posts, including the dividing up of directorates in order to form new organizational units (and thus new vacancies) as well as the insertion of an additional rank of 'alternate director general' between those of director and director general.[6]

In mid-1980s, under the government of PASOK, a new grade scale was established (under Law 1586/1996) which reduced the number of grades and separated function from grade, and pay from grade, and abolished a number of ranks. Movement up the payscale was quasi-automatic, and depended on length of service. Promotion in the hierarchy of posts depended on the decision of the Service Council of the relevant ministry and was granted for a three-year period only. Selected directors would serve as heads of units for a renewable three-year term, which meant that a rotating system was established to allow more qualified civil servants to serve as directors for a limited period of time before they stepped down to give their position to other qualified civil servants. As a consequence, equally qualified top civil servants would alternate in the roles of superior and subordinate in the same ministry, resulting in a situation in which within the same directorate a former director would receive orders from a new director who had been his subordinate for three years.

This system was abolished by New Democracy when it was in power between 1990 and 1993. In 1990, New Democracy re-established the general directorates and, in 1992, it extended the number of ranks by creating a new grade scale, relinked grade to post by making promotion dependent upon availability of vacant posts at the top, changed the composition of service councils, and altered the recruitment system to the civil service in general. Under this grade system a university graduate would take a longer time than before to reach the top grades, which were linked to particular positions in the hierarchy of posts.[7]

While New Democracy extended the grade scale, PASOK abolished it again after it returned to power in 1993. In 1994, without abolishing the rank of directors general, PASOK shortened the hierarchy of grades.[8]

---

6 Presidential Decree 611/1977 which codified all relevant legislation since Law 1811/1951 (which was the original Civil Service Code, voted in 1951). For details see Sotiropoulos, 1996*a*: 36–7 and 154. This decree was abolished by the new Civil Service Code, passed in early 1999 (Law 2683/1999).

7 The corresponding laws were 1892/1990 and 2085/1992, both passed by New Democracy. See Andronopoulos, 1994: 147–54; Spanou, 1996*b*: 107 and 109.

8 In 1994 PASOK created five ranks instead of ten according to the 1992 system, and instead of four according to the 1986 system. See Spanou, 1996*b*: 110. The last relevant law of PASOK is no. 2190/1994, which, in terms of recruitment of new civil servants, was modified in the same year by law 2247/1994. Current legislation is codified in the new Civil Service Code (Law 2683/1999).

Also, it severed again the links which associated promotion in the grade scale with promotion in the hierarchy of posts. Henceforth, a university graduate could attain the top grade in a shorter time than before, as well as be a candidate, along with other officials of the same grade, for a three-year term as head of a administrative unit. Finally, in 1999, with the new Civil Service Code, PASOK extended the hierarchy of grades (by creating seven levels in the grade scale) and linked the two highest grades (director general and director) with the two corresponding top posts. In contrast with past practice, today there are no directors without a directorate to supervise and the same, of course, holds for directors general.

As already mentioned, the process of filling the posts of directors general started in 1990. The process of filling the posts of head of directorate or of section is ongoing, given that each head serves for three years, after which he or she may be replaced by another qualified candidate.[9] Thus, it is difficult to measure the size of the Greek higher civil service because the occupants of such top ranks change frequently, and because there are disagreements over the exact size of the Greek public sector as a whole.[10] It is easier to establish the size of the subset of public employees who work in the central public administration.

Only a minority of public employees are civil servants employed in ministries. Specifically, in 1996, the last year for which *official* data is available, of all those employed in the public sector (408,992 people), a little more than a quarter worked in the central public administration (i.e. 113,355 civil servants worked in the twenty ministries of the Greek government in 1993). In 1999, there were nineteen ministries, since the Ministry of Commerce and the Ministry of Industry, Energy, and Technology have merged into a new ministry, the Ministry of Development. The central public administration consists of the nineteen ministries. In 1993, in the central

---

[9] However, re-election of the same person for a third time results in permanent occupation of the post by him or her. Under the new Civil Service Code of February 1999, this holds for heads of section.

[10] The most recently available *official* data were collected in December 1996 by the Ministry of the Interior, Public Administration, and Decentralization, which was created after the merger of the Ministry of the Interior and the Ministry of the Presidency of Government and which oversees public administration in Greece. On the basis of this source, we find that, in 1996, there was a total of 408,992 employees in the whole of the Greek public sector (including the employees of state-run enterprises, e.g. the national telephone company or Olympic Airways). In proportional terms, this means that in 1996 approximately 11% of the Greek labour force was employed in the public sector. See Ministry of the Interior, 1998: Table S1, p. 43. However, Greek experts report a much higher number, in the area of 600,000 to 700,000 employees. This last figure includes public employees on very short-term contracts and public employees hired for the duration of a project as well as the military, elementary and high school teachers, priests and doctors working in the public health system (*ESY*). See Makrydemetris, 1995: 188; Samatas, 1996: 97–8; Ministry of the Interior, 1998.

administration there were forty-four directors general and 1,369 directors. On a rough estimate, in 1997 there were sixty-two directors general and 1,456 directors.[11] In proportional terms, these two highest ranks of civil servants represented 0.01 per cent of the personnel of the central adminis- tration. If, however, one adds the heads of sections, the percentage rises to almost 0.09.[12]

The Methods of Recruitment and Promotion
in the Greek Higher Civil Service

The methods of recruitment and promotion in the Greek higher civil ser- vice are provided by the new Civil Service Code (Law 2683/1999), passed in early 1999. All recruitment to the higher civil service in Greece is internal. Minor exceptions are very recent efforts to attract private business man- agers to the top management posts of public enterprises, but there is no exception in regard to recruitment to the management posts of the central administration.[13] Only civil servants who fulfil certain criteria for promo- tion are appointed as heads of directorates general, directorates, or sections. There is no provision for outsiders (e.g. managers from the private sector) who might wish to be candidates for those top posts in the civil service, although the low pay of senior civil servants makes it unlikely that many such candidates would be attracted to the posts in central ministries. In fact, no civil servant may seek appointment to a higher civil service post in any ministry other than his or her own.

The service council in each ministry periodically evaluates all employees serving in the ministry and selects the heads of directorates and sections of the interdepartmental ministry. The heads of directorates general are selected by an interdepartmental 'special service council' (governed by Law 1892/1990 and Law 2683/1999). Each service council has five members: three heads of directorates (i.e. directors) of the ministry, appointed to the council by the minister himself or herself, plus two representatives of the

[11] Ministry of the Interior, 1998: 276. The estimate for 1997 is rough and was given to me in February 1997 during anonymous interviews with members of the Ministry of the Interior, Public Administration, and Decentralization. At that time the ministry's personnel was collecting information on the size of the higher civil service throughout the public ad- ministration system and did not have accurate data.

[12] There were 8,424 chiefs of section in the Greek public administration in 1993. The number has been calculated by the author on the basis of Ministry of the Presidency of Government, 1995: 276.

[13] Independent consulting firms assess candidates for the top management posts and present the government with a short list of the most highly qualified among them. However, this practice is not very common.

civil servants of the ministry, elected at ministry-wide elections according to Law 2190/1994 and Law 2683/1999. It is obvious that by appointing friendly directors to the council the minister can influence the selection of heads of directorates and of sections in the ministry. These directors tend to be of the same political persuasion as the minister.

In addition, the ministry-wide elections are also politicized along party political lines. They are usually won by a candidate of the labour union dominated by the governing party and a candidate from the labour union dominated by the opposition party. Independent candidates and candidates of the labour unions of smaller parties are rarely, if ever, able to take one of the two open seats in the service councils. As a consequence, a minister who would like to control the five-member service council can count on the three votes of the directors appointed by himself or herself plus the vote of the labour union representative elected with the list of the governing party. Each new service council is appointed for a two-year term.

The service councils have rarely, if ever, been enthusiastic about selecting graduates of the Greek National School of Public Administration for any posts of head of section or head of directorate. Graduates of the School were supposed to have a strong advantage in recruitment to these management posts, but due to resistance within all ministries this prospect was never realized. The School was founded in 1983 and started functioning in 1985, and was modelled on the French École National d'Administration. It continues producing young, highly qualified managers selected from a pool of university graduates who pass the competitive entrance examinations to the School, complete two years of courses and practical training, and then join the civil service. According to the School's founding law (1383/1983) its graduates should have followed a fast track to the top ranks of the civil service. In practice, bureaucratic obstruction by middle-aged civil servants—who are university graduates and candidates for higher posts but not graduates of the School—has blocked the way for the School's graduates. Instead, the latter are appointed to various directorates in a number of ministries but they are underemployed, in the sense that their skills (e.g. knowledge of foreign languages, familiarity with modern management methods) are seldom called upon by the directors and the directors general.

This is not surprising given the less than meritocratic selection processes applied by the service councils in each ministry. The selection process is a little more standardized when it comes to appointing directors general in a ministry. In this case, as mentioned above, it is not the ministry's own service council but a special service council which is convened to evaluate candidates for the post of director general. The special service council which selects the heads of the directorates general is composed of seven members: one senior judge, three university professors, two general directors (one from the Ministry of Finance and the other from the Ministry of the Interior), and the president of the Union of Civil Servants (ADEDY). One might argue that the special service council may be less influenced by political officials than ministerial service councils. Until 1998, the judges and university professors who served as members were hand-picked by the Minister of the Interior, but by 1999, with the new Civil Service Code, the minister no longer had jurisdiction. (Professors are appointed by the Rector of their university, and judges by the President of the Council of State.) This recent attempt to standardize the selection of directors general should not give the impression that promotions to top posts have gradually become more meritocratic. A non-random sample survey in 1996 among civil servants has shown that there is variation in their perceptions of distribution of spoils through promotions. In the Ministry of the Environment 51 per cent of the respondents believe that purely political criteria prevail in promotions, while in the Ministry of Commercial Shipping only 16 per cent believe so (Mylonopoulou-Mira, 1998: 109).

The total number of all civil servants who are card-carrying members of any political party is unknown and the same holds for the number of senior civil servants. Research conducted in 1989, and based on a sample of seventy-six top civil servants in four ministries in Athens, showed that 21 per cent of the respondents were registered members of a political party, usually the governing party (Sotiropoulos, 1996*b*: 93). These data should be read with caution, since they were collected through personal interviews and the sample was not random.

The percentage of higher civil servants who were then and remain political-party members must be higher, given the importance of party patronage for a successful career in the Greek public administration (Sotiropoulos, 1993). Party patronage is fuelled by the nature of promotion procedures described above, at least up to the level of director. Thus, it is reasonable to assume that most, but not all, senior civil servants will be affiliated with the governing party, but will conceal their political attachment.[14]

Despite the considerable influence of the government in selecting directors and heads of sections, there are senior civil servants who do not belong to the governing party. This may occur if the status of a senior civil servant in a particular ministry is too high or if he or she is very knowledgeable and thus valuable to any minister, regardless of political

---

[14] Some of the candidates for management posts may at least pretend to be supporters of the in-coming government by performing an about-face just before the new governing party comes to power.

persuasion. Above all, a senior civil servant who is not affiliated with the party of the latest in-coming minister may survive government turnover, if he or she has constructed personal networks of support among the ministry's personnel. Such networks constitute systems which link civil servants from different political parties, on the basis of membership of the same corps, long personal ties, kinship bonds, common regional origins, or even age similarities.

Interdepartmental Mobility of Civil Servants

There is no interdepartmental mobility of senior civil servants in Greece. It is even rare for a lower civil servant to change ministries, or even directorates within the same ministry, once hired in a specific, entry-level post. From time to time, when a public enterprise is privatized or abolished altogether, its personnel is allowed to petition for transfer to a ministry or other public enterprise.

However, there are provisions for compulsory transfers (although few have been made) as well as voluntary transfers, which may result from a petition by a civil servant. These provisions have been made because some ministries and public organizations have more personnel than they need, while others are sparsely staffed. For instance, state hospitals lack nurses and many elementary and secondary schools lack teachers. Also regional administration is understaffed, especially in the underdeveloped parts of Greece. This enables some *ad hoc* interdepartmental mobility among middle and lower civil servants. While more than one government has threatened to implement laws providing for compulsory transfers of personnel from one area of the state structure to another, in practice, mainly voluntary transfers have sporadically taken place. Such transfers seldom involve the movement of high-ranking civil servants.[15]

There is no mobility among members of the numerous corps either. Yet the recognition that intensive fragmentation and immobility reduce the efficiency of the civil service and increase bureaucratic rigidity has led to proposals for a number of interdepartmental corps. As things stand today,

---

[15] There are two kinds of transfers: temporary and permanent. Temporary transfers are three-year assignments, seldom sought by higher ranking civil servants but popular among lower civil servants who might wish to move to the same public agency where their spouse already works or to the Ministry of Finance where the average monthly salary is higher because of special allowances granted to the employees of this ministry. Permanent transfers are more rare than temporary ones. Permanent and temporary transfers are regulated by Laws 1735/1987 and 2266/1994. These laws sought to encourage voluntary transfers of civil servants to understaffed agencies of ministries in remote regions of Greece, close to the borders of the country, to no avail.

civil servants who work in the same area of activity but belong to separate ministries belong to two different corps. The creation of interdepartmental corps would unite all civil servants working in the same area of activity within a single homogeneous corps, regardless of the ministry in which they work. Such a development would have facilitated the mobility of civil service personnel among ministries. On the other hand, such a possibility would allow incoming governments to transfer civil servants from one ministry to another on political grounds.

Between 1986 and 1992 five different laws (1586/1986; 1735/1987; 1892/1990; 1943/1991; 2085/1992) provided for the creation of interdepartmental corps, but none has ever appeared (see Sfikas, 1995). The new Civil Service Code (Law 2683/1999) provides for the same possibility (art. 78). One may hypothesize that internal pressure by civil servants to maintain the current balance of power among various corps within ministries probably explains why no interdepartmental corps of senior civil servants has ever been formed.

Status in the Civil Service

Greek civil servants do not enjoy a high social status. The rather low social status of senior civil servants in Greece is also reflected in their level of pay. At the beginning of 1997, the gross monthly salary of a director general with a spouse and two children was approximately £1,933 (March 1999 exchange rates). The gross monthly salaries of directors and heads of section were £924 and £914, respectively.[16] Of course, one may add bonuses for participation in *ad hoc* committees or per diem payments for travelling abroad. However, the fact is that the gross monthly compensation of a director of a Greek ministry is only three times the minimum salary officially provided for private-sector newly hired employees with no job experience. Diplomats have traditionally enjoyed a higher social status than other Greek civil servants. They are paid more than other Greek civil servants, but substantially less than diplomats of other member-states of the European Union.

The level of remuneration is not a safe indicator of status. For instance, civil servants who are employed in the Ministry of Finance are paid better than their colleagues in other ministries, since they have allocated themselves some additional allowances from the state budget which is drafted in their own ministry. As a consequence, on the rare occasions when vol-

---

[16] My own research in the central headquarters of the Ministry of the Interior, conducted in March 1999.

untary transfers of personnel among ministries are arranged, there is a high demand for transfers to the Ministry of Finance. But, overall, that ministry's personnel does not enjoy any particular status, although the restraining power of its minister is felt whenever another ministry asks for additional funds beyond the ones annually allocated to it by the state budget.

Law-making power is not a safe indicator of status either. For instance, the Ministry of the Interior, Public Administration, and Decentralization (formerly the Ministry of the Presidency of Government) is responsible for drafting new laws on matters of administrative personnel, for amending existing relevant legislation, and for supervising administrative reform at all levels of the state structure. The higher civil servants of this ministry do not necessarily enjoy higher prestige among the administrative personnel and, in fact, sometimes their incursions into the organizational and personnel affairs of other ministries are resisted by other higher civil servants.

Social Background Characteristics and Social Status of Top Officials

Normally top officials are civil servants with university education. In 1996, university graduates made up 26 per cent of the total Greek civil service (Ministry of the Interior, 1998: 36). After the Second World War, the Greek higher civil service was staffed by male graduates of law schools and faculties of political science who came from Southern Greece, often from the peninsula of the Peloponnese (see Argyriades, 1963: 349; Langrod, 1965: 63–6). Today's higher civil service contains economics, engineering, and agronomy graduates, yet the legally trained civil servants probably remain preponderant. Very few have postgraduate degrees, with the exception of the Ministry of National Economy, where, according to a sample conducted in 1996, 30 per cent of the civil servants had a postgraduate degree (Mylonopoulou-Mira, 1998: 176). The vast majority of directors general and directors are men and, according to one source, they are aged between 50 and 65. However, there is great variation from ministry to ministry: thus, in 1996 in the Ministry of Finance, among the tax collectors with a university degree (who are primary candidates for management posts) only 18 per cent were 50 years or older. In the same corps of this ministry, among the civil servants of grade A there were only a few more men than women (54 to 46 per cent), while in the corps of tax collectors as a whole, regardless of grade, there were more women than men (56 to 44 per cent).[17] In 1996,

---

[17] Data supplied by the personnel directorate of the Ministry of Finance. Anonymous interview with a top civil servant in November 1996 and in January 1997.

75 per cent of all directors in all Greek ministries were male (Ministry of the Interior, 1998: 306).

The geographical origins of senior civil servants are not recorded in any official statistical source. On the basis of the little existing survey research it can be said that they probably come from the regions of Southern and Central Greece (see Vernardarkis and Papastathopoulos, 1990: 7–28; Sotiropoulos, 1996*b*: 64–78).

It is extremely difficult to document the social class origins of senior civil servants, using father's occupation or any other basis. Again, from limited survey research, it appears that a quarter to a third of senior civil servants come from rural backgrounds, i.e. the father was a farmer. Somewhere between a sixth and a quarter of the higher civil servants come from families of the employed urban strata. There are very few civil servants who come from working-class or upper-class families (Sotiropoulos, 1996*b*: 82–91).

In general, senior civil servants in Greece do not come from élite social backgrounds, nor do they themselves constitute a social élite. This is reflected in poems about the dreadful routine of work in the civil service; in the rampant absenteeism of lower and middle-level civil servants, and in the widespread conviction that segments of the civil service working in public agencies responsible for town-planning, customs regulations in port authorities, airports, and borders, and, above all, taxation, are easily corrupted by politicians and private businessmen (Nikolopoulou, 1998).

Organizations and Informal Contacts across Ministries

Senior civil servants do not interact together on a formal or regular basis, even if they are employed by the same ministry and work in the same building. As explained above, there are no interdepartmental corps of civil servants. Within ministries the only formal groups which cut across divisions and sections are the politicized labour unions, representing the two or three largest political parties.

There are no established regular channels of horizontal communication among all directors general or directors of a ministry, but there may be informal ones. The decision-making system involves vertical communication channels, linking directors with their supervising director general and directors general with the general secretary and the minister on an individual basis. In the ministries there are no collective bodies of decision-making, other than the service councils described above and the ministerial *cabinets* of ministers, which are composed of political appointees serving as advisors to the minister.

Most committees are created and disbanded in an *ad hoc* fashion by the general secretary or the minister.[18] There are ministerial *cabinets* along French lines, but the contacts between their members, who are advisors to the minister, and the senior civil servants are neither formal nor regular. Indeed, such contacts are not always welcome on both sides in view of the attempts by politically appointed advisors to shadow the work of senior civil servants in the early 1980s, at the beginning of the first term of the Socialist government of Andreas Papandreou (1981–5).

Informal contacts across ministries exist but are difficult to trace. It would appear that senior civil servants with common geographical origins, kinship bonds, or similar political beliefs, contact one another to ask for favours or speed up administrative processes which affect their personal interests. There are very few, if any, interdepartmental bodies, but top civil servants from various ministries may sit on the board of public agencies and public enterprises as representatives of their ministry.

The contacts between senior civil servants of the ministries and civil servants who work in the regional public administration and the prefectures do not assume any collective character either. Because of the high dependency of the regional and prefectural authorities on the ministries located in Athens, the relationship between national and subnational officials is a purely individual and hierarchical one. Orders and funds usually flow from the centre to the periphery, i.e. from each ministry to individual heads of its own corresponding directorates or sections in the prefecture, while information and enquiries go the other way.

Since at least 1994, the prefectural administration has been undergoing reform, mostly in the direction of delegating more powers from the central headquarters of ministries to their departments in the prefectures. The regional administration ideally encompasses several prefectures, but the organization of regional civil services has not made significant progress. Regional governments are still understaffed and they have not yet obtained clear jurisdictions, even though since 1996 there has been a concerted effort, undertaken by the Socialist government of C. Simitis, to organize the civil service of regional governments (Law 2503/1997) and to shape fewer and stronger units of local government out of a plethora of small and tiny municipal authorities which existed until 1997 (Law 2539/1997). However, by November 1997 only 7,473 civil servants had been transferred from the central services of the ministries to the administrative units of the thirteen regions of Greece, i.e. less than 7 per cent of the

---

[18] e.g. a committee to draft a new civil service code, regulating the career, the rights and duties of all civil servants, was founded and disbanded in the Ministry of the Interior, Public Administration, and Decentralization several times since 1987 but the new code was voted by the Parliament only in early 1999 (Law 2683/1999).

total of civil servants employed in the ministries (my research and calculations).

Political Party Policies Towards the Higher Civil Service

Throughout the twentieth century, political parties have monitored civil
servants individually and have controlled the civil service as a whole through
various mechanisms which have secured the cooperation of friendly civil
servants with incoming governments and the isolation of hostile elements
within the civil service. In the first three-quarters of this century these
mechanisms included the compulsory transfer and lay-off of scores of civil
servants considered political opponents. The civil service was a focus of
discord, an arena of intense political party competition between liberals
and royalists in the first half of the century, between conservatives and
centrists after the Second World War, and between conservatives and
socialists after the demise of the colonels' regime in the last two decades
(see Samatas, 1993; Sotiropoulos, 1993; Spanou, 1996*b*).

After the Second World War, all civil servants were systematically screened
to make sure that they were not voters of any political party of the left, or
sometimes even of the centre (Alivizatos, 1979: 370 and 378; Samatas,
1986). The conservative and right-of-centre government which won the
Greek Civil War (1944–9) checked on the political beliefs of any incoming
civil servants at the time of their appointment by resorting to security files
kept on every candidate for any job in the public sector.

Today, in terms of political beliefs, senior civil servants are expected to
side with the governing political party, particularly if the party stays in
power for more than one term. The policies of political parties are shaped
by two conflicting aims: on the one hand, to control the higher civil service,
by neutralizing any resistance from officials linked with the party which
ruled previously and by appointing party supporters to top-ranking positions; on the other hand, to reform the administrative system, as part of
reforms which attempt to make the Greek society adapt to the increasing
demands of economic globalization. It is hoped that the new Civil Service
Code, which is much less ideologically biased towards the right and much
less permeable to clientelistic practices than the preceding one (the Code
of 1951/1977), will restrain future party governments from intervening in
the civil service to the large extent that past governments have done.

One should not present top civil servants as innocent victims of the
whims of alternating ruling parties. In the well-founded party patronage
system which still permeates the civil service, mainly those civil servants
with personal or political contacts will stand a chance of gaining promo-

tion, a convenient transfer, or additional income through appointment to a temporary ministerial committee. Members of patronage networks benefit from relations of dependence between politicians and bureaucrats. Individual politicians may even become dependent on particular higher civil servants who possess vital information and technical knowledge useful in administrative battles waged among and within ministries. However, generally speaking, senior civil servants as a group are divided along the lines of political party competition and are unable to act in organized collective fashion.

Conclusion

It seems that there is a double bind for any Greek government which grapples with the administrative institutions. The double bind requires, on the one hand, the penetration of the higher civil service as a source of political spoils in order to promote the prospects for re-election and, on the other hand, the modernization of the public administration to meet the challenges of efficient and legitimate delivery of services, compounded by the additional pressures created by European integration. All governments elected to power after the transition to democracy in 1974 have been much more successful in developing the higher civil service as a source of political spoils than in modernizing it. There is an impasse: if reform-minded, incoming governments refrain from filling the higher civil service with party supporters, they might encounter strong resistance when they seek to modernize the public administration. However, by giving priority to political control of the higher civil service, the same governments reproduce the clientelistic patterns of relations between political and administrative élites which, to a large extent, have inhibited the modernization of the Greek administration.

In conclusion, in comparison with Greek political élites and with European administrative élites, the Greek higher civil servants as a group are and feel powerless. In their case it is legitimate to claim that they do not enjoy positions as powerful as the titles of their jobs indicate and that they have less influence than their counterparts in most other European countries. This reflects the fact Greek higher civil servants are in reality middle-level rather than top officials. The organization in which they serve, the Greek public administration, for the most part serves the interests of political parties alternating in power. The Greek higher civil service renders service, for the most part, not to the general public but to its elected political masters—to the governing political party, and to favoured clienteles among prospective voters.

REFERENCES

Andronopoulos, V. (1994). 'To Neo Vathmologio' [Law 2085/92], in Theodore Tsekos (ed.), *Dioiketitikos Eksygchronismos* [Administrative modernization], Conference minutes (Athens: National Centre of Public Administration).

Alivizatos, N. P. (1979). *Les Institutions politiques de la Grèce à travers les crises* (Paris: Pinchon).

Argyriades, D. (1963). 'An Ecology of Greek Administration Some Factors Affecting the Development of the Greek Civil Service', in John Peristiany (ed.), *Acts of the Mediterranean Sociological Conference* (Athens: Social Sciences Centre).

—— (1970). 'Some Aspects of Administrative Change in Four Mediterranean Countries', unpublished report (Paris: Organization for Economic Cooperation and Development).

Kapoulas, Z. (1995). 'Mia Anadrome sten Exelixe tou Ypallelikou Kodika' [A review of the evolution of the civil service code] *Dioiketike Enemerose*, 1: 101–4.

Langrod, G. (1965). *Reorganisation de la fonction publique en Grèce* (Paris: OECD).

Makrydemetris, A. (1992). *He Organose tes Kyverneses* [The organization of government] (Athens: Ant. N. Sakkoulas).

—— (1995). 'Paradoxes Asygehronies Exsygchronismou' [Paradoxes of modernization], *Oekonomikos Tachydromos* (22 June 1995), 188.

Ministry of the Interior, Public Administration and Decentralization (1998). *Deltio Statistikon Stoicheion Prosopikou Demosiou Tomea* [Bulletin of statistical information on public-sector personnel], Census of 31 December 1996 (Athens: National Printing Office).

Ministry of the Presidency of the Government (1995). *Deltio Statistikon Stoicheion Proso'pikou Demosiou Tomea* [Bulletin of statistical information on public-sector personnel], Census of 31 December 1993 (Athens: National Printing Office).

—— (1996). 'Table of Ministries and General Secretariats', Athens, October, unpublished mimeo.

Mylonopoulou-Mira, Polyxeni (1998). *Hoi Demarioi Ypalleloi* [The Civil Servants] (Athens: Ant. N. Sakkoulas).

Nikolopoulou, Alexandra P. (ed.) (1998). *Kratos kai Diafthora* [State and Corruption] (Athens: I. Sideris).

Samatas, M. (1986). 'Greek Bureaucratism: A System of Sociopolitical Control', unpublished Ph.D. thesis, New York School for Social Research.

—— (1993). 'De-bureaucratization Failure in Post-Dictatorial Greece: A Socio-Political Control Approach', *Journal of Modern Greek Studies*, 11(2): 187–217.

—— (1996). 'Opseis tou Laikistikou Grafeiokratismou' [Aspects of popular bureaucratism], *Epitheorese Dioiketikes Epistemes*, 2: 97–8.

Sfikas, Dimitrios (1995). 'He Organose tes Kratikes Dioikeses' [The organization of state administration], *Dioiketike Enemerose*, 1: 28

Sotiropoulos, Dimitri A. (1993). 'A Colossus with Feet of Clay: The State in Post-Authoritarian Greece', in Harry J. Psomiades and Stavros B. Thomadikis (eds.), *Greece, the New Europe and the Changing International Order* (New York: Pella).

—— (1996*a*). *Populism and Bureaucracy: The Case of Greece under PASOK, 1981–1989* (London: The University of Notre Dame Press).

—— (1996*b*). *Grafeiokratia kai Politike Exousia* [Bureaucracy and political power] (Athens: Ant. N. Sakkoulas).

Spanou, C. (1995). 'A la recherche du temps perdu: La Modernisation de l'administration en Grèce', *Revue française d'administration publique*, 75 (July–Sept.): 427–8.

—— (1996*a*). 'To Provlema tes Demosias Dioikeses: Mia Prote Proseggise' [The problem of public administration: a first approach], Working Paper, 4, *Idryma Oekonomikon kai Viomechanikon Ereuvnon*, Athens, Oct.

—— (1996*b*). 'Penelope's Suitors: Administrative Modernisation and Party Competition in Greece', *West European Politics*, 19(1): 97–124.

Tachos, Anastasios I. (1996). *Demosio-ypalleliko Dikaio* [Civil Service Law], 4th edn. (Thessalonika: Sakkoulas).

Tsekos, T. (1984). 'Rationalité et irrationalité dans l'administration hellenique: Recherches sur les origines d'un conflit', Mémoire DEA, Amiens: Université de Picardie.

—— (1986). 'Changement politique et changement administratif: La Haute Fonction publique en Grèce avant et après 1981', in Danielle Lochak (ed.), *La Haute Administration et la politique* (Paris: Presses Universitaires de France).

Vernardarkis, G., and D. Papastathopoulos (1990). 'He Anotate Demosioypallelia sten Hellada' [The higher civil service in Greece], *Dioiketitke Metarrythmise*, 41–2 (Jan.–June): 64–78.

Wilson, F. M. G. (1966), *The Machinery of Government in Greece* (Paris: Organization for Economic Cooperation and Development).

2

Spain: Still the Primacy of Corporatism?

IGNACIO MOLINA ÁLVAREZ DE CIENFUEGOS

Spanish Administration over the Last Two Decades

The general transformation of public administration in general, and the cadre of top officials in particular, over the last twenty years has been provoked by a combination of factors including the recent transition to democracy, regional decentralization through the creation of the so-called Autonomous Communities, European Union membership, and the long, uninterrupted presence of the same party (the Socialists) in office. The democratic impact is visible in the public policy outputs more than in the process of decision-making: public expenditure rose from 25 per cent of GDP in 1975 to 47.4 per cent in 1994 (INAP, 1996: 11) and the Spanish administrative state began to be replaced by a service state. According to the 1978 Constitution, the country is an 'Estado Social y Democrático de Derecho', that is to say, a welfare state and a democratic state (with parliamentary scrutiny and the rule of law). While in other European countries administrative systems were modernized, in Spain it was first necessary to adjust human resources to democracy (Constantino and Carrillo, 1994: 685).

Devolution of power to the Autonomous Communities has had profound impacts on the administrative structure and the way it works, as well as on the wider question of the organization of public employees (Ziller, 1990: 56). This process broke the centralist tradition and the reallocation of public spending and bureaucrats between the three different levels of government is still continuing (currently the regional level of government spends 25 per cent of total expenditure whilst local governments consume approximately 15 per cent). In addition, Spanish membership of the EU since 1986 incorporated a supranational dimension into the resolution of several public issues, and this too has had a significant impact upon the structures and processes of administration.

The extended period of Socialist rule—from 1982 to 1996—started when democracy was considered consolidated and, therefore, administrative modernization could be launched. The transition to democracy under a centre–right minority government had avoided major administrative reform for reasons of political priorities and opportunity. However, when the Socialists arrived in office, they began an incremental reform, starting with the creation of the Ministry of Public Administration (MAP) in 1986. Previously two Acts on the Civil Service (discussed more fully below) had been passed in 1984, with the objective of eliminating corruption and curtailing the power of the corps (*cuerpos*) in which civil servants were grouped. At that time, Spain lacked a modern, technologically advanced, and efficient public administration, but the strength of the bureaucracy discouraged radical change. From 1986 to 1990 the government sought to implement a step-by-step modernization programme, yet it faced so many obstacles that delays continued to mark the progress of Spain's administrative modernization. One author emphasizes that for Felipe González this was the greatest frustration of his premiership (Heywood, 1995: 138).

In addition to political changes, Spain had to face the problems that all Western administrations confronted during the 1980s: economic austerity, the transformation of the financial and industrial markets, new issues and priorities (such as the environment), neoliberalism and ideological prejudice against the state, technological challenge, and democratic pressure (Mény and Wright, 1994: 22–4). These problems produced similar responses across many nations, producing what many see as a converging trend towards 'New Public Management'—the search for efficiency by adopting private-sector practices. The redefinition of the role of the central administration included flexibility in human resources management (both in the recruitment and training of civil servants), and the idea of total quality applied to public administration.

Following these patterns, in 1987, the Instituto Nacional de Administración Pública (INAP) within the MAP was reorganized to train personnel and to modernize the administration, although it applied to generalist civil servants only, and did not cover the important specialized corps which will be discussed below. It is important to note that Spanish political culture displays a solid trust in the state (Bañón-Martínez, 1994: 231), although is also true that civil servants, often self-serving and corrupt, have never enjoyed a reputation for efficiency in Spain. Following a report in 1989 and a subsequent plan for modernization of the state's general administration (MAP, 1990b), a package of proposals was launched in 1992 to modernize the administration, replacing the legalistic approach and the hierarchical frameworks with the idea of 'management-by-objectives' and flexible organization. A new budgeting system (PPBS) was introduced and the recruitment procedures by competitive examinations (*oposiciones*) became more open, linking training and qualifications, although they were not substantially altered. Another aspect of the plan was an agreement with the unions representing administrative officials, and a series of legislative modifications was passed to separate politics and the administration (1992 Act on Legal Regime and Administrative Proceeding) and to adapt the latter to the new constitutional framework (the main administrative Acts had been passed in 1957 and 1958 under the Franco regime). A new Act concerning the organization and procedures of the general state administration was approved in 1997, during the first year of government of the conservative Partido Popular (PP). This envisaged the reduction of hierarchy and complexity, and divides the central public sector into three types of organization: central administration (ministries), autonomous agencies (*organismos autónomos*), and managerial public entities (*entidades públicas empresariales*)

The creation of autonomous agencies and public entities, within a more flexible framework of regulation, was one of the key points of administrative change. While central administration continues to focus on decision-making and regulation, the autonomous agencies implement or manage administrative activities (connected to promotion or production of services) and managerial public entities are organizations which produce goods and provide services (these are different from public enterprises, *socidades mercantiles estatales*, since the production of goods and services by the managerial public entities does not follow the logic of the market as it does with an organization like the Railway Company RENFE). The two first are regulated by public law and the latter predominantly by private law; but all of them are departmental and accountable (albeit a posteriori). The pilot experiment in the case of the autonomous agencies was the Executive Agency of Tax Administration (Agencia Estatal de Administración Tributaria). This tax agency was created in 1991 and its main functions are to provide assistance with income tax (IRPF) declarations and control tax evasion through inspection. It enjoys a substantial degree of flexibility and autonomy but remains accountable to the Ministry of Economy and Finance. Following the pilot, the General Post and Telegraphs Office was the first managerial public entity established under the new regulation (Subirats, 1994). However, ministerial organizations generally maintain a primacy in the governmental structure.

The fourteen Spanish ministries are divided, in most cases, into sectoral junior ministries (Secretarios de Estado) whose incumbents, although they do not attend the Council of Ministers, can also be considered to form part of the governmental élite according to the 1997 Act on Government. Besides this first level of political direction, there is an intermediate echelon of politico-administrative élites composed of the under-secretaries or general secretaries, the members of the private *cabinets* and the directors general. These posts are characterized both by the fact that they are political appointments, and by their technical profile, since most of them are recruited from among civil servants even though this is not a legal requirement. Finally, at the top level of the civil service, is the post of assistant director general, which must be filled by public employees. Our object of study, the bureaucratic élite, comprises not only this top level, but also the senior civil servants who hold political posts.

The Historical Legacy

The Napoleonic War, the liberal quasi-revolutions, and absolutist reaction during the first decades of the nineteenth century destroyed the Bourbon administration (in which professional bureaucratic posts were hereditary). After 1812, and throughout the last century, bureaucratic organization was based on a system of *cesantías*, that is to say, a spoils system whereby new governments institutionalized ideological purges in order to guarantee the loyalty of public employees. An attempt was made to compensate for the instability of this civil service by creating, within every ministry, specialized groups of officials (or corps) composed of people with a university degree, selected by objective examination and who could not be removed. The members of these corps had a monopoly of the most important posts in the administration and were relatively well paid. These specialized corps, which progressively fragmented the Spanish administration, enjoyed high social status, above all if compared with the *cesantes*, and sufficient power to maintain the privileges which were formally recognized by the Civil Service Statute of 1852 (for more detailed historical description see Ortega, 1992).

The élitist corps were efficient, but they were also an obstacle to any reform which would have facilitated the creation of a generalist bureaucracy. Moreover, the presence of the central state in the provinces was organized through the figures of the prefectorial Gobernadores Civiles, who were always highly politicized. Their traditional functions were police, control of local administration, and electoral fraud. During 1997 a historical change took place to adapt peripheral administration of the central state to Autonomous Communities. The fifty Gobernadores Civiles (with the rank of directors general and politically appointed by the government) were replaced by provincial subdelegates of the government who must be senior civil servants. This new administrative profile is counterbalanced by the political weight of the seventeen delegates of the government who are representatives of the central power in the regions (with rank of undersecretary). The politicization of the Gobernadores Civiles also helped obstruct any possibility that they might provide an alternative foundation for the creation of a senior civil service. Since the French model was the archetype to imitate, when the Spanish permanent civil service was created in 1911 (Statute of Maura), the spoils system was replaced by a permanent bureaucracy recruited through objective examination and structured in French-style corps. This reform ended the inefficient and politicized *cesantías* but fostered fragmentation by powerful corps in which every official could be promoted according to a career model in the respective ministry which was based on seniority rather than merit. The predominance of specialists over the very few generalists led to the patrimonialization of the most important posts of bureaucratic management by the former, with the subsequent emergence of several *esprits de corps*, and political and even social clientelism.

During the Francoist dictatorship, after the early years when public posts were filled on the basis of loyalties shown during the Civil War, élitist bureaucrats would control political power itself. This is explained by the low political profile of the authoritarian regime. The official party of the dictatorship, Movimiento Nacional, did not control effectively the machinery of government, and this allowed top civil servants to fill the political vacuum and to dominate decision-making and the implementation of policies in all the departments. Bureaucrats were a functional substitute for parties during the dictatorship (Constantino and Carrillo, 1994: 688), and the emergence of a civil service as the main instrument of political recruitment increased the power of the corps and their self-regulation with regard to the system of promotion, appointments to particular posts, and pay. Hidden under the label of technocrats (many of them sharing membership in the traditionalist Catholic organization Opus Dei), top officials were conservative and supported the dictatorship. In view of the lack of any legislation governing conflicts of interest, the importance of the public sector in the economy (through public firms or contracting-out to private ones) meant that bureaucrats could enjoy good contacts with business sectors—companies and firms offering outside work to bureaucrats could secure favourable treatment by the administration.

The modernization of the economy created pressures for the reform of the civil service in 1964. At that time the system of pay was reformed, the Presidency of the Government[1] acquired responsibility for regulating the

---

[1] With Franco as dictator, the Generalisimo was head of state and government: the post of President of the Government (or prime minister) was not filled until 1973, only two years before Franco died. However, a prime minister's and government's office existed under the label of Ministry of Presidency. This department was actually responsible (together with the particularly powerful Ministry of Finance) for civil service policy until 1986, when the Ministry of Public Administration was created.

civil service, posts were classified, and above all, generalist corps inspired by the British model were created to counterbalance the fragmentation caused by the specialization and departmentalization of the traditional corps. These new civil administrators were to be present in all ministries through the control of the Technical General Secretariats (advising staff). Economic progress and the capitalist reforms of the 1960s also involved the emergence of alternative paths of professional achievement for the upper classes in the private sector. At the same time, the middle classes could go to university, the prerequisite for a more democratized access to the élitist corps.

But the transition from the authoritarian regime at the end of the 1970s did not affect the administrative structure. The first political priority was to establish democracy. In addition, the peaceful nature of the process did not allow any kind of purge among civil servants who had collaborated with Franco. Moreover, many senior civil servants formed the nucleus of the first democratic governments (those chaired by the centre–right presidents Adolfo Suárez and Leopoldo Calvo-Sotelo) and thus the party supporting the government, the UCD, did not have to confront serious impediments to democratization within the higher bureaucracy. When the Socialists won power in 1982 they attempted to reduce the great power of the corps by establishing rules on conflicts of interest and other reforms included in an Act approved in 1984. Although some parts of this Act were concerned with democracy (the recognition of the right to strike or unionize, which affected the monopoly of the corps in representing their members), the failure of the Act to achieve its main goal of diminishing the power of the corps revealed the considerable resources which the most important corps could deploy to obstruct the reform, even though this was promoted by a determined majority government.

In fact, the Constitutional Court was the main body responsible for the failure of the reform, since part of the Act was annulled. Specifically, the Court did not accept the proposed replacement of the traditional, permanent, and corps-based bureaucracy by a system of posts which the government wanted to open to non-career employees. That is to say, the Socialists did not wish to reserve any particular post for the corps (something the Court accepted) and not even for civil servants (to which the Court objected). This radical strategy of promoting mobility was prohibited by Article 103 of Constitution that set out the general rule that a permanent civil service based on merit should be maintained.

Although the reform could not produce the radical rationalization of the Spanish civil service originally envisaged, it did produce a more incremental reclassification of officials into five groups (A to E according to educational background) and twenty-three levels (7 to 30) which correspond to the different stages in an individual's career. Moreover, reform weakened the corps to some degree. There were mergers of the more fragmented corps, generalists were encouraged, and positions in the public sector were reclassified to reduce the power of the corps. Under these reforms, pay was determined by the post occupied (thus it remained indirectly related to the corps because posts, although not reserved, tend to be filled by the same corps) and productivity. However, while the Socialist government fostered the relative politicization of the bureaucratic élite through the system of free designation among civil servants for top posts, powerful corps are still the main features of the administration.

Who are the Senior Civil Servants?

There are at least two types of public employees: civil servants (either permanent or temporary) and contractual public employees, who do not enjoy the security of tenure of civil servants. The Socialist government originally wanted to replace civil servants by fixed-term employees but, as mentioned above, the Constitutional Court limited fixed-term appointments to temporary or auxiliary posts, public jobs abroad, and those, requiring special qualifications, which are not able to recruit civil servants to carry them out. Table 2.1 presents the number of public employees and civil servants in the central administration, distinguishing between the number of group A officials as well as the most senior levels 28 to 30 (all level 30 officials have the rank of assistant general director).

In spite of its growth in recent years, the absolute number of Spanish public employees, and particularly civil servants in the central administration, is lower than that of many other West European countries. To establish the size of Spanish public employment, we must add to those working on administrative tasks (Table 2.1) employees in other service activities, such as defence, police, education, health assistance, universities, and the workforces of the regions (Comunidades Autónomas) and local governments (Table 2.2). The basic legal framework is identical to that described for the state employment. Article 149 of the Spanish Constitution stipulates that there is only one civil service model, and therefore autonomous communities have only a small margin for creating distinct systems. Moreover, many of the current regional civil servants previously worked in central administrative organizations (some of them also came from local government). The process of devolution involved the decentralization of many public employees working in those areas that were transferred to the regional level (particularly in agriculture, social services, health assistance,

TABLE 2.1. *Public Employees in Central Administration, 1997*

Ministry/Agency	Public employees	Civil servants	Group A	Levels 28–9	Level 30
Infrastructures[a]	67,058	51,194	1,777	414	123
Labour and Social Affairs	61,977	43,739	4,101	474	141
incl. Social Security	*36,026*	*26,841*	*1,893*	*176*	*31*
Economy and Finance[b]	49,905	37,710	3,886	2,151	511
Interior (excl. police)	31,111	24,159	1,408	213	74
Education (excl. state schools)	30,502	14,505	3,888	1,112	150
Environment	10,969	4,132	961	175	60
Defence (excl. armed forces)	7,078	7,069	252	86	25
Health (excl. health assistance)	6,940	4,810	1,358	182	80
Agriculture and Fisheries	5,805	4,055	1,147	253	112
Foreign Affairs[c]	5,669	2,342	798	335	201
Presidency	3,747	1,101	251	77	101
Industry and Energy	2,971	1,808	597	184	71
Public Administration	2,487	1,818	362	196	70
Justice	1,750	1,560	327	217	29
TOTAL	287,969	200,002	21,113	6,069	1,748

[a] Includes 55,029 employees in the General Post Office (56 of them in the three top levels).
[b] Includes 27,629 employees in the Tax Administration Agency (1,172 of them in the three top levels).
[c] Excludes 107 ambassadors.

education, public works, and industry).[2] They still belong to their original corps and share the majority of features with their former colleagues in the central administration, but the situation is completely different for those new recruits who have not been transferred from the centre and who

[2] e.g. within group A corps, 45% of agronomists work for the regional administrations. For the generalist Civil State administrators the figure is 9%. It is planned to transfer all school teachers and public doctors to the regions within a few years. Public education and health assistance are already managed by the autonomous communities which have special local autonomy statutes (such as the Basque Country, Catalonia, Galicia, Andalusia, Navarre, Valencian Community, and Canary Islands), but the other ten are in the process of gaining new functions in these two very important areas. Table 2.2 shows the relative importance of these two groups of public employees both in the aforementioned seven autonomous communities and in the central state (those waiting for the next decentralization). They all belong to group A, but normally do not perform bureaucratic functions and, consequently, do not belong to the so-called top officials (level 26 in the case of high-school teachers). The Social Security Institute, Central Post Office, and Tax Administration Agency are the other three large clusters of public employees, but these agencies will remain substantially within the central administration.

TABLE 2.2. *Public Employment in Spain, 1997*

Employer	No. of employees
Central State	858,407
Ministries and autonomous agencies	*287,969*
Armed forces	*117,435*
Police	*122,569*
State schools	*133,914*
National Health Service	*133,186*
Other public agencies	*63,334*
Autonomous Communities	636,559
Departments and public agencies	*240,322*
Schools	*226,312*
Regional health services	*169,925*
Local Administration	425,470
Universities	82,568
Judiciary	33,346
TOTAL	2,036,350

started their careers in regional government. The bureaucratic élite in regional administrations is much less politically powerful. Nevertheless, the generalist corps of administrators tend to dominate top positions within it.

The higher Spanish civil service consists of officials organized in the senior corps.[3] The structure and size of the various corps are very different —some of them have few members, whilst others have more than 100,000 members (e.g. elementary school teachers). The corps that control the most important executive functions may be either generalist (for example, state civil administrators) or specialist (for example, financial and tax inspectors, state commercial experts and economists, or labour and social security inspectors). The specialist corps is normally departmental while the generalist corps are interdepartmental and trained in general public-sector management skills such as human resource management, organizational analysis, and budgeting. However, state civil administrators do not monopolize the top posts—only 20 per cent of such posts are filled by them. Rather they share these functions with other specialized and traditional corps, thus reinforcing fragmentation and lack of mobility. All these powerful corps were self-regulating in terms of recruitment (through spe-

[3] We consider only administrative civil servants; therefore, we have not included senior officials in the judiciary (judges, judicial secretaries, prosecuting attorneys), parliamentary advisers (*Letrados de las Cortes*), and other semi-public jobs such as notaries or real estate registrars.

cific merit examinations in each corps), duties, rights (including, to some extent, salary), and promotion.

The Socialist government's hostility towards the corps led it in 1984 to embark on a reorganization aimed at weakening their powers by reclassifying public employees according to their educational background. It produced five groups of employees according to the academic qualifications required for entry into each: group A for officials with a university degree (levels 20 to 30), group B for those with a technical school degree (levels 16 to 26); group C for those with a high school degree (levels 12 to 22); group D for those with a junior high school diploma (levels 9 to 18), and group E for those with an elementary school education only (levels 7 to 14).

The senior civil servants are in group A (for which a university degree is required). Nevertheless, not all officials in this group can be considered as 'top'. Top officials consist of the élite corps (which must be distinguished from the large number of other officials in group A occupying less important posts and enjoying lower social status) and those who occupy levels 28 to 30. This excludes senior civil servants without executive functions (e.g. university professors and school teachers, public works engineers, doctors, and other professions requiring a university degree). In practice officials in levels 28 to 30 tend to be members of the élite corps, whose members are normally appointed by the government to fill political posts.

Until 1984 posts were legally assigned, according to their character, to specialized corps. The 1984 reclassification arose from the desire to encourage the generalist corps (the state civil administrators), to promote interdepartmental mobility, and to weaken the extraordinary power of the élitist and departmentalized corps. However, the legal measure designed to open up the top posts to any senior civil servant has not altered the fragmentation of the Spanish bureaucracy. Corps currently operate only *de jure* as a vehicle of recruitment, since posts can be filled by any interested civil servant in group A. The 1984 reform did not succeed in reducing the power of the corps because the interest of financial inspectors in economic matters or government attorneys in legal advice, has tended to perpetuate the specialization and the concentration of corps in particular departments. Not even the ability of the government freely to appoint level 30 officials, therefore allowing it to disperse the corps more evenly across departments, could produce radical change. The corps still exert *de facto* powerful influence in the administration of the Spanish ministries. Thus, four of them alone (state civil administrators, diplomats, financial and tax inspectors, and state commercial experts and economists), which represent only 15 per cent of all civil servants in group A, excluding teachers and physicians, occupy more than 50 per cent of all level 30 posts and 45 per cent of the politically appointed directorates general.

It is important to remember that not all top officials in Spain are civil servants. The administrative career ends at the rank of assistant director general (level 30). The merit criterion is replaced by the political appointment in higher posts (although to designate level 30 posts the government can choose from among suitably qualified civil servants). Many of them are, however, bureaucrats (80 per cent of the directors general), and the 1997 Act on the functioning of the general state administration requires the status of civil servant for all officials but advisors in the ministerial *cabinets*.

We can, therefore, distinguish between three different circles of senior bureaucrats. A *political circle*, consisting of members of the core executive including the President of the Government and ministers as well as junior ministers (Secretarios de Estado); a *politico-administrative circle* of political bureaucrats including under-secretaries, general secretaries, and delegates of the government, directors general and subdelegates of the government, and members of the ministerial *gabinetes* and a *bureaucratic circle* of senior career civil servants including assistant directors general at level 30 and levels 28 and 29 in regional and central administration.

Sociological Characteristics of Senior Officials

The Spanish administrative élite is relatively young: 78 per cent of directors general, 77 per cent of level 30 civil servants, and 61 per cent of all group A officials are under 54. The recent history of Spain explains the youth of its political and administrative élite. This was accentuated during the Socialist period of government due to the retirement of civil servants linked to the Francoist regime (see Baena del Alcázar, 1993: 462). Therefore, a third of top officials are in their thirties, whilst only one-fifth are over 54. The effect of the departure of Francoist officials is more evident when we consider that those aged 54 or over account for only 35 per cent of all group A civil servants. The female quota is still quite low (approximately 15 per cent of top posts, when the total proportion of women in group A is 24 per cent and nearly 40 per cent among lower civil servants), but the gender balance is improving, so reproducing the general social changes amongst the youngest public managers.

Corps members also share a common background. Not only do they have the same kind of academic degree, having all passed identical examinations, but they also belong to a social class which, due to the long period required for preparation for entry into the higher civil service, is usually relatively wealthy. Family tradition is often decisive in the selection of the corps, and geographic origin is also significant. Unlike Italy, and also contrary to a commonly held belief, the predominant geographical origin of senior officials is not the poorest regions (Andalusia or Galicia) but Madrid and Castille-Leon. This results from a traditional feeling of loyalty to the central power in these regions, combined with fewer private job opportunities (precisely the opposite reasons explain the low number of senior civil servants from Catalonia and the Basque Country).

It is also important to note that this regional origin of bureaucrats corresponds with the large number of them working in Castille and Madrid. Top officials are strongly centralized in Madrid (more than a half of them work in central ministries), while historically few of them work in areas with a nationalist tradition. In Catalonia and the Basque Country there is less enthusiasm for the central state but also more opportunities for qualified and well-paid jobs in private firms. This also explains the higher social status of senior officials in the former regions and the lower prestige in the latter ones, where professional success is more closely linked to private employment. This reinforces precisely the problems of loyalty to the state and also demonstrates the tendency for civil servants to seek appointment in their own region, as well as the civil service's consent to such an irrational allocation. Moreover, the strong presence of senior bureaucrats in the Castillian provinces reveals their social power in this region with a weak civil society.

With regard to the university background of senior civil servants, a solid majority hold degrees in law (45 per cent), followed by economics (20 per cent) or technical diplomas (20 per cent). The low proportion of those who studied humanities (7 per cent) or politics or sociology (5 per cent) reflects the obstacles already mentioned to the development of generalist top officials with a capacity for interdepartmental mobility. Furthermore, the strength of the lawyers reflects and explains the predominantly legalistic administrative culture among the senior managers, a characteristic criticized by the government and the bureaucrats themselves (Serrano, 1993: 49). The Spanish university system, with its enormous and overcrowded centres, and the methods of recruitment to the élitist corps (through examinations for which an individual prepares over three or four years) prevent the emergence of dominant universities, such as Oxford or Cambridge, or the development of specific training administrative institutes where different corps can intermingle.[4]

The majority of senior civil servants come from wealthy families and

---

[4] Short periods of training, once the entrance examination is passed, take place in particular administrative schools but, once again, there is no intercorps common experience. Generalist administrators go to the Instituto Nacional de Administración Pública, tax and financial inspectors to the Instituto de Estudios Fiscales, diplomats to the Diplomatic School.

have chosen the corps because of family traditions. This produced minimal social mobility in the 1960s when, for a member of a non-wealthy economic and social class, it was easier to become a great entrepreneur than a senior civil servant. Nevertheless, top officials are also linked to business: during the 1970s, 20 per cent of big businessmen were bureaucrats. This percentage has declined because of the increase in the number of businessmen in Spain and the process of privatization (many former public firms were managed by civil servants although there was not any legal requirement for it), but there is still an important presence of them in banking, steel, or construction firms. These sectors maintain permanent contacts with the administration through subsidies and public contracts.

The Senior Civil Servant in the Organization

There exists no institutionalized system of recruitment. Each corps regulates competitive examinations (*oposición*) of outsiders, who prepare for the tests by themselves, although corps members cannot be a majority on the selection board. Once the examination has been passed, successful candidates go to the different administration schools (one for each corps) for a very short period of training. A true administrative career has never existed in Spain, except for a small increase in pay every three years of experience or promotion through appointment as manager, which has involved a traditional inflation of top posts (Baena del Alcázar, 1993: 470). The personal grades (1 to 30) introduced in 1984, and which partially coincide with the classification of posts (7 to 30), try to solve this problem. When the candidate passes the exam and arrives in the civil service, he or she acquires a personal grade, according to the post.

Careers start when newcomers opt for vacancies in their group and level (élite corps members start at level 26). The promotion to a new post, both by merit competition or by free appointment (which has become the routine for top posts) would be the career path.[5] Each grade can be consolidated in the personal record after two years in the post at the same level or at a higher level.

There are four main components of the payment system: basic salary and *trienios* represent from 30 to 50 per cent of total remuneration depend-

---

[5] The free designation of top levels (28 to 30) among civil servants (posts of assistant general director, provincial delegates, etc.) requires, however, the prior publication of the availability of the post and the possibility of any qualified senior official applying for the position. There is also the possibility (but it is not very common) of opting for a designation by open merit competition instead of the free politicized appointment by which patronage is practised.

ing on the administrative level and post held. *Trienio* is a fixed amount granted every three years of service. Guaranteed allowances form the second major component of the salary. These include allowances for rank (depending on the personal grade or on the level of the occupied post), for post held (depending on the job), and individual allowance (similar to the concept of performance-related payment). For all hierarchical levels, salary and rank allowance are set down in the Annual Budgetary Act, whilst posting allowance and individual allowance are determined by each ministry.

This rational system of career and payment has, however, been irrationally implemented. The particular post occupied has a greater impact on the level of pay than personal grade—allowances for post are so large that officials with lower personal grades can earn more than some of their grade superiors. Therefore competition (and inflation) for top posts has not disappeared. Since, as we have seen, merit is not the main criterion for appointment to these top posts, and since there is no right to promotion, bureaucrats who are not politically loyal can easily become disillusioned.

Traditionally, low wages were prevalent amongst the public employees, even the top ones, and this led to corruption as officials sought to top up their incomes. Many public employees also held jobs in the private sector or they resorted to semi-legal practices of seeking additional payments for the provision of public services: the so-called *tasas* which senior bureaucrats charged until 1963. Remuneration was composed by a basic wage that was multiplied by a coefficient according to the corps (ranging from 1.3 to 5.5). Furthermore, there existed small increments for experience, post, or full-time dedication. This system, combined with the small basic wage, provoked competition among the corps to gain the highest coefficient and increased the number of department heads. In consequence differences in pay and status grew wider. The corps coefficient disappeared in 1984 and members of the same corps can nowadays have big pay differences because of the range of available allowances. These allowances do not ultimately depend on objective calculations but on the decisions of politicians who have, therefore, a powerful instrument to attract personal and ideological loyalty. The career system has been distorted because officials do not look for promotion to higher levels but rather seek specific posts with a high allowance attached to them (some level 28 posts can earn more than level 30 posts with a low allowance).

The overall pay of top officials is more or less equivalent to between 60 and 70 per cent of the pay of a manager with comparable responsibility in the private sector, although their social security coverage through the mutual benefit society MUFACE is regarded as generous. Furthermore, the 1983 Act on the Incompatibility of Offices among Senior Officials has limited traditional *pantouflage* (the practice of using one's job as a senior official as a springboard for a lucrative job in the private sector) and has engendered full-time commitment to the public job. This important reform prevents officials from holding multiple posts—either two wages from the state budget or one within the administration and one in private firms deemed to affect the impartiality of the official. These two inconveniences and the extremely rapid promotion available to senior civil servants (many of them start at level 26 and consequently it is possible to reach the highest levels between the ages of 30 and 40) explains why large numbers of bureaucrats decide to leave the civil service when they receive a job offer in the private sector.

The marked loss of financial and social status brought about by these changes not only provokes this exodus of high-ranking public servants to the private sector looking for higher remuneration, but also impedes the recruitment of candidates from the private sector into senior administrative posts. Political conviction rather than the attractions of a well-paid career account for the presence in the senior civil service of some officials with a background in the private sector. Some work in the public sector as external experts, advisers in the private *cabinets*, or managers in public firms. However, the relatively poor pay and recent legislation bringing the whole of the politico-administrative élite within the civil service strengthen even further the monopoly of bureaucrats in public management.

While senior officials enjoy lower incomes, their position within state organizations has been maintained. Senior civil servants exert near total control of under-secretary posts which are found in every ministry. In addition, they still monopolize systems of recruitment in their respective corps, and regulate the conditions governing access to them. This is a major reason for the persistence of a highly legalist culture in Spanish administration—the large number of officials with a background in law leads to the perpetuation of the requirement of legal expertise as the main component in the mix of subjects applicants are required to study in order to prepare for entrance examinations.

However, the main consequences of the corps system are that it gives a dominant role to the élite corps and that it engenders fragmentation within the Spanish administrative system. Recruitment and promotion patterns remain largely self-regulated by the corps which tend to promote the particularistic interests of their members. The consequence of this dominance by the corps is a collection of sectoral executives limited to their small jurisdictions and which are largely uncoordinated from a political centre. The specialization of the corps and the fragmentation of departments are illustrated in the Table 2.3. Among level 30 officials the percentage from departmental corps ranges from just over one half (Infrastructure Ministry)

TABLE 2.3. *Specialization of Corps in Ministries*

	Level 30 officials		Directors general	
	N	% from specialized corps	N	% from specialized corps
Foreign Affairs	191	89	21	100
Economy and Finance	378	79	47	81
Public Administration	78	65	12	50
Labour and Social Security	92	62	15	73
Infrastructures	164	52	17	47

to nine-tenths (Ministry of Foreign Affairs). Around one half of directors general are members of specialist corps in the Ministries of Infrastructure and Public Administration while in Economy and Finance, Labour and Social Security, and Foreign Affairs it is over three-quarters.

Until 1984 ministries formally limited top posts and senior managerial positions to members of specialized corps. Since 1984 these positions remain occupied largely by members of specialized corps, as some corps have managed to monopolize managerial functions in different ministries. The dominance of the specialized corps varies from one ministry to another (Table 2.3)—in Foreign Affairs and Economy and Finance there is a near monopoly, but the hold is weaker in Labour and Social Security and Infrastructures. It is also paradoxical that the fragmentation that results from the dominance of specialized corps coexists with a very unitary political core executive in which the Prime Minister, encouraged by constitutional and political factors, has an extremely powerful influence. Nevertheless, recent years have seen some shift away from the dominance of the corps. Party patronage has increased in importance in distributing top posts, as favours, among party sympathizers, the 1984 legal reform formally ended the reservation of posts, and *gabinetes* (technical and political advising offices similar to the French *cabinets*) were created in all ministries and for junior ministers during the 1980s.

Until 1984, the preparatory work for any decision was undertaken solely by members of the particular corps involved. The creation of the *gabinetes* meant that for the first time political decisions were adopted by accountable ministers who were supported by advisers in whom the minister had trust. However, *gabinetes* are not able to control all important issues or follow through by shaping the implementation of their own decisions. Moreover, there are many routine aspects of ministerial work which are entirely decided within the directorates general and without political intervention. Furthermore, many of the members of *gabinetes* are themselves senior civil servants who, however close to the particular incumbent of the ministerial post, remain part of their respective corps.

The existing *esprit de corps* does not mean an equally strong solidarity between different corps. On the contrary, there are interdepartmental tensions and different specialized corps contend for the most important posts *within* each department. There are also ministries which are monopolized by just one corps (e.g. diplomats in Foreign Affairs, labour inspectors in Labour) or ruled by non-élitist corps (Interior). In these cases, rivalries are between these specialists and the generalist state civil administrators who, for example, traditionally control the technical general secretariats—the general secretariats are primarily advisory staffs, and their influence has diminished with the development of the *gabinetes*. When the different corps intersect, something that rarely happens in spite of the 1984 measures to promote mobility, interdepartmental and consequent inter-corps tensions may come to the surface. For example, within the Secretariat of State for European Union, the members come from the different ministries and maintain personal ties with their original departments rather than with the coordinating organ in which they work (Dastis, 1995: 331). In this case, when any issue becomes politicized, each ministry decides how to negotiate within its own domain. The Permanent Representation in Brussels is composed of permanent or temporary officials who come from different ministries and has many problems of jealousy surrounding their respective tasks, strategies, and remuneration.

Although there are no legal differences in status between the departments, the ones with the highest number of top civil servants are Economy–Finance and Foreign Affairs, which both contain a large number of posts requiring specific educational qualifications. Moreover, the large number of top posts in these two ministries also means that they attract members of élite corps.[6] Indirectly, the formal legal equality of status among ministries is again circumvented by the trend among each corps to maintain its own importance. However, the creation in 1986 of the Ministry of Public Administration, where the generalist administrators dominate (Table 2.3), has at least caused the incorporation of this politically encouraged corps into the élite of traditional ones. This new ministry monopolizes the management of human resources and supervises the structure and modernization of central administration thus exercises authority across the whole range of government activities. This in turn gives generalist administrators

---

6 Diplomats, financial inspectors, and state commercial experts are, additionally, the only corps which maintain, as an exception to the general rule, a legal reservation for some posts (coinciding with those with a high posting allowance in the pay).

in the Ministry of Public Administration relatively higher status among Spanish bureaucrats.

Another interesting feature of Spanish public administration is the conflict between élitist corps and the lower levels of the civil service. Traditionally, the control by bureaucrats of the administrative organization has largely explained why there are so many senior civil servants in comparison to medium and poorly qualified ones (which has absolutely restricted the capacity for promotion). This antagonism between senior and lower levels has been strengthened by the emergence of the unions, supported by the Socialist government in its anti-corporatist strategy, and their growing importance in matters such as pay and working conditions (including those of top officials). Unionization is not very important in the civil service (nor among the Spanish private workers) but at least low-grade public employees are more heavily unionized. Nevertheless, the generally low rate of unionization limits their capacity to negotiate in questions such as working conditions or the pay of top officials. Above all, we must bear in mind that the senior bureaucrats themselves negotiate in the name of the state with lower civil servants, who have very different problems.

Spanish Civil Servants and Politics

The Socialist civil service reform combined an attempt at rationalization (the merger of corps and the unification, in a department of human resources, of policy for reducing the particularism of the corps) with political objectives connected with democratic transition, such as dealing with the inheritance of a Francoist administration with many conservative, or even authoritarian, top officials (Baena del Alcázar 1993: 467). The lack of a tradition of collaboration between political and civil service élites (because of the relatively short experience of democratic government) also provoked lack of trust, which reinforced an anti-bureaucratic strategy. However, the 1984 reform failed, if we consider that only some corps were merged (although they were particularly important among small élitist ones in the autonomous agencies), or that the new Ministry of Public Administration lacked the power for such an operation. It was not possible to transform the status quo by legal measures alone in the face of such important constraints. Nevertheless, the enduring political will of the Socialist government to reduce bureaucratic power produced some results.

In spite of being in theory 'exceptional', in practice the massive use of the method of free designation among civil servants for posts 28 to 30 (they were rarely opened to public competition except for the particular cases of Education and Health where merit criterion were usually observed), and the political appointments of bureaucrats such as directors general and secretaries general, led to a gradual replacement of senior officials by loyal ones.[7] This also involves risks of patronage, lack of independence, and an inherent instability in public management as a change of party in government, or a change of minister within the same government, means a general replacement of the all top-level officials. This would mean that the abuses of corporatism could be replaced by other equally harmful political abuses (Baena del Alcázar, 1993: 469).

The advent of the PP to office in 1996 has not meant a substantial change in civil service policy, and particularly with regard to senior managers. The issue, however, has become sensitive and politicized because of an acute controversy between PSOE and PP about the number of top officials. The Conservatives had promised to reduce the number of top officials in order to save money, in view of the EMU convergence criteria, and to diminish politicization and patronage. However, by 1998, after two years of right-wing government, levels 28 to 30 had increased in size as top officials were replaced and as the personal grades of those appointed to political posts were maintained to allow them to return to their administrative posts. This general change not only reveals that this electoral promise was imprudent but also demonstrates the continuity of patronage methods by the PP. By April 1997 (one year after the PP electoral victory) only 16 per cent of the directors general appointed by the Socialists had not been changed and more than 3,000 civil servants had been dismissed.

That is to say, the conservative electoral victory has not brought about a dismantling of the Spanish senior civil service, since the government of José María Aznar used the traditional methods of politicized appointments to replace top posts. In any event, a renewed trust in the senior civil service, politically closer to the Popular Party, was illustrated by the 1997 Act of Organization and Functioning of the General State Administration.[8] This limited candidates to the spoils system of directors general and under-secretaries to career civil servants. The difficult balance between politicians and bureaucrats, spoils system and technocracy, was struck by the functionarization of all politico-administrative posts (except for the 'political circle' discussed above, including ministers and junior ministers) and the consolidation of the private *cabinets* where the politicians can freely

[7] However, this pattern is not followed in the higher education sector since autonomous universities recruit tenured professors (with civil service status) according to co-option practices that often tend to corruption and nepotism.

[8] This underlines the fact that the Socialist reforms were not radical although, in 1998, the conservative minister of Public Administration did agree with the unions a bill that would completely replace the fragmented legislation on Civil State Officials (in 1964, 1984, and 1997 Acts). However, these plans are currently blocked due to opposition of regional governments, opposition parties, and many senior civil servants themselves.

designate advisers, civil servants or not, according to criteria of confidence and trust.

This recent reform, however, will not produce substantial changes if we bear in mind that already in 1996 80 per cent of the incumbents of these politico-administrative élite posts were civil servants, despite the absence of any legal requirement to appoint civil servants to these posts. This significant degree of professionalization with both parties can actually hide a 'closed circuit spoils system' (Quermonne, quoted in Jiménez Asensio, 1996) since neither the PSOE nor the PP have difficulties in filling these posts from highly qualified civil servants who are politically close to them when they are in office. As a result of this, Spain will continue to combine a political process of promotion to all senior posts with a high degree of functionarization among the politico-administrative élite in the central state. This generates a very similar profile between politicians and top officials in levels 28 to 30 (Serrano, 1993: 14). It also contrasts with the Autonomous Communities where a very politicized administrative system leads to a low percentage of career civil servants appointed as top officials (Matas, 1996).

Senior civil servants are also present in the two big political parties although not in small ones: we have to note their small number and importance in the case of regionalist and nationalist parties or the former communist United Left. Old boys' networks in Spain are not very important within the administration, due to the tendency to departmentalism and the specialization of corps. Corps structures also play a role outside the administration, above all in Parliament where civil servants interact with others and facilitate communication among members of Parliament belonging to different parties but to the same corps. In the core executive, around 50 per cent of ministers (and a higher proportion of junior ministers) are senior civil servants. However, this percentage is lower than that during the Francoist technocratic dictatorship.

Conclusions

The main structural problems of the Spanish civil service are caused by the control of the bureaucrats over the organization (Baena del Alcázar, 1993: 461). Officials belonging to group A (university studies) monopolize the top posts (28 to 30), since it is impossible for other civil servants to be promoted beyond level 26; but the senior posts are even more limited, to those belonging to the élitist corps.

Élite corps were indeed weakened following democratization, by legislation limiting the number of offices they could hold, abolishing the monopoly of posts, free designation methods, and instability. Yet they have managed to maintain their power and remain a key factor in understanding Spanish bureaucracy. Furthermore, there is no real tradition of generalists in the Spanish bureaucracy—the senior general corps was created only in 1964. Every ministry has created and maintained its own specialist corps, often with very similar functions to those carried out by other corps belonging to different ministries. The corps seek autonomy from the civil service authorities, formally the Ministry of Public Administration, and compete among themselves for privileges. The resulting factionalism and the tacit exclusive reservation of public positions and functions for these corps diminish their relations with public officials in other corps, and hence their *esprit de corps* is reinforced at the expense of reducing the cohesion and political coordination of Spanish administration.

Demands for transformation of the civil service have been a constant during the last two centuries but all the different governments have been incapable of engaging in real change. Incremental and reactive reforms have been the usual responses, but at least the political will of the democratic governments has ultimately avoided the risk of the Spanish administration becoming a mere federation of bureaucratic groups (Baena del Alcázar, 1993: 465). Senior bureaucrats are powerful in the political system as they occupy senior positions in political parties, the core executive, and Parliament; and they have power within the economic system. The incremental Socialist strategy of weakening the corps—following the launch in 1995 of the idea of creating an open structure of senior officials where both high civil servants and private executives could access and be freely removed—has been abandoned by the PP which places greater trust in corps. The conservatives will continue to make political appointments from within the corps, and the Spanish administration is characterized by the persisting primacy of corporatism.

REFERENCES

Álvarez, J. (1980). *El origen geográfico de los funcionarios españoles* (Madrid: Instituto Nacional de Administración Pública).

Baena del Alcázar, M. (1984). *Estructura de la Función Pública y Burocracia en España* (Oñati: Instituto Vasco de Administración Pública).

—— (1993). *Curso de Ciencia de la Administración*, i, 3rd edn. (Madrid: Tecnos).

—— and N. Pizarro (1983). 'The Structure of the Spanish Power Elite 1939–1975', *EUI Working Paper*, 55 (Florence: European University Institute).

Bañón-Martínez, R. (1994). 'La modernizzazione dell'amministrazione pubblica spagnola: Bilanci e prospettive', in Y. Mény and V. Wright (eds.), *La riforma amministrativa in Europa* (Bologna: Il Mulino).

Beltrán, M. (1977). *La élite burocrática española* (Barcelona: Fundación Juan March/Ariel).

—— (1985). *Los funcionarios ante la reforma de la administración* (Madrid: CIS-Siglo XXI).

—— (1988). 'Spain', in D. C. Rowat (ed.), *Public Administration in Developed Democracies: A Comparative Study* (New York: Marcel Dekker).

—— (1990), 'La administración pública y los funcionarios', in S. Giner (ed.), *España: Sociedad y política* (Madrid: Espasa-Calpe).

Botella, J. (1994). 'The Spanish Ministerial Elite in a Period of Changes (1976–1993)', paper presented at the ECPR Joint Sessions of Workshops, Madrid.

Canales Aliende, J. M. (1996). 'El directivo público', *Actualidad administrativa*, 7: 151–61.

Centro de Investigaciones Sociológicas (1993). 'Imagen social de los funcionarios', *Estudio 2054* (Madrid: Centro de Investigaciones Sociológicas).

Constantino, J., and E. Carrillo (1994). 'Dalla gestione del personale al management del capitale umano', in Y. Mény and V. Wright (eds.), *La riforma amministrativa in Europa* (Bologna: Il Mulino).

Dastis, A. (1995). 'La Administración española ante la Unión Europea', *Revista de estudios políticos*, 90: 323–49.

Heywood, P. (1995). *The Government and Politics of Spain* (London: Macmillan).

INAP (1996). *La misión del INAP: Modernización y cambio en las Administraciones Públicas* (Madrid: Instituto Nacional de Administración Pública).

Jiménez Asensio, R. (1996). *Altos cargos y directivos públicos* (Oñati: Instituto Vasco de Administración Pública).

MAP (1990*a*). *Estudio Delphi sobre la modernización de los procedimientos de actuación de la Administración Pública* (Madrid: Ministerio para las Administraciones Públicas).

—— (1990*b*). *Reflexiones para la modernización de la Administración del Estado* (Madrid: Ministerio para las Administraciones Públicas).

—— (1994) 'Informes de la Dirección General de Organización, Puestos de Trabajo e Informática', unpublished reports.

—— (1997*a*). 'Base de Datos del Registro Central de Personal', unpublished report.

—— (1997*b*). *Guía de la Administración del Estado. Organigramas* (Madrid: Ministerio para las Administraciones Públicas).

Matas, J. (1996). *Las élites políticas de la administración* (Barcelona and Madrid: Cedecs Editorial, Rupérez and C. Moro, and Ediciones Encuentro).

Mendoza, X. (1990). 'Técnicas gerenciales y modernización de la Administración pública en España', *Documentación administrativa*, 223: 261–90.

Mény, Y., and V. Wright (eds.) (1994). *La riforma amministrativa in Europa* (Bologna: Il Mulino).

Núñez Pérez, M. (1992). 'Remodelación de la administración del Estado', *El decenio González*, ed. Javier Ruperez and Carlos Moro (Madrid: Encuentro).

Ortega, L. (1992). 'La reforma de la alta burocracia en España', *Sistema*, 107: 5–20.

Parrado, S. (1997). *Las élites de la Administración Central: Estudio general y pautas de reclutamiento* (Seville: Instituto Andaluz de Administración Pública).

Pernaute Monreal, Maria Angeles (1978). *El poder de los cuerpos de burócratas en la organización administrativa española* (Madrid: Instituto Nacional de Administración Pública).

Serrano, T. (1993). 'Características básicas de los directivos de la Administración del Estado en España', *Papeles de Trabajo*, 293 (Madrid: Instituto Universitario Ortega y Gasset).

Subirats, J. (1990). 'Modernizing the Spanish Administration or Reform in Disguise'. *ICPS Working Paper*, 20 (Barcelona: Institut de Ciències Polítiques i Socials).

—— (1994). 'La modernizzazione amministrativa in Spagna: Flessibilità organizzativa e cambiamenti nelle procedure di attuazione della pubblica amministrazione: azioni intraprese', in Y. Mény and V. Wright (eds.), *La riforma amministrativa in Europa* (Bologna: Il Mulino).

Ziller, J. (ed.) (1990). 'Les Fonctions publiques de l'Europe des douze: Annexes', special issue of *Revue française d'administration publique*, 55.

3

Italy's Senior Civil Service: An Ossified World

SABINO CASSESE

Even after more than a century of political unification, Italy is still characterized by a lack of economic unification. The political union of the country was achieved in 1861, and was the result of the merging of various pre-existing states (among them the Kingdom of Sardinia, the Grand Duchy of Tuscany, the Papal State, and the Kingdom of the Two Sicilies) which had enjoyed different degrees of economic and social development. The demarcation line fell mainly between the regions of the North (Piedmont, Lombardy, Venetia, Liguria, Emilia-Romagna), economically developed regions with a long-standing tradition of civic culture, and those of the South and the Islands (Abruzzi and Molise, Campania, Puglia, Basilicata, Calabria, Sardinia, and Sicily), economically underdeveloped regions which were socially fragmented and, generally, without established civic traditions, with a Centre (Tuscany, Umbria, Marche, and Latium) placed half-way between development and underdevelopment.

Instead of bringing about a reduction in these differences, unification accentuated the economic backwardness of the South, which witnessed the collapse of its weak industrial base in the face of fiercer competition from the North. The South was also confronted with a fiscal regime and an investment policy which drained its resources while favouring the North, not to mention customs tariffs which took a heavy toll on southern agriculture.

By the middle of the twentieth century this situation had not improved. As the country's economy shifted from a predominantly agricultural to a mainly industrial base, emigration to other countries was steadily replaced by migratory movement within the country. The Italian economic miracle

The author wishes to thank Francesco Battini (Corte dei Conti and Presidenza del Consiglio dei Ministri), Raffaele Iuele and Antonella Trifella (Presidenza del Consiglio dei Ministri) and Stefano Tomasini (Ragioneria generale dello Stato, Ministero del Tesoro) for the material provided and for their suggestions, as well as Stefano Battini and Giacinto della Cananea for their comments on an earlier draft of this chapter.

saw a massive flow of unskilled workers from the South into the rich indus-trial heartlands of the North. Meanwhile, a different pattern developed in the recruitment to the public-sector workforce. Unification had taken place under Piedmont and the administration had remained in the hands of the Piedmontese. However, the beginning of the twentieth century saw a pro-gressive southernization of jobs in the public sector.

Three figures provide an overview of this phenomenon—with the proviso that they are not homogeneous and, therefore, chronological category series cannot be deduced from them. In the 1950s, 78 per cent of high-ranking civil servants came from the South; in the 1960s, the number of southerners within the senior ranks of the civil service rose to 84 per cent; in 1995, 73 per cent of state civil servants (1.2 million employees in total) came from the Centre and South. In order to put these figures in context, they should be compared with the distribution of the population of 55 per cent in the North and 45 per cent in the Centre and South.

Consequently, therefore, a sizeable migration of personnel from South to North has taken place. Since 35 per cent of civil servants work in the North and 65 per cent in the Centre–South, 27 per cent of civil servants in the North come from the Centre–South, which, in this way, contributes to the administration and the provision of public services in the North.

In general terms, we may see an asymmetry within the civil service with three-quarters of public employees coming from just over half of the population. When we consider the top echelons of the state administra-tion, the disequilibrium grows even stronger. In 1995 the Centre–South provided 93 per cent of directors general, while the North provided only 7 per cent. This disequilibrium at the top has increased in the last few years: in 1962, the directors general coming from the Centre–South, comprised 89 per cent of the total, in contrast to only 11 per cent from the North. It is also interesting to compare these figures with a relatively homogeneous category in terms of size and income, like that of magistrates: in 1995, the South contributed 75 per cent of judges, the North 25 per cent of the total.

This leads to state employees in general, and senior officials in particular, not being representative in territorial terms. While people from the North have been involved in the conquest of the economy and the market, those from the South have dedicated themselves to the conquest of the state. This has produced the paradox of a senior civil service that administers the nation, but which is not national. Italian senior officials are not at the centre of the country but rather at the centre of its main disequilibrium

This chapter aims to illustrate this paradox. It is divided into four parts. In the first part, I shall present the subject to be analysed (the senior civil service) and its organizational context. In the second, I will define a profile of senior officials, then illustrate the characteristics of the category in which they are found. In the third, I shall analyse the two (failed) attempts of reform. Finally, I shall offer some concluding remarks.

The Senior Civil Service in Italy

In order to identify the senior civil service, we need to select the categories of personnel which have a dominant role within key state organizations. This process is simplified in Italy by legal provisions which, since 1972, give recognition to the top echelon of the administration with the qualification of director general: at present there are approximately 1,300 directors general. From this category we need to exclude about 150 non-state directors (from non-economic bodies and research institutes), 250 diplomats, about 200 prefects, over 260 directors of armed forces and the police, and about twenty directors of autonomous companies. In fact, the first of these groups are not state directors, the second and the third are positioned mainly in the periphery; the others have specific sectoral competences. This leaves about 400 administrative directors who staff the highest places in the state administration, mainly those of directors general in the ministries.

Considering that central ministries now number nineteen, and the Prime Minister's Office (which has a large administrative structure, including some departments which correspond to ministries under ministers without portfolio), there is an average of twenty key positions per ministry, a number which corresponds to that needed to control the administrative apparatus.

These directors general are positioned at the top of the administration. They are directly under the minister and the minister's private office or *cabinet*. The minister is politically responsible to Parliament, issues guidelines, and controls the administration, taking the most important decisions in the ministry. The private office supports the minister and, in fact, constitutes the interface between the minister and the top echelon of the administration (the directors general). However, directors general are career officials and, as such, hold permanent posts, while ministers and their private offices change with the change of government. It can be said, therefore, that the 400 people identified constitute the most important level of the permanent administration of the state.

In order to take a 'snapshot' of directors general, we shall now examine six elements: their place of work; age and length of stay in office; gender; professional qualifications; origin (internal or external); and mobility. As far as the place of work is concerned, 65 per cent of directors general are located in the region of Lazio and, therefore, in Rome. The concentration in the capital is the natural consequence of the fact that directors general in the ministries constitute the highest rank of the central state machinery. The average age of directors general is high: 71 per cent are over 56. The situation has worsened over the last few years: in 1961 only 55 per cent of directors general were over 56: in 1979 the percentage had increased only slightly to 57 per cent. Age explains a further phenomenon: the fact that directors general stay in office for an average of only ten years. In fact, given their relatively high age, they reach their retirement after only a few years in office.

A further characteristic of the group under analysis is the very low representation of women: they make up only 5 per cent of directors general, compared with 20 per cent of directors, the category immediately below. Qualifications are almost invariably of university level: 95 per cent hold a university degree. Data relative to the distribution of degrees per subject area are not available. Taking as a sample the 65 directors working within the Prime Minister's Office (16 per cent of the total) we find 53 per cent holding law degrees (and this figure climbs to 66 per cent if we include those with degrees in political science, a discipline that in Italy has a large law component). These figures may be compared with that of only 3 per cent for engineering degrees. A further element of comparison is the evolution of the dominance of law backgrounds in the whole of the civil service: in 1954, the figure amounted to 36 per cent of the total, in 1961 it was up to 40 per cent. The predominance of those with law degrees is even more marked in control bodies: access to the Corte dei Conti, in particular, has long been reserved to law graduates.

As for their origin, directors general promoted from the lower grades of the administration comprise 83 per cent of the total. Horizontal mobility is almost non-existent. There are very few cases of directors general who, on reaching retirement, are appointed as chairmen of public or private companies. These are limited, on the whole, to directors from the Defence Ministry or from the diplomatic service. The French phenomenon of *pantouflage* is unknown in the Italian administration.

The presence of directors general in politics is also extremely limited. In post-1945 legislatures, the presence of public employees in Parliament has been between 3 and 5 per cent. After the 1996 election, 6 per cent of MPs had been public service directors (from the state civil service or other public bodies), a low figure compared with the 10 per cent for teachers, 10 per cent for university professors, and 11 per cent for lawyers in Parliament.

The elements presented above suggest a senior civil service strongly anchored in public administration, regulated by a system of promotion linked to the length of office. It is, therefore, important to analyse the category immediately below, that of the directors, from which the directors general are recruited. In this category there are approximately 4,200 people.

A recent survey, based on a sample of 82 directors, showed that 90 per cent never change the geographical location of their workplace; 48 per cent are over 55 years old and 44 per cent are between 41 and 55; 46 per cent have been in office for over thirty years and 45 per cent between sixteen and thirty years; 88 per cent entered the civil service before the age of 30 and 46 per cent started in the ministry where they still were at the time of the survey, indicating an internal and closed job market. The survey did find evidence of some internal mobility, with 62 per cent of respondents having changed administration at least once. On the other hand, 68 per cent never changed their rank, and 44 per cent never even changed their type of activity and tasks.

The emerging picture from this brief overview of the senior civil service is that of an ossified structure, where access is restricted through internal promotions and progress on the hierarchical ladder is conditioned by age, length of service, and, maybe in part, by merit. The senior civil service in Italy is, therefore, aged, with little professional or geographical mobility, with a marked underrepresentation of women and a high percentage of law graduates. Moreover, the profile of the level immediately below that of directors general (which for the reasons outlined above can be seen as the recruiting ground for senior civil servants) reflects the same patterns and characteristics.

Two different kinds of pressure have come to bear on this ossified world. The first is a negative pressure exercised through political patronage on the senior civil service. The second is a positive pressure for stronger autonomy and better selection procedures. Italian bureaucracy has successfully managed to fend off both kinds of pressure.

In the post-1945 period, the Italian administrative-political system has been dominated by the influence of political parties. One indication of this control is that the weakness and short duration of governments (an average of nine months) have always been determined by the control of parties' secretariats over the governments.

Political parties in control of governments could have also used the legal means at their disposal to take hold of the bureaucracy. In fact, directors general are appointed by the Council of Ministers and, until 1993, the Council was not limited in its choice. Parties in government were able to select and appoint some of their members or sympathizers, at least to gain control of key posts. If they did not do this, or were not able to do this, it is thanks to the resistance of the ossified world of the senior civil service.

There has been equal resistance to the second pressure, this time positive, to reform the senior civil service in response to the economic and social development of the country. This attempt at reform has developed over a period of more than thirty years, and it deserves closer scrutiny. We may identify two phases, one starting at the beginning of 1972 (Andreotti government) and the other in 1993 (Amato government and Ciampi government). Both reforms were characterized by a series of common elements, including: the passing of the government's legislative decrees (delegated legislation) for the reform of the higher reaches of the national bureaucracy; the devolution of some powers to the senior civil service; the imposition, in exchange, of a new mechanism for promotion based on merit (increasing fast-streaming and vertical mobility) and of interdepartmental mobility, through the creation of a common framework for the higher civil service (horizontal mobility). In both phases of reform amendments to the original projects resulted in a considerable watering down of their ambitions, and the limited implementation of the reforms to those elements considered favourable to the senior civil service.

The first attempt goes back to the decree of the President of the Republic of 30 June 1972, no. 748. The decree had been adopted after two years of debate and controversy. It was considered as a partial 'compensation' for the senior civil service after the transfer of some administrative functions from the state to the regions in 1970. The reform envisaged the division of the senior civil service into five levels: from the lowest to the highest ranks, these were defined as director, higher director, director general (the latter category subdivided into three categories of directors general c, b, and a). The 1972 decree assigned to the senior civil service, and in particular to the directors general, autonomous powers of supervision and coordination, decision-making, and control. These duties had to be fulfilled within the guidelines set by the minister, based on lists of acts to be presented by the senior civil servants to the minister. The minister could then overrule, amend, or reform the acts of directors general.

In exchange for the new tasks, the senior civil service was asked to become more mobile, vertically and horizontally. Vertical mobility was to be guaranteed through entry competitions and courses, common to all the ministries. These selection processes for entry into the senior civil service were to be overseen not by the ministries but by the High School for Public Administration, linked to the Prime Minister's Office. A first competition would have opened access to specific training programmes, with a further final competition to establish the eligible candidates. The selection was open to all employees of managerial rank.

Horizontal mobility was introduced by the law of 29 July 1975, no. 382, which provided for a common definition of the role of higher civil servants irrespective of their department, with the following four exceptions: the Ministry of the Treasury, the Home Affairs Ministry, the Ministry for Foreign Affairs, and the Ministry of Defence. In this way, even with the four exceptions listed, the management of the career of senior civil servants was not under the control of individual ministries and the door to horizontal mobility between ministries was opened. Lastly, the law provided for the appointment of outside directors general on two-year or permanent contracts.

All these reforms were modified during their implementation, were made ineffective, and undermined. Too many people were admitted to the selection for the higher civil service: 8,000 people for an administration which counted at the time twenty-two ministries and two million employees. Senior civil servants never made use of the autonomous powers assigned to them. On the one hand, senior officials preferred not to take responsibility for autonomous acts to be submitted to the minister. On the other hand, laws continued to provide for a majority of decisions to be taken through ministerial decrees. In addition, the autonomous powers of top officials, linked to the value of the decision (for example: contracts could be signed only up to a certain total sum), were quickly eroded by the double-digit inflation of those years. Very few directives were ever passed, they had vague aims, the lists of acts to be communicated to the minister were never prepared, and in consequence, ministers did not have to overrule, amend, or reform any proposals from the directors general. Moreover, private offices of ministers continued to overstep their duties and/or invade the sphere of competence of the civil service.

A similar failure characterized the new selection procedures. It was not until 1978 (six years after the redefinition of the career of senior civil servants) that some attempts were made to bring about the creation of the High School for Public Administration, but the envisaged competitive entry and training periods were quickly replaced by short non-competitive training courses under the control of individual ministries. Competitive selection based on merit was rejected, and the old method of promotion linked to length of service was continued. Moreover, the provisions for external recruitment were never implemented. The selection of outside directors general for two-year periods was never carried out, while the appointment of outside candidates to permanent positions numbered less than a dozen cases in the first ten years of the implementation of the law. Lastly, the provisions for the definition of a common framework for the role of the senior civil servants, though never formally abrogated, was never implemented: a curious fact for an administration with a strong legalistic culture.

The second attempt at reform, initiated with a legislative decree of 3 February 1993, no. 29 (modified three times in the course of the same year) has made advances with respect to the definition of powers of senior officials. The decree envisages that the government should set the objectives and the programmes and verify the results and effectiveness of the action of the administration with reference to the general guidelines. Senior officials have responsibility for the technical, financial, and administrative implementation of all guidelines, including all decisions which involve contact between the administration and the outside world. Senior officials have autonomous powers over resources, personnel, and control. They are responsible for policy implementation and its results. It follows that, on the basis of the 1993 reform, senior officials have control over expenditure, the management of personnel, and the control of employees. The minister can take specific decisions only when there is a clear need or urgency and, in any case, in agreement with the Prime Minister.

In exchange for this decisive shift of powers in favour of the senior civil service, the law envisages two other fundamental changes: on the one hand, a strong reduction of the number of top officials by 10 per cent and, on the other, the introduction of the competitive training courses and competition. Such training should be common for all departments, it should last two years and it should not be restricted only to those already employed in the civil service (as foreseen in 1972) but to all those under 35 years of age with a university degree. The training course would be open to all those passing an initial competition; there would then be an intermediate examination followed by a six-month internship in the public or private administration, leading to a final competition.

This second reform, too, has not been implemented (although it is still too early to draw more definite conclusions). The number of senior officials has not decreased. Their new powers have not been made use of, and directors general have preferred not to take full responsibility for the management of their departments, especially as a result of the increase in the *ex-ante* control through the Corte dei Conti, a protection which many directors general would want reinstated. And, in this context, their fears can be linked with the growing dynamism of magistrates: embezzlement charges in Italy amounted to approximately 450 a year until 1989 and have climbed to more than 1,000 a year since 1991; extortion charges amounted to 100 a year until 1989 and up to 500 since 1992; corruption charges, which were less than 100 a year until 1991, have remained over 400 since then; and charges for abuse of authority have numbered between 6,000 and 10,000 since 1992. Faced with such an aggressive stance on the part of magistrates, senior officials have retreated into a defensive position, avoiding the assumption of new powers and responsibility. As far as open competition is concerned, by late 1997 only one had been initiated.

Fernand Braudel, in his *La Mediterranée et le monde mediterranéan à l'époque de Philippe II* (Paris: Colin, 1949), refers to the *insigne faiblesse de l'Italie*, which he identifies in the wealth and density of cities. The negative side of this lies in the absence of a state, so that Italy is characterized by an administration without a centre. The French high civil service presents an élitist model of administration: the North American a representative model; Italy corresponds to another model, defined by the following elements:

1. The senior civil service is not a homogeneous group, given the absence of a common training on entry, a common culture, or the feeling of an *esprit de corps*, but it is united by geographical origin (and, in part, by its social origins in the middle class).

2. The nature of the senior civil service reflects the division of the country into North and South, with only part of the country represented among senior officials, in spite of their responsibility for the administration of all of the national territory.

3. The senior civil service, given its origins in the *Mezzogiorno* (the south of Italy), mirrors the characteristics of Southern Italy which can be summed up as follows: (i) coming from regions characterized by unemployment, job security takes precedence over efficiency and service; (ii) coming from relatively non-industrialized areas (or where industry has not managed to establish firm roots in society and the economy), legalistic and formalistic attitudes tend to dominate, without reference to the objectives of public administration; the mentality is far from managerialist; there is a rejection of competition.

4. The senior civil service is not integrated into the political class or into the economic management structures of the country, due both to its different origins, and to the lack of osmosis between civil service and private firms and between administrative management and political control.

5. The senior civil service pays a price for this isolation, refusing to take on an autonomous policy-making role and preferring the bureaucratic supervision of secondary administrative management.

6. But the senior civil service has been able to survive the political turbulence produced by government instability.

It remains for us to wonder why reforms have failed and, furthermore, why the southernization of the civil service is on the increase. The answer lies not so much in the higher civil service as in the echelons below it: it is these groups which oppose any reform attempt, fearing a reduction of their career prospects without any accompanying benefits. In other words, the trade-off contained in the reforms remains asymmetrical. It gives more powers to the bureaucracy in exchange for mobility. But the benefit is to the advantage of senior officials, while the burden lies on the shoulders of middle-rank categories, those of directors, who have cultivated hopes of promotion and oppose any interference of merit over age and years of service. This asymmetry explains why the reforms remain blocked.

REFERENCES

On history, see G. Melis, *Storia dell'amministrazione italiana* (Bologna: Il Mulino, 1996). On the impact of economic dualism on the administrative élite, see S. Cassese, *Questione amministrativa e questione meridionale* (Milan: Giuffrè, 1977). On the higher civil service in the 1980s, see S. Cassese, 'The Higher Civil Service in Italy', in Ezra N. Suleiman (ed.), *Bureaucrats and Policy Making* (New York: Holmes & Meier, 1984), 35, and in the 1990s, see M. D'Alberti (ed.), *L'alta burocrazia* (Bologna: Il Mulino, 1994).

Law 29/1993, E. Zaffaroni, 'Il decreto legislativo n. 29/1993 e la dirigenza', *Quaderni regionali*, 3 (1995): 933. For the mobility of civil servants, see G. Bonanomi (ed.), *La mobilità del personale statale* (Bologna: Il Mulino, 1995). On the role of penal judges, Camera dei deputati, *Rapporto del Comitato di studio sulla prevenzione della corruzione*, Presentato al Presidente della Camera il 23 ottobre 1996. 'Southernization' of civil servants is covered in Ministero del tesoro-Ragioneria generale dello Stato, *I dipendenti dello Stato per regione di origine e di servizio*, Quaderni RGS, Analisi dei fenomeni gestionali-Personale, 3 (Nov. 1996).

On civil servants in Parliament, *Rivista Italiana di Scienza Politica*, 3, special issue on 'Elezioni politiche 1996', ed. Roberto D'Alimonte and Stefano Bartolini (Dec. 1996). For proposals of reform, Commissione di studio per la definizione delle caratteristiche, del ruolo e della tipologia dell'alta dirigenza dello Stato e di quella ad essa equiparata, 'Relazione finale', *Funzione pubblica*, 1 (1996). A comparative approach is found in Barbara Wake Carroll, 'Bureaucratic Élites: Some Patterns in Career Paths over Time', *International Review of Administrative Sciences*, 62 (1996): 383–99.

Further reading: Alessandro Taradel, 'La burocrazia italiana: Provenienza e collocazione dei direttori generali', *Tempi moderni*, 6(13) (Apr.–June 1963); Franco Ferraresi, 'Modalità di intervento politico della burocrazia in Italia', *Studi di sociologia*, 6(3) (Sept. 1968), 247–8; by the same author, *Burocrazia e politica in Italia* (Bologna: Il Mulino, 1980); Robert D. Putnam, 'The Political Attitudes of Senior Civil Servants in Britain, Germany and Italy', in Mattei Dogan (ed.), *The Mandarins of Western Europe: The Political Role of Top Civil Servants* (New York: Sage, 1975), 111; Stefano Passigli, 'The Ordinary and Special Bureaucracy in Italy', in Mattei Dogan (ed.), *The Mandarins of Western Europe: The Political Role of Top Civil Servants* (New York: Sage, 1975), 233; Vittorio Mortara, 'Tendenze conservatrici e rapporti con la politica degli alti burocrati', in Sabino Cassese (ed.), *L'amministrazione pubblica in Italia* (Bologna: Il Mulino, 1976), 263; Sidney Tarrow, *Between Center and Periphery: Grassroots Politicians in Italy and France* (New Haven: Yale University Press, 1977).

4

The Senior Civil Service in France

LUC ROUBAN

Introduction

It is not easy to define the French higher civil service or to draw precise boundaries around a social group whose existence is largely self-regulated. The notion of 'senior civil servant' is a social rather than a legal one. Thus, senior civil servants may be defined through their role as privileged partners of political power and by their participation in government decision-making. The two simplest and most useful criteria of definition are functional and organic ones. The higher civil service is made up of civil servants responsible for managing administrative departments and of members of the *grands corps* (the Financial Inspectorate, the Council of State, the Court of Accounts, the prefectoral corps and the diplomatic corps). If the two groups are statistically similar, it is necessary nevertheless to underline the fact that many public managers do not necessarily come from the *grands corps* (most central administration directors, for example) and that many members of the *grands corps* participate in technical or supervisory tasks outside ministries. In this study, I shall therefore define senior civil servants as being senior managers of the state public administration (local managers differ noticeably from this group). Within this group, one finds members of the *grands corps*, central administration directors, departmental heads of ministries but also managers of field offices. It is, therefore, a heterogeneous category whose members share neither the same careers nor the same prestige nor the same professional culture. Thus, any generalization, such as those frequently presented in the rather paranoid popular or journalistic literature, would be misleading: the higher civil service in France does not constitute a unified group, an integrated élite that shares the same vision of the world or the same political opinions. Nevertheless—and it is the paradox of the French situation—the higher civil service is certainly a political force, having often fulfilled regulation or mediation functions during major political crises. History clearly shows that senior civil servants have been able to moderate political passions or to launch innovative programmes when politicians were bogged down in ideological posturing. For instance, the senior civil service enabled the state to continue its task of social modernization during the Fourth Republic while the political class was torn by its divisions. Of course, there is competition within the higher civil service for the most prestigious jobs. But senior civil servants know also that social solidarity and common interest unite them. One of the most powerful ties is probably the awareness of belonging neither to the world of politics nor to the world of routine management.

In order to understand the French higher civil service, it is necessary to keep in mind the fact that its members regard themselves generally as intellectuals and not as managers. Since the second half of the eighteenth century, they have participated actively in the intellectual controversies around the institutional evolution or the development of French society. Behind the hierarchy of the various jobs of the civil service, there is an implicit social hierarchy according to which decision and control functions are the most prestigious while functions of management are interesting only during the initial stages of an administrative career, when it is necessary to learn the rules of thumb and the art and craft of personnel management.

The relationship between senior civil servants and politicians is certainly more ambiguous and closer in the 1990s that it was during the 1960s. The politicization of the senior civil service has been considerably strengthened, but senior civil servants still consider themselves as representing the permanence of the state, and they are still reluctant to talk freely about their political involvements. Whatever the social changes that have occurred during the last fifteen years and whatever the political changes, the senior civil service remains strong. Therefore, a careful overview of the higher French civil service has to take into account three variables which interact simultaneously: (*a*) the fundamentally individualistic culture acquired during years of professional training; (*b*) the decisive role of the corps in the career path and in the representation of what is 'good administrative work'; and (*c*) the privileged social rank of the higher civil service. I shall present here the main characteristics of senior public managers in France by trying to highlight signs of an evolution since the 1960s.

Senior Public Managers

There are some 5,000 senior public managers in the French civil service according to the Direction générale de la Fonction publique (Civil Service Directorate General). Statistical data show that the population of senior managers tends to be aged between 41 and 60 (78 per cent). Women con-

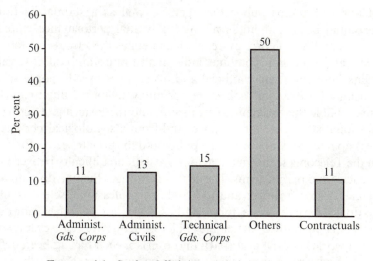

FIGURE 4.1. Senior Officials and their Various Corps

stitute less than 1 per cent of officials in the technical *grands corps* and 11 per cent of those in administrative *grands corps*.[1] But this population breaks down into professional subgroups, i.e. large categories of corps and functions, that do not offer either the same careers or the same social environment (Figure 4.1). Corporate barriers, as well as recognized models of professional success, undermine the fluidity and the mobility that any transformation of the senior civil servants into managers would require. Nevertheless, it would be unwise to stress the contrast between a so-called 'typically French bureaucratic' model, that would be strongly integrated and dominated by collective norms, and a 'typically Anglo-Saxon managerial' model, resting on an individualization of careers. This individualization is very present within the French civil service but rests both on the corporate career regulation and the individual capacity of each civil servant to manage his or her personal resources (as exemplified by the difficulty of organizing careers for functional jobs, i.e. positions of *sous-directeur, chef de service*, and *directeur d'administration centrale*). Symmetrically, one may argue that managerial norms, as they are currently implemented in the Australian or British systems, involve a strong pressure on the whole

---

[1] The following data come from a secondary analysis of a sociological study completed in 1991–93 of a representative quota sample of 500 senior public managers. For more details and more developed typologies of senior public managers: see Rouban (1994). Other secondary analyses focusing on the civil service culture or the implication of senior civil servants in government reform have been published in English (Rouban, 1995a, 1995b). One will find equally precise data about the sociology and the careers of central department directors in Rouban (1996).

population of senior public managers as well as a standardization of professional behaviour undermining 'individual performance' appraisal systems. The French corps system, which defines the successive steps in a bureaucratic profession, combines individualist values and collective values. The link between a senior official and his corps is based upon a specific knowledge, history, and collective or family memory. But many legal features enable the weakening of this link and the fostering of individual professional strategies: for instance, and from a sociological perspective, there is no real barrier between the public and the private sector. Engineers from the Telecoms sector manage to move with no difficulty between public agencies and private firms. The corps encourages them to do so in order to create a rapid turnover and to avoid any professional sclerosis. Other corps do not have the same opportunities. The world of state senior public managers is, therefore, particularly heterogeneous. In fact, several socio-political worlds coexist and (partially) overlap, each having been defined by a set of administrative tasks as well as by particular social or historical characteristics.

Recruitment and Promotion Methods

It is necessary to distinguish between the recruitment and the appointment processes to higher positions. Recruitment in the corps is organized through professional training schools: the École Nationale d'Administration (ENA) for the administrative *grands corps*, the École Polytechnique and other schools of engineers such as the École des Ponts-et-Chaussées or the École des Mines for the technical *grands corps*). There are, in fact, two steps in the selection process. A first competitive examination selects the candidates, who become civil servants during their period of study. A second competitive examination grades the student at the end of the training period and this grading remains crucial for the rest of his or her career. The most prestigious administrative corps (the State Council, the Court of Accounts, the Finance General Inspection) recruit 'the best' as they are ranked. This recruitment remains very limited each year so as to protect the *élitisme* of these corps (approximately 10 per cent of each ENA promotion a year, i.e. no more than fifteen persons). Most former ENA students who cannot gain access to the *grands corps* become *administrateurs civils*, that is to say, managers able to be assigned to various ministries. There is a real social hierarchy to the competitive entry examination. At the top, ENA and Polytechnique provide all members of the *grands corps* who will work in ministries or will assume headquarters or supervisory tasks; then there are the various competitive examinations for the civil service A category (the civil service upper category) which do not give access directly to the higher civil service. These are technical, professional examinations and most of the ministries' field offices managers are recruited in this way: the National Tax School, the National School of the Police, the National School of the Magistrature, the National School of Public Health. Regional administration institutes (IRA) recruit and train managers for central services (*attachés d'administration centrale*) and for field offices. But the former students of the IRA are not senior public managers.

There is also a social hierarchy between civil servants recruited in a corps through 'external' examinations (i.e. students from universities or political science institutes) and those recruited through 'internal' examinations (from among serving civil servants). Most members of the *grands corps* have been recruited through the ENA external examination process. Each corps admits a very low proportion of direct recruitments, without any examination, *au tour extérieur*. These direct recruitments are generally operated on political criteria. Very precise rules have been established so as to check that these recruitments are not totally arbitrary. Candidates must generally prove that they have some professional experience in public administration and that they are qualified enough to take the job. These constraints have been more strictly observed through legal controls since 1990, because strict observation suited many corps associations eager to defend their social identity and their professional value. These corps, and noticeably the Court of Accounts, felt insecure after the early 1980s when drastic political changes accelerated the rate of recruitment through the *tour extérieur*. In 1983, such appointments to the Ministry of Foreign Affairs caused a real revolt of members of the corps who collectively re- fused some appointments imposed by the Presidency. The appointment to 'functional' positions within ministries (ministerial directors, department heads, under-directors, heads of ministerial field offices) is made in ac- cordance with mixed political and professional criteria. Appointments are generally decided upon by the ministerial *cabinet*, sometimes after long negotiations in order to find jobs for those who have been asked to leave. Higher positions within ministries are considered as functional jobs, that is to say, the appointment as well as the dismissal can be made at any time without reasons having to be given.[2] The civil servant leaving such a position may rejoin the ranks of his corps or find another job in another ministry or elsewhere. However, he keeps always his *grade*, that is to say his hierarchical level within the corps.

[2] To be precise, positions of ministerial directors are purely discretionary, that is to say that, unlike those of departments' heads or under-directors, politicians may choose anyone to occupy this position even from outside the civil service.

As a general rule, appointments to higher positions within the ministries are made from within the ranks of the civil service even when the recruitment is largely open, as is the case for the positions of ministerial directors (from a legal point of view, the minister could choose anyone who shares his political convictions or proves to be skilled enough). About 40 per cent of directors come from within the relevant ministry. A third of them were inspectors or fulfilled management functions in other ministries or come from various corps of the civil service (*grands corps*, academics, etc.). Less than one-fifth comes from the outside, i.e. public or private enterprises, public agencies, the administrations of the city of Paris or the Île-de-France region (but this does not necessarily mean that they are not civil servants). It is necessary to underline the fact that the very frequent political changes that have occurred in France since 1981 have fostered important movements within the ranks of the higher civil service. Each government, however, has its own style and one cannot truly distinguish the politicization of the right from the politicization of the left.

Rules of promotion within each corps depend both upon criteria of seniority and upon the choice made by the hierarchical superior. For technical and administrative *grands corps*, promotion and career advancement are decided through a peer review institutionalized by professional councils. For a corps such as that of *administrateurs civils*, promotion is based upon the decision of the hierarchical superior, on the advice of professional

TABLE 4.1. *Institutional Origins of Ministerial Directors* (%)

	1984–85	1986–87	1988–89	1992	1993–94	Average population
A service within the same ministry	26.4	18.6	21.3	12.2	22.1	19.2
Cabinet	31.9	15.7	28.0	17.1	11.6	22.6
Public enterprise or agency	2.8	12.7	9.3	17.1	14.0	11.1
Private firm	5.6	8.8	5.3	0	5.8	4.9
Another corps	4.2	11.8	13.3	4.9	14.0	10.4
General inspection	0	1.0	1.3	0	5.8	2.1
Director in another ministry	8.3	2.9	5.3	12.2	4.7	7.8
Grand corps member	2.8	7.8	5.3	12.2	9.3	6.7
Director within the same ministry	5.6	2.9	1.3	9.8	2.3	3.7
Paris/IDF	0	7.8	0	0	5.8	2.3
Foreign service	12.5	9.8	9.3	14.6	4.7	9.2

committees, within the ranks of each ministry. The management of careers is, therefore, difficult for civil administrators because members of this corps are tempted to seek a top position in another ministry (for example, a department head position) that will allow them to obtain a senior hierarchical rank.

It should be emphasized that promotion in the world of senior public managers is not organized, from a sociological viewpoint, as it is in that of middle-level civil servants. Even if the rules of the civil service general statute apply to all civil servants, some of them are more equal than others. Specific corps rules may give room for more individual freedom. Senior public managers must plan their careers carefully, which may involve seeking posts in prestigious ministries, political friendships that enable participation in a ministerial *cabinet*, professional networks that facilitate vertical and horizontal professional mobility. To have occupied a top position within a ministry is likely to change one's career prospects—as it opens up the possibility of moving into a top management position in public or private enterprise. Career management is an individual skill that distinguishes the good professional from the real senior civil servant. There again, the difference is of a social nature. The real senior civil servant learns and knows about the positions open to him/her at each moment of his career. For instance, it is necessary to be neither too young nor too old to become department head if one wants to retain a chance of being appointed ministerial director later. It is necessary to be a good professional but also a good diplomat if one hopes one day to enter into a *grand corps* through the *tour extérieur*. It is always good to enter a ministerial *cabinet*, provided that you are not too much involved in controversial political choices. It is necessary especially to acquire specific skills about timing and strategic relationships, to know when it is necessary to say to the minister that he is wrong, and when it is better be quiet, when to negotiate or not with the unions, whom to contact or to avoid in order to take a decision. Careers of the senior civil servants are shaped by social skills and do not depend exclusively on professional merits. For example, nearly half of ministerial directors find a position in the public administration after they quit, either in a ministry or in the corps: only a tenth remain within the same ministry. More than a fifth, on the other hand, go into the private sector or into the banking or business public sector. A position of ministerial director offers a springboard for assuming responsibilities outside the world of ministerial bureaucracies with new social resources if, and only if, you are skilful enough to enjoy them.

The professional future of senior officials is largely defined and modelled by positions previously occupied. For instance, we may observe that up to 40 per cent of ministerial directors coming from a corps outside the central

TABLE 4.2. *Professional Future of Ministerial Directors* (%)

	1984–85	1986–87	1988–89	1992	1993–94	Average population
Post within the same ministry	23.9	10.0	15.3	16.0	1.2	12.0
Post in another ministry	3.0	4.4	1.7	4.0	0	3.1
Public enterprise or agency	14.9	20.0	6.8	4.0	2.4	11.6
Private firm	13.4	15.6	6.8	0	0	8.4
Back to the corps	6.0	13.3	22.0	8.0	1.2	11.2
General inspection	7.5	6.7	6.8	8.0	0	6.9
Adm. *grand corps*	17.9	12.2	8.5	12.0	0	10.4
Foreign service	9.0	11.1	11.9	4.0	0	7.5
Elected representative	0	1.1	0	0	0	0.6
Paris/IDF	1.5	0	1.7	0	0	0.6
Retirement	1.5	0	1.7	4.0	0	2.0

administration rejoin it again when they quit. A similar pattern prevails among most members of the administrative *grands corps*, general inspections, Foreign Office counsellors, or diplomats (*ministres plénipotentiaires*) appointed as directors within the Foreign Office. It should also be noted that most ministerial directors coming from public agencies or private enterprises tend to rejoin them. The diversification of career prospects is real only for those directors coming from ministerial *cabinets*. Unless there is a clear and complete political involvement, a career is largely determined from its first steps and during the first years of professional life.

The Political Activity of the Senior Civil Servants

It is very difficult to gain detailed knowledge of the political involvement of senior civil servants. In France, civil servants have the right to participate in political parties or to compete in national or local elections. If elected, they can be committed to a real political career or they can return to the civil service. Political militancy is relatively rare and, when assumed, it is very discreet. Senior civil servants are politicized through clubs or personal relationship systems. When they are interviewed or questioned through mail surveys, senior civil servants generally prefer not to say anything about their political preferences and they invoke the legal prescription of discretion that forbids civil servant to express political opinions during working hours or in the line of duty. As a result, rates of reply exceed rarely 50 per cent. A 1992 survey shows nevertheless that such reticence is less marked today than thirty years ago (the figures in the right-hand column are percentages):

Communist Party	0.8
Extreme left	0.6
Socialist Party	32.3
MRG (moderate left)	4.2
Environmentalists	5.6
UDF (centre right)	11.4
RPR (Gaullist)	6.0
No reply	39.1

Not surprisingly, this reveals that a majority of senior public managers felt close to the Socialist Party in 1992, at the end of the Edith Cresson government. It might be assumed that figures would be inverted in 1997, at least before the legislative change of June 1997, in favour of the parties of the right, given that senior public managers are appointed according to political criteria. It is more interesting to measure the degree of involvement in political activities. If senior civil servants are discreet, there are, nevertheless, objective signs of serious political involvement in unions and interest groups: senior civil servants share a representation of the administrative world as a specific professional world in which the dominant features are collective interests and intellectual commitment. Indeed, one observes that their participation in the various kinds of political activity is always higher than the average political involvement of French citizens, as well as higher than the average political involvement of business managers and liberal professions.

Another criterion of politicization can be researched by exploring the political functions fulfilled by senior civil servants. One distinguishes here between political functions as such (participation in a political party, in an electoral campaign) and politicized functions, implying at least a basic agreement with the general orientations defined by the government

TABLE 4.3. *Comparative Active Socio-Political Involvement* (%)

	Senior officials	Private-sector manager	French citizens
Environment Protection Association	8	5	2
Human Rights Defence Association	10	5	2
Union or professional association	38	16	10
Political party	7	5	2

(participation in a ministerial *cabinet*, a post within the Government General Secretariat or the Elysée General Secretariat). The survey on ministerial directors shows that politicized functions are more frequent than political functions. Up to 36 per cent of directors have had politicized functions. These responsibilities concern principally participation in a ministerial *cabinet* or the occupation of upper positions in *cabinets* such as those of *cabinet* director or cabinet chief. Political involvement as such is especially visible on the left: 6.8 per cent state that they are members of the Socialist Party as opposed 1.4 per cent for the neo-Gaullist RPR and less than 1 per cent for the centre–right UDF.

The Mobility of Senior Civil Servants

The career of senior civil servants is organized within their corps. To each ministry corresponds one or several specialized corps. Interdepartmental mobility is, therefore, limited by the career system. There are two exceptions. First, *grands corps* may have a 'home base' within a ministry, but their members are extremely mobile inside and outside public administration. For example, most upper positions within the Ministry of Industry are occupied by senior civil servants who have come through Polytechnique and the School of Mines (the *X-Mines* in administrative colloquial language). But the *X-Mines* appear no less frequently in upper management positions in private business as well in public enterprises. The same could be said for most Telecoms engineers or engineers belonging to the *corps des Ponts-et-Chaussées* or members of the administrative *grands corps*. If members of the General Inspection of Finance occupy most upper positions within the Treasury Department, an important proportion of them are scattered throughout the public or private banking sector. The mechanism of *pantouflage*, which allows round trips between the public sector and the private sector is one of the defining characteristics of the *grands corps*. One may again quote the case of the State Council, the final court of appeal for administrative justice. In 1997, the State Council included 317 members, of whom only 205 (64 per cent) were involved in the various legal sections of the Council or as presidents of regionally based Administrative Appeal Courts, while eleven members (4 per cent) occupied positions in ministerial *cabinets*, and 101 other members (32 per cent) were working outside the State Council, assuming various management responsibilities in public administration, private or public enterprises.

In order to understand clearly Figure 4.2, it is necessary to stress the fact that several legal measures enable French civil servants to stay within the civil service while they work outside the corps where they have been ap-

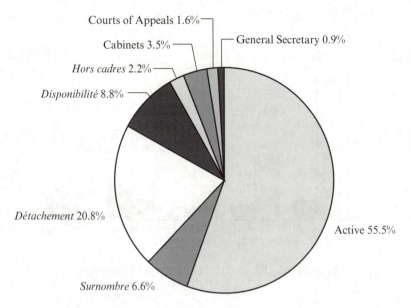

FIGURE 4.2. Professional Position of State Council Members in 1997

pointed. These legal measures are called *positions statutaires*. Apart from being active in post, a civil servant may be *en détachement* (he or she is appointed elsewhere in public administration or in various public bodies and his or her remuneration is paid by the public entity where he or she is appointed). When a civil servant is *en détachement*, he or she continues to benefit from his or her retirement and seniority rights within the corps. Another position is the *disponibilité*, when the civil servant is working outside the public sector and does not benefit any more from his or her retirement pension rights or seniority within the corps (this is generally the position of most civil servants working in private business). The position *hors cadres* means that the civil servant no longer benefits from the pension and seniority rights of his or her corps but from the legal rights offered by the entity where he or she is working (especially when senior civil servants work within international organizations); when a civil servant is *en sur-nombre*, he or she is generally waiting for a specific appointment within the corps (civil servants coming back to their corps after having spent a few years in private business or in ministerial *cabinets*). External experience is decisive in the pursuit of the career. While members of administrative *grands corps* prefer traditionally to participate in ministerial *cabinets*, until recently, other senior public managers preferred to work in private business firms (Figure 4.3).

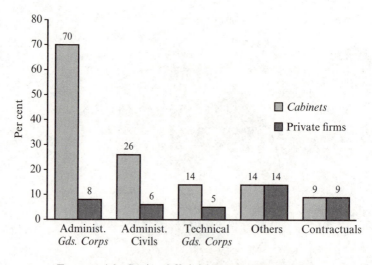

FIGURE 4.3. Senior Officials' External Experience

The question of professional mobility is somewhat different for *admini-strateurs civils*. The civil administrator corps is an interdepartmental corps whose general management is in the hands of the Civil Service Department. But the civil administrators' careers depend in practice upon the ministries to which they are appointed. Interdepartmental mobility is difficult to man-age because civil administrators naturally try to join the most prestigious ministries. Measures have been taken recently with the aim of improving the management of this corps, by setting job descriptions for positions of ministerial under-directors in order to define useful guidelines for profes-sional mobility. Until recently, mobility depended largely on individual wishes and did not match the requirement of a long-term and coherent policy. As a matter of fact, the professional environment as well as remun-eration (given the weight of bonuses) can be appreciably different from one ministry to another.

The Internal Hierarchy of the Civil Service

Not all senior civil servants share the same social status. A real hierarchy exists at the top of which one finds the administrative and technical *grands corps*. These two groups can be themselves in competition for access to ministerial top positions, as is the case within the Ministry of Industry. Members of the technical *grands corps* are often rather critical of their colleagues who come from ENA. At the second rank of the hierarchy are the civil administrators. This group is divided by a secondary hierarchy according to the ministerial sector to which they have been appointed (they have chosen this sector in accordance with their rank at ENA). The most prestigious ministry, which enables the most rapid careers, is the Treasury Department. At the bottom of the list, one finds the Welfare and Human Services Ministry or the Labour Ministry. This social hierarchy corresponds obviously to various professional cultures but also to the social significance attached to some administrative and political questions. When an official manages budget questions he is likely to take part in the final decision concerning the launching of some government policies. By way of contrast, social questions are regarded as technical, specialized questions, even if they absorb an important proportion of the national budget.

In order better to understand the culture of the higher French civil service, it is necessary to keep in mind the fact that the social hierarchy is defined according to the degree of functional polyvalence, that is to say, the degree to which higher officials use generalist skills. Polyvalence, which facilitates a strong mobility, is always regarded as more prestigious than professional specialization. When a senior civil servant describes one of his colleagues as a specialist, it is generally to signify a certain form of disdain. This is why most critics of the ENA miss their target and reform plans rapidly prove to be impracticable. The transformation of senior civil servants into managers would imply the learning and, above all, the *practice* of a specialized knowledge that do not match the cultural criteria associated with the pursuit of successful careers. In other words, a young ENA student knows that he has a lot to lose if he starts his career as a specialist. In the long run, specialization might indicate that he is unable to occupy a wide range of functions and that he will therefore never be regarded by his colleagues as a member of the élite. The hierarchy of ministries affects not only the culture and the career of senior civil servants—it may also determine pay levels, which can differ by as much as 100 per cent within the same rank. These differences are due to the system of bonuses which can generate important variations in the final annual remuneration, according to corps and responsibilities. These bonuses are not necessarily linked to a systematic evaluation of performance (appraisal systems are relatively rare, with the noticeable exceptions of the Ministry of Infrastructure, the Postal Service, and France Telecom) but are based on levels set for each position through negotiations between individual ministries and the Budget Ministry.

It is possible to establish a hierarchy of ministries by analysing for each ministry the mode of entry in the corps. The higher the proportion of senior public managers having entered their corps through internal examinations the lower the social profile of the ministry. Conversely, the higher the proportion of managers having entered through an external examination the more prestigious the ministry. Surveys show that there are three groups of ministries.

In the first group are those posts of the administration in which managers have gained entry through the internal examination system and to which there is little recruitment through the *tour extérieur*. In this group are the technical ministries, in which one finds also a relatively well-established managerial culture: the Ministry of Transport (47 per cent of managers come from external examinations and 42 per cent from internal examinations), the Postal Service (respectively 45 and 38 per cent), France-Telecom (61 and 35 per cent).

In the second group, the social profile of senior public managers is still modest, but politicization is more sensitive. The proportion of managers coming from internal examinations is important but recruitment through the *tour extérieur* has increased. This especially the case for the Ministry of Labour (65 per cent through external examinations, 31 per cent through internal examinations, 7 per cent from the *tour extérieur*), the Ministry of Education (respectively 49, 33, and 7 per cent), the Ministry of Welfare and Human Services (respectively 51, 18, and 13 per cent, with 11 per cent having followed a specific seniority procedure).

The third group comprises ministries dominated by the *grands corps*. There is much less recruitment through internal examinations. It is particularly the case of the Ministry for Infrastructure (73 per cent through external examinations and 24 per cent through internal examinations), the Ministry of Industry (respectively 59 and 18 per cent, with 13 per cent through the seniority procedure), the Ministry of Economy (respectively 78 and 12 per cent), the Ministry of Agriculture (respectively 66 and 8 per cent). The Ministry of Interior is characterized by a relatively low rate of internal examinations (11 per cent) and by a high rate of *tour extérieur* (14 per cent). One may note finally the case of the administrative *grands corps* where the low rate of internal examination (5 per cent) is combined with significant recruitment through the *tour extérieur* (25 per cent). The hierarchy of ministries matches obviously the social hierarchy prevailing within the whole population of senior public managers.

Sociological Characteristics of Senior Public Managers

A majority of senior public managers come from the upper social classes, that is to say, they may be children of senior public managers from the public or the private sector, of manufacturers or merchants, or of members of the liberal professions (Figure 4.4). However, it is necessary to pay atten-

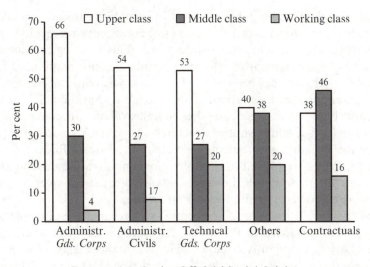

FIGURE 4.4. Senior Officials' Social Origins

tion to the relatively high proportion of senior public managers coming from the middle class. In fact, one can distinguish generally three groups. Members of the administrative *grands corps* have clearly higher social origins than the average. They are distinct from members of the technical *grands corps* and from civil administrators who come in a larger proportion from the middle class. Finally, a third group is composed of the other corps and contractual public agents who, on average, are of modest origins. In these three groups, the proportion of higher civil servants originating from the lower classes is rather limited. Many debates have taken place in France concerning the fact that administrative schools such as the ENA serve as social filters and eliminate candidates on a social basis. In fact, the question is more complex. Social origins do not affect the examinations so much as the subsequent career path. Senior civil servants benefiting from large personal relationship networks will be able to advance more rapidly than their colleagues who may have more educational qualifications but fewer contacts. It is also necessary to underline the fact that this debate always focuses on the ENA and the administrative *grands corps*. As a matter of fact, scientific schools and technical *grands corps* are a force for real upward social mobility. Moreover, in a country such as France, where the state still occupies an important role in the regulation of the economy and social life, it is not surprising that social élites are attracted to the civil service.

By contrast, one may raise genuine questions about the future of the professional culture of the senior civil servants. Surveys have shown that managerial values were shared particularly by middle-class civil servants and, therefore, by senior public managers within the technical *grands corps*. Members of the upper social classes are rather reticent with regard to public management and managerialist doctrines. This sociological difference explains why administrative reform in France has not really used managerial formulae but has been largely based upon incremental changes and 'soft' techniques (such as experimental contracts, strategic planning on a volunteer basis) which require neither an upheaval of careers nor a radical transformation of administrative structures. This variable could also explain why some Socialist governments (especially the Michel Rocard government in 1989) have proved to be more reforming than some Neo-gaullist governments: these political changes involve a rapid turnover of senior civil servants with rather different social origins.

Did the social structure of the central services and the administrative *grands corps* (localized in Paris, and therefore limited here to the State Council, to the Court of Accounts, and to the Finance General Inspection) change between the 1967 survey by Alain Darbel and Dominique Schnapper (1969) and my 1992 survey? The answer is negative. Except for some statistical variations, which might be determined by minor differences in samples (the ministerial organization has changed in twenty-five years), social origins are on the whole very stable (Table 4.4). Nevertheless, within the limits of statistical interpretation, one may observe that the Ministry of Finance seems to be more élitist than it was in the 1960s. The proportion of senior civil servants originating from the upper classes increases by 11 per cent while the proportion of those coming from middle and blue-collar classes is lower. A similar change can be observed within the Ministry of Education where the proportion of top managers coming from the upper classes climbs from 46 per cent to 56 per cent, at the expense of the middle-class representatives who decrease from 41 to 22 per cent. Technical ministries have experienced a noticeable process of democratization, since the proportion of managers originating from the upper classes has been reduced

TABLE 4.4. *The Evolution of Senior Officials' Social Origins, 1962–1991* (%)

	No answer 1962/1991	Working class 1962/1991	Middle class 1962/1991	Upper class 1962/1991
Finance Ministry	4/0	6/5	41/33	50/62
Justice and Interior Ministries	1/3	6/3	31/28	62/65
Technical Ministries	1/2	7/19	30/30	62/50
Social Ministries	3/0	14/16	32/25	52/59
Education Ministry	0/6	14/17	41/22	46/56

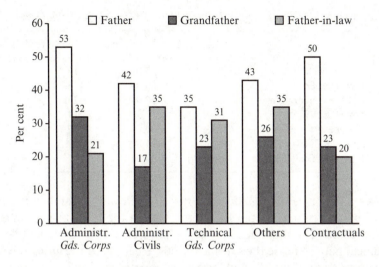

FIGURE 4.5. Socio-Professional Heredity: Civil Servants' Parents

from 62 per cent to 50 per cent while the proportion of managers coming from the lower classes climbs from 7 per cent to 19 per cent. The proportion of middle-class representatives declines everywhere and, with the exception of technical ministries, every ministerial sector tends to be more élitist.

A third characteristic of the higher civil service in France relates to the very strong socio-professional heredity. On average, up to 40 per cent of senior civil servants are themselves children of civil servants (Figure 4.5). This heredity implies that the professional socialization does not begin with the preparation for civil service exams or the training in professional schools. Its roots are to be found in the family sphere. To be brief, the children of senior civil servants know better than others the most prestigious and the most useful routes of access to the higher civil service. The children of senior civil servants, in a huge proportion, are likely to choose a specific academic channel which generally starts in the law schools, continues through political science institutes, before entering the ENA competition. Senior civil servants with middle-class origins or the children of private-sector managers will have rather a pronounced tendency to go into law studies (Table 4.5).

As one may observe, the access through Sciences Po. (the prestigious political science institute in Paris) is always more socially selective than law studies. In contrast, it is difficult to decide at first view whether the access through Sciences Po. is socially more selective than access through the ENA. If the ENA filters the middle classes, Sciences Po. filters the lower

TABLE 4.5. *Senior Officials' Social Origins by Course of Study* (%)

	Upper class	Middle class	Working class
Only Law	35.7	47.0	16.5
Law + Sc.Po.	41.7	50.0	8.3
ENA + other cursus	46.7	30.0	23.3
Law + ENA	52.4	33.3	14.3
Sciences Po.	61.5	30.8	7.7
Sc.Po. + ENA	71.4	19.0	9.5
Law + Sc.Po. + ENA	75.0	20.5	2.3

classes. This reveals a functional system, which was certainly not antici-
pated by the framers of the 1945 reform when the ENA and Science Po.
were created. The most democratic course seems to be the scientific and
technical path, outside the specific selection leading to the *grandes écoles*.
The proportion of middle and lower class representatives is then preponderant. The choice of any education depends appreciably on heredity. Among
all the senior civil servants who used a way other than the traditional path
law school/Sciences Po./ENA, 47 per cent have a father and a paternal
grandfather who have worked in the private sector. Only 22 per cent have
a civil servant father and 12 per cent have a civil servant father and paternal
grandfather. As for the group of senior civil servants who only entered a
law school, the observation is clearly similar: 41 per cent of them have a
father who has worked in the private sector, 24 per cent have a civil servant
father and 18 per cent have a civil servant father and paternal grandfather.

The Senior Civil Servants' Professional Relationships

The work of the senior civil servants may be analysed as a translation of
political demands, whether they come from elected élites, pressure groups,
or citizens. The central point of connection in each ministry is, of course,
offered by the minister's *cabinet*. Senior civil servants have generally more
relationships with members of the minister's *cabinet*, or with the Prime
Minister's *cabinet*, than with their colleagues working in other ministries.
Contacts with colleagues are generally organized within departmental
committees and commissions. Each senior civil servant is generally eager
to defend his organizational autonomy and his area of influence, so free
riders are relatively rare. As a general rule, vertical contacts are more
frequent than horizontal contacts. One of the major purposes of administrative modernization projects launched since 1989 has been to favour
informal contacts between senior public managers within each ministry so

as to accelerate administrative procedures. In some ministries, the setting up of *projets de service* (strategic plans based on mutual agreement between the managers and the employees) in 1990 was the first opportunity for under-directors, working sometimes on each side of the divide, to meet and talk.

Two major points of contact are, therefore, offered: on the one hand, by ministerial *cabinets* and, on the other hand, by prefects who play a crucial role in the exchange of information between central administrations, field offices, and local government administrations. One of the most notable changes over the last twenty years is the opening up of the professional relationship system. Senior civil servants now have more frequent interaction with representatives of the various pressure groups, professional interest groups, or public interest groups (consumers defence, environment protection). The development of the European Union plays a very important role, since senior civil servants often have to serve as representatives of industrial or economic national interests in Brussels. The European Union is not, therefore, perceived as a threat but rather as an opportunity to strengthen the functions of mediation. One has also to stress the fact that the more senior civil servants participate in the negotiation of European rules the more interaction they have with political staffs and interest groups. Table 4.6 shows that relationships with ministerial *cabinets*, with the Prime

TABLE 4.6. *Relationship System and Participation in the Negotiation of EU Rules* (%)

	No negotiation of EU rules	Negotiation of EU rules
Contacts with the Prime Minister's Cabinet		
Permanent	—	—
Frequent	4.5	29.6
Rare	26.8	37
None	68.5	33.3
Contacts with the cabinet		
Permanent	11.9	44.4
Frequent	26.4	38.9
Rare	45.9	16.7
None	14.2	—
Contacts with professional groups		
Permanent	15.7	31.5
Frequent	37.4	48.1
Rare	33.6	14.8
None	13.2	5.6

Minister's *cabinet* as well as with professional pressure groups are more intense when senior civil servants participate in the negotiation of European rules.

The Absence of Any Higher Civil Service Policy

The higher civil service has never truly been the subject of government policy. The senior civil service has been largely self-regulated and controlled since the nineteenth century. The multiplication of corps, the real expertise level of senior civil servants, their presence within the ranks of ministerial *cabinets*, their individual as well as collective prudence about any change concerning their career would make any external political intervention in higher civil service management very sensitive and be likely to raise powerful opposition. For instance, measures were proposed by the government at the end of 1996 systematically to send newly appointed managers from the ENA, whatever their corps, to field offices for a two-year period, in order to give them practical experience of day-to-day management. Senior members of the administrative *grands corps* protested loudly, saying that this training was already offered within their ranks and that they needed these young managers immediately. The measure was buried.

In fact, two factors may explain why most civil service ministers are reluctant to take unilateral reform measures. First, senior civil servants are at the heart of the decision-making structures affecting the civil service organization (Prime Minister's *cabinet*, Civil Service Ministry, State Council, and even Parliament, since 40 per cent of MPs are former civil servants). Secondly, it is necessary to underline the fact that, although the higher civil service always attracts the attention of the media and many fantasies in public opinion, it does not cost much from a budgetary perspective. The cost of 5,000 state senior public managers is not comparable to the cost of the other 2.5 million state civil servants. The budgetary stakes are, therefore, very low, and savings that one might expect from a managerial reform are not comparable to the political threats that any government would have to face if a radical reform was to be launched. The game is not worth the candle.

Things have, nevertheless, changed since the end of the 1980s because governments of both the left and the right have understood that administrative modernization requires a clear definition of the professional role of the various categories of civil servants. To put it simply, the ambition would be to give up the traditional notion of 'senior civil servant' that evokes high social status, and to adopt a modernist notion of 'public manager' that evokes steering functions within the administrative system. The main governmental preoccupation is, therefore, to adapt the training of managers to the changes in the external environment, including the European integration process, the evolution towards a new political pluralism with more localized group and citizen participation, and the decentralization process calling for more negotiations with elected leaders and private business firms. Another important topic for reform relates to the capacity of senior civil servants to manage their personnel and to lead their services so as to increase the overall efficiency of public administration. These changes involve the development of new management techniques (strategic internal contracting, personnel and programme evaluation), as well as a cultural change toward some kind of charismatic leadership. A general assessment of modernization plans over the last ten years shows that field office managers, coming from the middle class and belonging to relatively common *corps*, have been the most involved in this change of role.

The various political parties are, therefore, generally not very forthcoming about measures they would recommend for the higher civil service. The political alternation between the Socialist Party and the RPR–UDF alliance since 1981 has pushed the leaders of the left, themselves coming very largely from the ranks of the lower and middle civil service, to the view that the higher civil service had to be spared and that it could be a precious ally in launching social reforms with the blessing of the ruling class. Extremist parties are alone in adopting clear positions: the Communist Party has always criticized the higher civil service, considered as an 'objective ally' of big business. But the four Communist ministers in government between 1981 and 1983 finally developed good relationships with the senior civil servants of their ministry (notably Anicet Le Pors who became the Civil Service Minister). The National Front denounces the bureaucracy and the civil service in general terms (but not the higher civil service) in the name of budget savings and because of all the waste, abuse, and fraud produced by the welfare state; but it supported the pro-public-service groups during the 1995 strikes against European deregulation, in the name of national values.

The Erosion of the Higher Civil Service Social Status:
A Debated Question

Senior civil servants are incontestably a major part of the French social élite, in sociological as well as in cultural terms. Opinion polls on the civil service reveal that civil servants as a whole are regarded by a majority of respondents as honest and competent. Critics focus much more on the bureaucracy, that is to say, the slowness of the administrative system, than on people. Recent polls also show that a majority of the French favour the existence of a large public service.[3] One cannot argue that privatization is currently regarded as a panacea. Questions directly related to senior civil servants are rarely asked in opinion polls because most people do not know much about them and have no direct contact with them. When the media talk about senior civil servants it is generally within debates concerning the social élites at large, which does not make things clearer. Senior civil servants are often criticized as technocrats but, at the same time, they exert an undeniable attraction because they represent a social success model which is much more legitimate than the model offered by private business—even if they are part of a closed élite, even if they are technocrats, paying too little attention to popular protests, they work nevertheless for the future of the country and not for money. When asked, most French reply that they would like their children to enter the civil service.

Senior civil servants are certainly somewhat more pessimistic (but they always are). They feel under pressure today from new élites, such as businessmen and local elected leaders. The former have obtained a new legitimacy in recent years (under left governments) by asserting that they lead the fight against unemployment. The latter have tried to demonstrate, not always with much success, that they now hold important decision-making power and that they could handle local government management without the assistance of the state. Senior civil servants have other matters of equal concern. The politicization of the higher civil service is sharply criticized and, to tell the truth, the arguments of the critics are empirically founded. Officials are especially critical of the worsening of their work conditions. With the exception of members of administrative *grands corps*, many of them think that the level of their remuneration is neither comparable with their professional responsibility nor with the average level obtained in the private sector: 65 per cent of officials in field offices were dissatisfied with their pay, 60 per cent of the civil servants in central services and 37 per cent of the administrative *grands corps*.

One major and almost obsessional concern for senior civil servants is to compare their social status (and their level of remuneration) with those of

[3] Recent polls show for instance that very few people support the idea of a privatization of major public services. At the most, only 13% think that the Postal Service should be privatized. Globally, scores of satisfaction with the performance of public services are very high: 92% of people are satisfied with France Telecom, 80% with the Postal Service, 65% with the SNCF, the national railway public enterprise, 57% with the school system. The worst score is obtained by the Social Security (only 49% satisfaction) whose agents are not civil servants (cf. SOFRES, 1997).

private-sector senior managers. This comparison always gives rise to passionate controversies. The truth is that it is impossible to compare levels of remuneration in the two categories because sociological differences are very important. Moreover, any debate on remuneration depends on the basis of calculation. Comparing average monthly net incomes is favourable to the civil service. In 1996 this amounted to FF 23,803 for administrators or people of similar status and FF 31,460 for upper management positions, as compared with FF 22,500 for private-sector senior managers. But these are only average data. They mean very little, since for real salaries the variation is much larger in the private sector than in the civil service (which is why senior civil servants tend to compare their own situation with one of the few private big business managers earning FF 500,000 a month). Nevertheless, to complicate the comparison further, the average dispersion between the estimated highest and lowest pay levels is more important in the civil service than in the private sector, due to seniority and career progression: a beginner subprefect earns on average an annual income (salary and bonuses included) of FF 133,236 while a *Trésorier-payeur général* (the head of the Treasury services in each *département*) working in the Paris region at the end of his career may earn up to FF 900,000. By way of comparison, a product manager of a private firm with an annual turnover of 200 million FF earns on average FF 273,000 while the general manager of a firm with an annual turnover of more than 2 billion FF may earn up to FF 1,078,000. The gap is, therefore, 575 per cent within the civil service as opposed to 295 per cent in the private sector. Any serious comparison should be widened to include other features, such as fringe benefits, job security, promotion prospects, retirement pensions within the private sector, profit-sharing bonuses, the distribution of stock-options, and other perks.

Critics within the ranks of the higher civil service have sharply increased since the early 1990s. Modernization (such as the Plan Durafour signed between the government and the civil service unions in 1990) has especially benefited the middle and lower ranks of the civil service. The purchasing power of senior civil servants has declined while they have been called upon to behave as managers do, with smaller budgets and additional constraints. During the period 1982–92, civil servants of category A saw their purchasing power decrease by 7.5 per cent, while that of category B civil servants remained stable and that of category C civil servants increased by 2.9 per cent. It is necessary, however, to draw distinctions within the ranks of category A, because the smaller group of senior public managers suffered much more, with an average 14 per cent decrease in purchasing power. Associations of the alumni of administrative schools worry, therefore, about the future of the higher civil service, because its social status is no longer what it was in the 1960s. The use of the *pantouflage* to obtain better salaries in the private sector cannot be a long-term policy, nor it is available for everyone in all circumstances, since it has been more severely regulated since 1994 (with the creation of ministerial commissions verifying questions of conflicts of interest). A real reform would certainly involve an upheaval of the internal hierarchy of the civil service. The policy of 'state reform', inaugurated by the Juppé government in 1995 was based upon a systematic devolution of administrative authority to prefects and, along the lines of managerialist reforms experienced elsewhere in Europe, upon a clearer separation between those who regulate and evaluate and those who implement. This policy will prove useful and coherent only if the professional situation of field office managers is improved and if careers in the central administrations of ministries are more precisely evaluated and structured. For the time being, it is hard to predict the fate of the state reform. The Socialist Party returned to power in June 1997 with its Communist allies but without a precise programme for administrative modernization.

Conclusion

Any study of the French higher civil service raises the question of change within public administration. At first glance, the world of these *grands commis de l'État* seems rather archaic, coming from the political and social world of pre-Revolutionary Europe. However, such a conclusion would be misleading. After all, these upper managers have adapted quite well to the tremendous changes occurring in their professional environment since the 1960s. They have proved to be rather flexible when confronted with the emerging power of big business, the decentralization process, or the consolidation of the European Union. The strongest corps have deployed new social strategies: *pantouflage* within the private sector or taking over management positions in the new local administrations, especially at the *département* level where many former ENA students serve as general managers. Even the European integration process, which seems rather opposed to statist-minded people, was an opportunity to renew their power and to play on their favourite ground of institutional engineering. Europe is not a matter of concern for the members of the *grands corps*, who can easily exploit their legal or financial expertise, as it is a real new professional resource for the managers of central ministries who may at last negotiate successfully with pressure groups and industry representatives. This is the final paradox: there is change without change. French higher civil servants have not imposed a drastic neo-liberal diet, a complete set of managerialist tools, and they have not listened to the advice of Michel Crozier (1979: 260) to invent a new style of management in France. They are still living in a complex and fragmented world, which is not based on professional performance but on a mixture of social and intellectual ability. They still compete with one another and many of them suffer from the inequities of the professional examination system. Of course, these higher managers are no longer able to impose economic choices or to decide public policies unilaterally. But who is able to do so today? As a matter of fact, politicization is spreading throughout public affairs, and everything is debated at length. Nevertheless, higher civil servants are still able to penetrate the political staffs and the economic task forces. They have to share their power, but this is not an indication that they are powerless. Corporatist networks have offered them a specific combination of rigidity and adaptiveness, a high degree of decentralization in a centralized political sphere, and a good knowledge of the intricacies of power. In a world in which the state seems to be vanishing, confronted with open markets, a European Union, and changing notions of citizenship, the corps model may still be one of the best structures to keep alive both professional solidarity and individual career paths.

REFERENCES

Crozier, Michel (1979). *On ne change pas la société par décret* (Paris: Grasset).

Dabel, Alain, and Dominique Schnapper (1969). *Morphologie de la haute administration française* (Paris: École Practique des Hautes Études).

Rouban, Luc (1994). *Les Cadres superieurs de la fonction publique et la politique de modernisation administration* (Paris: La Documentation française).

—— (1995*a*). 'Public Administration at the Crossroads: The End of French Specificity', in Jon Pierre (ed.), *Bureaucracy in the Modern State* (London: Edward Elgar).

—— (1995*b*). 'The Civil Service Culture and Administrative Reform', in B. G. Peters and Donald Savoie (eds.), *Governance in a Changing Environment* (Kingston: McGill-Queen's University Press).

—— (1996). 'Les Directeurs d'adminstration centrale 1984–1994', *La Revue administrative* (Feb.): 18–31.

SOFRES (1997). *L'Opinion publique en 1997* (Paris: Seuil).

5

Senior Officials in Austria

BARBARA LIEGL AND WOLFGANG C. MÜLLER

Introduction

As elsewhere in Europe, a strong and powerful central administration was created under enlightened absolutism under Maria Theresia (1717–80) and Joseph II (1741–90) in Austria. Top civil servants upheld the ideals of enlightenment even under the successors of Joseph II who did their best to reverse his reforms (Heindl, 1991). Given the important role of the state in a relatively economically backward country (Gerschenkron, 1962) the bureaucracy remained very important throughout the Habsburg monarchy. Metternich's dictum, *Österreich wird nicht regiert, sondern verwaltet* (Austria is not governed but administered), puts this in a nutshell (quoted from Kneucker, 1981: 261). It is probably even more true for the aftermath of the Habsburg empire (Megner, 1986; Schimetschek, 1984; Wandruszka and Urbanitsch, 1975). The emerging representative institutions remained weak and were stalled by the nationality conflict. As a consequence, many cabinets were of administrative origin. During the fifty-eight years' reign of Franz Joseph (1848–1916), seventeen civil servants were appointed prime minister and seventy cabinet minister out of a total of twenty-six prime ministers and 157 cabinet ministers (Schimetschek, 1984: 8). Power was accompanied by social prestige, though the salary of a top civil servant could by no means provide the living standard equivalent to it (Megner, 1986). The civil service of the Habsburg monarchy is still held in high esteem in those parts of the monarchy which were exposed to quite different experiences afterwards. This applies to the countries which came under communist rule but also to Northern Italy.

Writers have often held a less positive attitude towards the old Austrian bureaucracy. Franz Kafka's famous *Das Schloß* (The Castle) is a case in point. Likewise, in 1909 the Austrian writer Hermann Bahr let one of his characters say, 'No one can understand Austria who has not before understood our bureaucracy. It is the key to everything. And no one can help us who has not put to an end its dreadfulness. But it burns out the light of

each and everyone who tries it. Because it has power above everything'
(quoted from Megner, 1986: 9). The breakdown of the Habsburg empire
was a serious blow to the Austrian bureaucracy in many respects (Heindl,
1995). Civil servants suffered most from the severe economic problems of
the new republic and the resulting drastic cut-back programme which was
forced on Austria by the League of Nations. However, according to the
Austrian writer Franz Werfel's brilliant novel *Eine blaßblaue Frauenschrift*,
senior officials were still in command of the country. This novel is set in
1936. Indeed, the inter-war years were characterized by a high degree of
cabinet instability, both in terms of the classic institutional definitions and
in terms of cabinet members (Müller *et al.*, 1995: 81–6), which would lend
credence to Werfel's claim. Likewise, Peter Huemer's (1975) excellent case
study of the destruction of democracy in inter-war Austria centres on a
civil servant of the same rank as Werfel's main character, *Sektionschef*
Robert Hecht. Hecht was the architect of the 'legal' transition from democracy to dictatorship, which was completed in 1933/4. This case, however,
also indicates the party politicization of senior officials which took place
during the inter-war period. This process was completed in the post-war
Second Republic. We will return to this topic later.

This chapter first provides an overview of the structure of the civil
service in post-war Austria and the position of senior officials within it.
This includes a discussion of recent changes which aim at making the civil
service more flexible and effective and their impact on the top layer of the
permanent bureaucracy. In the following two main sections we are concerned with the incumbents in these positions. We provide information on
the demographic and educational background and career patterns of the
top civil servants and members of the *cabinets ministériels* who served in
the 1970–95 period. We then turn to the political role of senior officials.
The penultimate section discusses the impact of party politics on the civil
service. In the concluding section we summarize the main points of this
chapter.

Formal Structure

1. Senior Officials Defined

What are senior officials? Two kinds of answers are possible, one based on
formal positions in the permanent bureaucracy, the other based on influence on political decisions. In this subsection we provide a top–down
description of the executive and identify the relevant groups.

Austrian government ministries are all headed by a cabinet minister.

There are no non-cabinet ministers in Austria. However, there may be one or more junior ministers.[1] A junior minister (*Staatssekretär*) is a political position. Appointment and removal follow exactly the same rules as in the case of cabinet ministers. Junior ministers are legally subordinate to the minister. Until 1988 their task was limited to assisting the minister and standing in for him in Parliament. In practice, this meant that they were not allowed to stand in for their minister in running the ministry. They were not even legally entitled to direct parts of the ministry. Since 1988, a minister can delegate certain ministerial tasks to a junior minister, if he or she agrees. However, the latter remains bound by the minister's instructions. Ministers and junior ministers constitute the political layer of government ministries. In this chapter we will not be concerned with them.

In 1997 the Austrian civil service at the national level comprises a total of about 200,000 people (this data was made available to us by the Ministry of Finance and is taken from the Personalinformationssystem des Bundes, PIS). This figure relates to a wide range of different state activities, including the armed forces, the police, academic personnel at the universities, and teachers in higher education. These all enjoy civil service status. However, only about one-third of civil servants work in the general central administration. Of those, 8,389 belong to the higher service (A type positions; see below). This is the group from which senior officials are recruited.

The administrative structure of federal ministries consists of four levels, only two of which are obligatory. From top–down they are the department (*Sektion*), the subdepartment (*Gruppe*), the division (*Abteilung*), and the subdivision (*Referat*). While the organization into departments and divisions is obligatory, ministers are free to subdivide departments and divisions. Table 5.1 on pages 94–5 provides an overview of the numbers of these organizational units in the 1966–95 period. According to Table 5.1A the number of departments per ministry has been between three and eleven. Department heads make up a total of roughly eighty people. The number of subdepartment heads has varied considerably and in 1995 was almost six times the level in 1966. Altogether there are a few hundred heads of divisions and subdivisions. Summing up all four levels, in 1995 about 1,700 civil servants held leadership positions in the 40,000 strong central administration (4.3 per cent).

Table 5.1 also provides an answer to the question of whether the overall numbers of senior officials and staff members are increasing, as would be suggested by the thesis of the steady growth of governmental tasks. Or,

---

[1] In practice most ministries do not have junior ministers. Only the Federal Chancellor had more than one.

conversely, whether their number is decreasing because of privatization and deregulation, which have been on the government's agenda for about a decade. While the total number of leadership positions continuously increased in the 1966–95 period, from 546 in 1966 to 1,738 in 1995, their number dropped for the first time in 1997 to 1,383. This is below the level of 1990. Thus, both theses are supported by the Austrian figures.

A typical ministry consists of several departments. Typically, one of them is the presidial department, responsible for the ministry's personnel and finance. While the department heads are generally equal, the head of this department is 'more equal' than his colleagues in internal affairs. The Ministry of Foreign Affairs is a deviant case. There, a director general exists who is the equivalent of a British permanent secretary in being superior to all other civil servants, including the department heads. However, the Foreign Ministry is distinguished from all other ministries by the fact that appointments are not permanent. As a rule, senior officials in the ministry and embassies serve four-year terms. Only occasionally an ambassador or civil servant may stay longer in a specific post for special reasons. The Ministry of Interior also deviates from the pattern of all other departments in having a director general for public security who is head of an extraordinarily large and important department, but who is not formally superior to his colleagues heading normal departments.

If political influence is the defining criterion of senior officials the members of the *cabinets ministériels* have to be taken into account in addition to section, subsection, and division heads. Ministers and junior ministers are free to appoint their personal staff. In practice, many of their staff members are civil servants and are recruited from the ministry itself. Others come from the party, the media, and other occupations, and become public employees under contract (see below). Occasionally, the appointees maintain their original employment, with their employer seconding them to the ministry. Appointees typically prefer this somewhat odd construction if they are already employed in the public sector on quite good terms, e.g. in the public broadcasting system or the central bank. According to media reports, a young minister who hired a more senior journalist from the public broadcasting corporation earned less than his press secretary.

2. Appointment to Senior Official Positions

Austrian civil servants are employed in a vertical system consisting of five types: (A) higher service, (B) senior service, (C) specialist service, (D) middle service, and (E) assistant service. The same vertical system applies to state employees who do not have civil service status, the employees under contract (*Vertragsbedienstete*). Their employment categories parallel those

TABLE 5.1. *Number of (A) Departments* (Sektionen), *(B) Subdepartments* (Gruppen),

(A)	1966	1970	1976	1984	1985	1990	1995
Chancellery	5	5	6	5	4	7	5
Foreign Affairs	5	5	6	6	7	7	7
Economics, Trade, Construction[a]	9	10	11	12	12	9	11
Finance	6	6	7	7	7	6	6
Health, Environment, Family, Youth[b]	—	—	4[c]	4[c]	4[c]	5	9
Interior	4	4	4	4	4	4	4
Justice	6	6	6	6	6	5	6
Defence	4	5	5	5	5	5	5
Agriculture	6	6	6	6	6	6	7
Social Affairs	7	7	6[c]	6[c]	6[c]	6	6
Education	7[d]	7[d]	7[d]	7[d]	7[d]	5	6
Transport	3	4	5	4	5	6	6
Science	—	—	4[d]	4[d]	4[d]	4	5
TOTAL	62	65	77	79	80	75	83
(B)							
Chancellery	3	1	1	2	1	8	4
Foreign Affairs	0	0	0	0	0	1	5
Economics, Trade, Construction[a]	0	1	5	7	7	11	14
Finance	0	0	0	9	8	7	6
Health, Environment, Family, Youth[b]	—	—	6	6	6	8	25
Interior	6	5	5	6	7	5	7
Justice	0	2	1	0	0	0	0
Defence	10	9	9	11	11	14	15
Agriculture	0	—	11	12	12	17	14
Social Affairs	0	2	6	6	6	8	12
Education	0	2	2	3	8	12	13
Transport	1	1	2	1	1	5	5
Science	—	—	1	1	1	2	4
TOTAL	22	24	55	68	75	98	124

Source: 1966–85: Pabst *et al.* (1986); 1990–95: *Amtskalender der Republik Österreich.*

[a] We have combined the Ministry of Trade and Industry (which existed throughout the whole period and the Ministry of Construction and Technics (which was a separate ministry for the 1966–97 period)

[b] We have combined the Ministries of Health, Environment, Family and Youth which, in different portfolio combinations, existed as two or even three separate ministries after 1970.

[c] Joint presidial department of the Ministry of Social Affairs and the Ministry of Health and Environmental Protection.

[d] Joint presidial department of the Ministry of Education, the Arts, and Sport and the Ministry of Science and Research.

(C) Divisions (Abteilungen), *and (D) Subdivisions* (Referate), *1966–1995*

(C)	1966	1970	1976	1984	1985	1990	1995
Chancellery	26	22	32	36	27	67	48
Foreign Affairs	17	25	32	35	39	50	55
Economics, Trade, Construction[a]	68	77	95	96	103	91	108
Finance	47	50	56	70	68	73	71
Health, Environment, Family, Youth[b]	—	—	34	51	56	31	94
Interior	30	29	32	32	34	38	44
Justice	26	35	37	39	39	39	40
Defence	41	49	38	53	53	66	53
Agriculture	31	38	45	53	53	60	63
Social Affairs	43	49	46	46	47	47	54
Education	34	44	49	57	66	86	77
Transport	20	18	40	31	38	57	73
Science	—	—	32	35	36	42	52
TOTAL	383	436	568	634	659	747	832
(D)							
Chancellery	0	5	3	8	8	40	28
Foreign Affairs	2	4	—	28	25	43	74
Economics, Trade, Construction[a]	7	4	19	44	49	53	64
Finance	0	0	1	6	10	20	25
Health, Environment, Family, Youth[b]	—	—	21	21	23	16	95
Interior	7	8	7	6	7	6	18
Justice	0	0	0	0	0	0	0
Defence	2	2	3	18	19	27	47
Agriculture	4	3	41	52	52	58	72
Social Affairs	44	38	15	17	18	30	21
Education	2	22	32	70	69	88	100
Transport	11	5	6	13	13	84	104
Science	—	—	5	9	9	29	51
TOTAL	79	91	153	293	305	494	699

of the civil service and are indicated by small letters (a–e). Employment in the A/a service type requires a university degree, employment in the B/b service type a school graduation (*Matura*) which allows university entry. Both formal qualifications can be compensated for by special courses at the administrative academy.

Appointment to head of department, subdepartment, division, and subdivision normally requires A status. Under exceptional circumstances especially qualified civil servants with B status can be appointed head of divisions and subdivisions (Bundesministeriengesetz, 1973, 1986). People who do not have civil service status can be appointed to any of the four types of leadership positions, provided that these positions are not permanent ones or other important reasons prevent giving civil service status to the appointees. In practice, this clause means that they have qualifications, for instance, in computing, which would, in the private sector, earn a salary so much higher than the salary for civil servants that it would be impossible to recruit them as civil servants. They are, therefore, hired as employees under contract which allows the state more flexibility in terms of payment.

According to the Constitution (Art. 65) it is the President who appoints civil servants. Article 66 of the Constitution, however, allows the President to delegate the appointment of certain (unspecified) categories of civil servants to cabinet ministers. In practice presidents indeed have delegated most types of civil service appointments to cabinet ministers since 1924 (Bundesministeriengesetz, 1924, 1930, 1995*d*). They have reserved only appointments in the two highest service classes (VIII and IX) for themselves. All these appointments have to be agreed unanimously by the cabinet before they are formally proposed to the President.

Since a constitutional amendment in 1994 the President may allow cabinet ministers to further delegate the appointment of certain (unspecified) categories of civil servants to heads of large administrative units (Bundesministeriengesetz, 1994). This amendment merely ratified existing though unconstitutional practice. Ministers generally have not been concerned with the recruitment of low-ranking civil servants to these units. Since the constitutional amendment they have officially delegated their appointment power (Bundesministeriengesetz, 1995*a–c*, 1996).

Appointments to head of department, subdepartment, and division are made only after the vacancies have been publicly advertised in a formal procedure. The advertisements are published in the official government paper, the *Amtsblatt zur Wiener Zeitung*. They detail the qualifications and abilities required for the specific positions, e.g. a degree in law, the command of foreign languages, and management abilities. All applications are scrutinized by commissions which are established for each vacancy individually. Commissions consist of four members. Two members are appointed by the minister, one by the civil servants' trade union and one by the central civil service representative body, the Zentralausschuß (which normally works closely with the trade union). A constitutional clause determines that members of this kind of commission are autonomous and independent, i.e. their decisions in this capacity are made outside the ministry's normal chain of command. The commission is chaired by one of the minister's appointees. The commission distinguishes qualified from unqualified applicants and ranks the qualified ones. In so doing the majority principle is applied. In the case of ties the chairman casts the decisive vote. Dissenting opinions are reported along with the majority's decision. The commission's review is not legally binding on the minister. If the minister decides not to appoint the applicant who was ranked first by the commission the central civil service representative body is entitled to be informed about the minister's reasons for doing so (Ausschreibungs- gesetz, 1989, 1991).

Positions in *cabinets ministériels* need not be advertised (Bundesminis- teriengesetz, 1991). Normally the ministers have clear ideas about whom they want to hire and do so without any formal procedure. Appointment to a staff position from outside the civil service, however, is not the equi- valent of access to the civil service. Members of *cabinets ministériels* who wish to continue their career in the regular civil service have to go through the procedure as outlined above.

3. Accession to the Civil Service and Tenure

Appointments to senior official positions are normally made from within the civil service. It is, therefore, necessary briefly to review accession to the civil service and acquiring tenure (a *definitives Dienstverhältnis*; the act of acquisition which is referred to as *Pragmatisierung*). Once a civil servant has tenure he or she can no longer be made redundant. Civil servants with tenure enjoy a great amount of protection also in other respects. In par- ticular, they cannot be removed from their positions easily (see below). There is an ongoing discussion on limiting tenure to those civil servants involved in state jurisdiction (*Hoheitsverwaltung*).

Since 1989, all civil service positions and positions for employees under contract need to be publicly advertised. Any position must be contained in a specific ministry's official plan of positions (which is part of the budget). The annual budget negotiations between the individual ministries and the Ministry of Finance are paralleled by negotiations about personnel posi- tions. Until 1997 personnel matters rested with the Federal Chancellery. This competence and the respective department were transferred to the Finance Ministry when the former Minister of Finance Viktor Klima became Chancellor in 1997. In these negotiations the individual ministries normally try to increase or at least to maintain their numbers of personnel.

The hiring decision itself rests with the individual ministries. Applicants for A/a positions are typically screened in a job interview in which the applicant faces several top civil servants of the hiring ministry. Alternatively, hiring decisions are made in so-called assessment centres where several applicants are interviewed simultaneously and in a competitive atmosphere. The ministries are free to decide whether they hire their personnel already on the civil service track (*provisorisches Dienstverhältnis*) or whether they hire personnel as employees under contract. In practice, the latter method is the much more frequent one. Both tracks can lead to civil service status with tenure. Until 1996 probation was four years: now it is six years. During this time employees who do not fulfil the ministry's expectations can be made redundant. A formal requirement for acquiring tenure is the civil service examination (*Dienstprüfung*), although there are exceptions for officials in the higher medical and technical services whose special training exempts them from an extra civil service examination. The examination is preceded by training in the administrative academy. Large ministries typically have their own training institutions such as the federal finance school belonging to the Finance Ministry. There is a similar training institution in the Ministry of the Interior. The examination is held by permanent examination commissions some of which are entirely ministry-based while others also contain representatives of the central personnel department (i.e. the Chancellery until 1997 and the Finance Ministry since then).

The Foreign Ministry is a special case. Accession to the foreign service requires the passing of the *examen préalable*. In this exam the applicants have to prove their ability to understand political, economic, cultural, and legal matters in international relations and they have to demonstrate their language skills (German, English, and French). The *examen préalable* is held by a commission of five senior civil servants of the Foreign Ministry. A precondition for being accepted as candidate is graduation from law, political science, or any discipline of the social science and economics faculties. Candidates who hold a different university degree can compensate for this by graduating from the Vienna diplomatic academy or an equivalent postgraduate institution. The diplomatic academy is the training institution of the Foreign Ministry and, in practice, most candidates for the *examen préalable* go through it.

Being eligible for leadership positions in the civil service in practice also requires further training. Though there is no legal obligation, applicants for head of division and higher positions are expected to have gone through the leadership course of the administrative academy. Likewise, courses in rhetoric, law-making, and other subjects (for instance, the European Union) may be demanded for certain leadership positions, or having taken these courses may constitute an advantage in the competition for these positions.

4. Payment

Until 1996 civil servants of A status were paid according to their position in a system of service classes, ranging from III to IX. Promotion led from a lower class to a higher class. This system was not in practice performance-related, nor did it offer incentives for good performance. Although there were performance-review procedures in which an individual's job perform-ance could be rated, in practice this system was never properly applied: almost all civil servants were rated 'excellent' by their superiors, suggesting that that the civil servant concerned has 'by special achievements, gone beyond the line of duty'. To avoid potential conflict, the top civil servants hardly made differentiations in their ratings. Since the system did not dis-criminate, individual performance had no effect on promotion within the administration or on pay (Müller, 1994). Consequently, promotion de-pended largely on seniority. After the reforms of the late 1980s, appointees to a few top civil service positions could be paid on the basis of special contracts. They were: the head of the constitutional service in the Federal Chancellery (which checks the constitutionality of draft bills and has other important tasks), the director general for public security, the director gen-eral of the postal services, the secretary general for foreign affairs, and the heads of large ministerial departments and very large subdepartments which have coordination tasks for all ministries, e.g. the head of the per-sonnel department.

The 1996 payment regulation has replaced the old service classes by a system which distinguishes nine groups of functions (I–IX). The payment of civil servants consists of their basic salary plus extra pay for their func-tions. The extra pay is substantial. Only those civil servants who occupy a leadership function are entitled to receive it. Once a civil servant is removed from a leadership position, the extra pay is immediately cancelled. If the leadership positions are abolished due to the ministry's reorganization, the extra pay will be paid for another three years.

The new payment system automatically applies to all civil servants ap-pointed since 1 January 1996. Those appointed before this date remain under the old system but have the right to opt for the new system. Incum-bents of those few top leadership positions who have a special contract providing them with substantially higher payment than the normal civil service payment scheme had to opt for the new payment system until

1 January 1998. Likewise, appointments of civil servants to leadership positions are tied to the appointees' opting for the new system.

5. Accountability of Senior Officials and the Politics of Ministerial Reorganization

Legally, each minister has organizational power over his or her ministry. This means that the minister can create or abolish departments, subdepartments, divisions, and subdivisions. The precondition for new organizational units, or at least the adequate payment of appointees to these positions, was that they had been provided for in the personnel plan. Under the pre-1996 system incumbents could be removed from leadership positions provided that they were offered a position of the same rank. If this was not the case an 'urgent official interest' was required. Civil servants could appeal to the Administrative Court which then had the last word. The Court as a rule accepted ministerial reorganizations as a reason for the removal of incumbents (without further questions about the reasons for the reorganization) but frequently rejected other justifications. As long as the case remained undecided new appointments remained provisional. Although the chances of succeeding in the Court were good for ministers who removed incumbent civil servants in the course of a ministerial reorganization, only a few of them went down this path. Having undecided Court cases has generally been seen as having a negative impact on the ministry's organizational culture, and many ministers feared they might lose more in terms of having an effective ministry than they might win by making such changes. However, the old system to some extent offered a suitable alternative, provided the Federal Chancellery and the Ministry of Finance cooperated. A minister could tailor-make the ministry for his or her needs by creating new organizational units, giving them the most relevant tasks (which were removed from the old units) and by appointing heads who were in tune with the minister. While the creation of new departments was more tricky, subdepartments could be established relatively easily. If a minister wanted to deprive a department head of power the trick was to establish a large subdepartment. The most frequent reason for ministers to engage in the politics of ministerial reorganization was related to the party affiliation of senior civil servants (see below).

The new system, which became effective in 1996, has changed the accountability of senior civil servants considerably. They can no longer appeal to the Administrative Court. They can appeal to a court-like commission which decides quickly (within four months). Moreover, the reform of the payment system has increased flexibility. Under the new system, a minister may not only offer a leadership position but also, without increasing the number of administrative units, adequate payment. An unintended consequence of this system, however, has been to make civil servants much more hostile towards ministerial reorganizations, in particular those which decrease the number of administrative units.

The most relevant difference between the old and new systems, however, is that many appointments to positions of the three highest function groups (VII–IX) are made only temporary, for a period of five years. These positions include function group IX containing, among others heads of large ministerial departments, the director of the federal president's *cabinet*, the head of the Austrian mission in the European Union, and the governor of the post office bank; function group VIII for, among others, heads of smaller ministerial departments and the administrative directors of the parliamentary parties; and function group VII for officials such as the deputy director of the president's office, the heads of departments in Parliament, and the heads of large ministerial subdepartments.

Demographic and Educational Background

In this section we look at the demographic and educational background of both the heads of departments and the members of the *cabinets ministériels*. As we could not find any ready-made statistical data on these two groups, we have generated the empirical data from the Austrian *Amtskalender* (a handbook published annually since 1702), extracting information for the 1970–95 period. Within these twenty-five years there were 298 incumbents of the position of head of department and 527 ministerial staff members. We can examine the general characteristics of these groups, the major trends in their development over the past twenty-five years, and set out significant differences between ministries.

1. General Trends

Compared to the heads of departments, the number of members of the *cabinets ministériels* was quite low during the 1970s (see Figure 5.1). In 1970, there were thirty-two of them and their number even dropped to twenty-eight in 1971. This probably was due to the change of government in 1970 from the People's Party (ÖVP) to the Social Democrats (SPÖ), who had criticized the emerging *cabinets ministériels* when in opposition. However, once in power the Social Democrats recognized the need for personal staffs of cabinet ministers. During the next fourteen years the number of the members of the *cabinets ministériels* more than doubled, rising to sixty-six—and of course, this increase was now criticized by the opposition

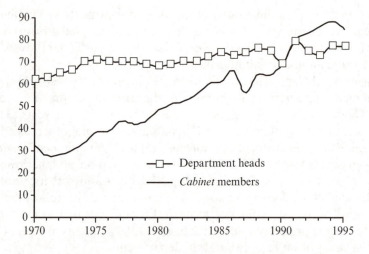

FIGURE 5.1. Numbers of Department Heads and Members of the *Cabinets Ministériels*, 1970–1995 (absolute numbers)

ÖVP (Engelmayer, 1976; Pabst *et al.*, 1986). Only in 1987 were they temporarily reduced by ten, which might be explained by the cabinet reshuffles which took place in 1986 and 1987. From 1988 onwards the numbers of *cabinet* members rose from sixty-four to eighty-eight in 1994, which is an increase of more than one-third. The rapid growth in numbers following 1987 might be due to another change of government from the coalition of the Social Democrats and the Freedom Party (FPÖ) to the grand coalition of SPÖ and ÖVP. Having been out of office for sixteen years, the ÖVP probably had a relatively strong demand to staff the *cabinets ministériels* well.

If we relate the number of members to the number of their masters, i.e. the politicians who serve in minister or junior minister positions, we see that the *cabinets ministériels* are very small. While the total number of staff members has varied between thirty-two and eighty-eight in the 1970–95 period, the number of ministers and junior ministers has varied between fifteen and twenty-four (Müller, 1997: 124). This means that on average each of the politicians had two to four staff members. While the average was two in the early 1970s, it was four in the mid-1990s.

2. Status and Educational Background

According to the Federal Ministries Act of 1973 only bureaucrats with an academic degree should be appointed to leadership positions, although civil servants belonging to the level of senior service (B level, with the prerequisite of secondary school graduation) have the possibility of promotion to a higher rank (A level) by taking a special examination. As we have seen, according to the Ministry of Finance's PIS figures there are slightly more than 8,000 civil servants holding A positions in the general administration in 1997. In 1996 about 7,000 civil servants with A status in the general administration held an academic degree. Although these numbers cannot be compared on a one-to-one basis, as they are taken from two different years, we still may conclude that about one-eighth of the civil servants in A positions have been appointed after having taken special exams at the administrative academy. Only very few of the administrative academy graduates acquire top leadership positions, however. There were only three of them among the department heads in the 1970–95 period. Until 1994 all heads of department were civil servants. In 1995 the first employee under contract was appointed head of department (in the Ministry of Economic Affairs).

As mentioned above, staff members may be recruited internally (i.e. from the civil service) or externally (i.e. as employees under contract). In the 1970–95 period the vast number of them was recruited from the civil service. While initially almost all staff members were civil servants, the percentage of employees under contract rose from 3.6 in 1971 to 23.3 in 1979. In the 1980–94 period their share went up and down, with a minimum of 16.7 per cent and a maximum of 26.7 per cent. In 1995, they peaked at 32.9 per cent.

It is common wisdom that the Austrian bureaucracy has traditionally been dominated by law school graduates. The reason for this is seen in the rule of law. This is established in Article 18 (1) of the Federal Constitution: 'The entire public administration shall be based on law.' The courts have insisted on a very strict application of this rule. In addition, the training of the law students at Austrian universities used to comprise a more general education centred not only on law. The strict application of the rule of law has not changed during the last decades. What has changed is the training at law schools. Law graduates nowadays get a much more narrow law-centred training than in previous decades. As rule-making and rule-adjudication have turned into very complex matters due to technological, social, and economic changes it might be expected that non-legal experts are also needed in the top layers of the bureaucracy. This might have given people from other educational backgrounds the chance of becoming civil servants and reaching top positions in the civil service. Therefore, we proceeded from the assumption that the number of law school graduates would be declining both in the *cabinets* and in the permanent bureaucracy during the twenty-five years we observed. Empirical data, however, provide ambiguous evidence (see Figure 5.2).

Today there is no 'monopoly' of law school graduates among civil servants with A status, though, accounting for 45 per cent, they constitute

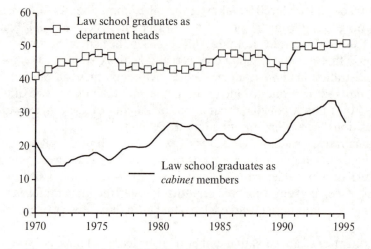

FIGURE 5.2. Number of Law School Graduates Among Department Heads and Members of the *Cabinets Ministériels*, 1970–1995 (absolute numbers)

by far the single most important group. Law school graduates are more important in the top ranks of bureaucracy, however. In the 1970–95 period, they have accounted for nearly two thirds of the department heads: 66 per cent of the heads of departments were law school graduates in 1970 and the same was true for 1995. In the 1970–95 period their overall share never dropped below 60 per cent but also never reached 70 per cent (see Figure 5.2). It is no longer accurate to refer to a 'monopoly' of law school graduates, if it ever was, but they still have a predominant position at the highest level of the central administration. Law school graduates are followed by technical, agricultural, and drainage engineers.

Law school graduates also constitute the single most important educational group among the members of the *cabinets ministériels*, however their predominance is less obvious. 227 of our 527 *cabinet* staff members in the 1970–95 period have held a law degree (43 per cent). In any one year, the proportion of law graduates in the personal staffs of ministers varied between 32 per cent and 66 per cent in the period under consideration. While the data on members of ministerial *cabinets* are harder to interpret as they list a higher proportion of academic qualifications which do not unambiguously relate to a particular discipline, law school graduates still accounted for nearly one-third of the ministerial staffs in 1995. They are followed by economists (ranging from 5 to 23 per cent), social scientists/ arts scholars (varying from 6 to 22 per cent), and technicians (ranging from 0 to 13 per cent). People without an academic degree are much more common in the *cabinets ministériels* than among the heads of departments (varying from 0 to 18 per cent). Most of them served as press secretaries. It is interesting to note that the number of non-graduates peaked in the 1971–7 period; these were the early years of social democratic government.

3. Gender

If we look at the very top layer of the bureaucracy, the heads of department, ministries seem to be typical male institutions. It was not until 1985 that the first woman became head of department (in the Ministry of Agriculture and Forestry). It took another four years for a second woman to be promoted to such a position (in the Ministry for Labour and Social Affairs). In 1993, a third woman reached the top ranks of the civil service in the Ministry for Environment, Youth, and Family. In 1995, only two of the seventy-seven heads of departments were women—fewer than 3 per cent. Women headed only 10 per cent of the subdepartments and 15 per cent of the divisions (Neyer, 1997: 197). Despite their still marginal representation in the top civil service, the share of women has substantially increased among subdepartment and division heads over the last decade, as Neyer (1997: 197) has shown. The severe underrepresentation of women in the top ranks of the civil service to a large extent is due to its rigid promotion system (automatic biannual advancement). Most of the well-educated female bureaucrats do not stay in office long enough to be up for promotion to the highest civil service ranks. The recent flexibilization of appointments has potentially improved the career chances of women. If we take a look at the number of women holding A positions in the general administration in 1996 and 1997, there is indeed a large number of women in waiting positions. Women account for a quarter of those who have acquired tenure and 45 per cent of the employees under contract.

In the *cabinets ministériels* women are less represented than among civil servants in A positions, but they do much better than in the top layer of the permanent bureaucracy. During the 1970s they constituted between 6 and 14 per cent of *cabinet* members. In the 1980s between 14 and 23 per cent were women. In the first half of the 1990s the share of women peaked at 27 per cent in 1993, dropping to 19 per cent in 1995.

4. Comparison of Ministries

In order to avoid effects from ministerial restructuring we have grouped the ministries into thirteen categories according to their subject (see Table 5.1). Especially the fields of Environment, Family, and Health have seen much restructuring. In addition to these policy fields there were several ministers who did not have a ministry of their own, but were hosted in the Federal

Chancellery. Their only human resources were the members of their *cabinets ministériels*. These ministers included the Minister for Federalism and Administrative Reform, the Minister for Health (1987–91), and the Minister for Women's Affairs. In addition to these ministers there were several junior ministers, who had a staff of their own.

5. Heads of Departments

As Table 5.2 shows, the general predominance of law school graduates has been a monopoly indeed in two ministries: the Ministries of Finance and Interior. There, law school graduates have amounted to 100 per cent over the period 1970 to 1995. The Ministries of Justice and Public Economy were dominated by law school graduates, too. Law school graduates outnumbered heads of departments with different educational backgrounds in the majority of ministries except the Ministries of Education, Agriculture, Defence, and Economic Affairs. In the Ministry of Economic Affairs engineers and technicians held a significant position, perhaps resulting from the merger of the Ministries for Trade and Industry and Construction and Engineering in 1987. Economists were not only outnumbered by the engineers but also by law school graduates. Men from the army clearly dominate the Ministry of Defence and agricultural engineers the Ministry of Agriculture. In the Ministry for Education law school graduates and social scientists/ arts scholars are equal in number. So we may conclude that the outliers, the Ministries of Defence and Agriculture, appoint bureaucrats according to relevant subject-matter rather than a legal background.

6. Members of Cabinets Ministériels

Law school graduates enjoyed a very prominent position in the Ministries of Foreign Affairs (89.7 per cent) and Justice (91.7 per cent), and a less significant but still dominant position in the Ministry of Interior (63.2 per cent) (see Table 5.3). In the Federal Chancellery, in the *cabinets* of junior ministers and in the Ministry of Economic Affairs they ranged from 43.2 per cent to 58 per cent. In the offices of junior ministers they were followed by economists and social scientists/arts scholars, in the Ministry of Economic Affairs by engineers (20.6 per cent) and economists (19.1 per cent), who were almost equal in number. The Ministry of Finance was dominated by economists (43.9 per cent), the Ministry of Agriculture by agricultural engineers (34.6 per cent), the Ministry of Defence by officers (36.8 per cent), and the Ministries for Women's Affairs and for Education by social scientists/arts scholars. So, the outliers of the ministries were also dominated by staff members especially qualified for these areas.

TABLE 5.2. *Characteristics of Department Heads According to Ministries, 1970–1995 (absolute numbers)*

Ministries	Total (employees under contract)	Women	Law graduates	Economists	Engineers/ technicians	Social scientists/ arts scholars	At least two academic degrees incl. law	Others
Federal Chancellery	23 (0)		17	1		1	2	2[a]
Foreign Affairs	44 (0)		35	4		1	3	1
Labour and Social Affairs	22 (0)	1	16		1		1	4[b]
Economic Affairs	43 (1)		13	7	16	1	5	1[c]
Finance	27 (0)		27					
Interior	15 (0)		15					
Justice	24 (0)		23				1	
Agriculture and Forestry	20 (0)	1	8		9	1	2	
Defence	19 (0)		4					15[d]
Education, Arts, and Sports	19 (0)		6		3	6	3	1[e]
Science and Research	11 (0)		8			3		
Public Economy and Transport	17 (0)		14		1		2	
Health, Environment, Family/Youth, and Consumer Protection	14 (0)	1	9		3			2[f]
TOTAL	298 (1)	3	197	12	33	13	19	25

[a] One medical doctor.
[b] One medical doctor, two without academic degree, one with at least two academic degrees excluding law.
[c] At least two academic degrees excluding law.
[d] Army/army plus academic degree.
[e] No academic degree.
[f] Medical doctors.

TABLE 5.3. *Characteristics of the Members of Cabinets Ministériels According to Ministries, 1970–1995 (absolute numbers)*

	Total (employees under contract)	Women	Law graduates	Economists	Engineers/ technicians	Social scientists/ scholars of the arts	Academic degrees (unknown origin)	No academic degree	Others
Federal Chancellery									
Cabinet of Federal Chancellor	36 (5)	4	18	6		3	7		2[a]
Cabinet of Vice-Chancellor[b]	21 (1)	2	6		1	3	9	1	1[c]
Minister for Federalism and Administrative Reform	5 (2)	3	2			2			
Minister of Health	5 (3)	1	3	1		1			1[d]
Minister for Women	13 (13)	12	2			7	4		
Cabinet of secretaries of state	37 (15)	16	16	5	1	9	5		1[e]
Ministries									
Foreign Affairs	39 (0)	2	35	3		6			1[f]
Labour and Social Affairs[g]	26 (3)	8	10	2		2	2	4	2[h]
Interior	19 (1)	2	12	1		2		2	2[i]
Justice	12 (0)		11					1	
Economic Affairs[g]	78 (10)	8	37	15	16	5		2	3[j]
Finance[g]	57 (16)	7	21	25		2	3	2	4[k]

Agriculture and Forestry[g]	26 (0)	1	9	1	9	1	1	3	2[l]
Public Economy and Transport	27 (2)	3	6	2	5	2	9	2	1[m]
Defence	19 (4)	1	3	2	1	4	1	4	9[n]
Education, Arts, and Sports	34 (9)	6	11	2	1	14	3	2	1[o]
Science and Research	21 (3)	8	7	2		7	3	2	
Health, Environment, Family/Youth, and Consumer Protection[g]	52 (26)	22	18	2	2	6	11	8	5[p]
TOTAL	517 (109)	110	227	69	36	74	55	31	35

[a] One with at least two academic degrees including law, one with at least two academic degrees excluding law.
[b] At the same time Minister for Federalism and Administrative Reform (1989/90–1991/92), plus office of secretary of state for sports (1995/96).
[c] One graduate from an arts college.
[d] One medical doctor.
[e] One with two academic degrees of unknown origin.
[f] At least two academic degrees including law.
[g] Including advisers of state secretaries.
[h] One with at least two academic degrees including law, one doctor of divinity.
[i] One 'graduate engineer', one officer.
[j] One professor, two 'graduate engineers'.
[k] Three with at least two academic degrees including law, one doctor of divinity.
[l] One 'graduate engineer', one with two academic degrees including law.
[m] One with at least two academic degrees including law.
[n] Two with at least two academic degrees including law, seven army/army+academic degree.
[o] One professor.
[p] Three medical doctors, one 'graduate engineer', one interpreter.

There are striking differences between the ministries in terms of staffing the *cabinets ministériels* with employees under contract. According to Table 5.3 there were some ministries that did not have any employees under contract or only very few of them. Another interesting aspect of these ministries is that they employed either no or at least fewer women than other ministries. Among them are the Ministries of Foreign Affairs, Justice, Interior, and Agriculture.

Female ministers and junior ministers seem to increase the number of female advisers. Especially during the years of Johanna Dohnal, who was junior minister for Women's Affairs between 1983 and 1989, the proportion of female advisers of the secretaries of state in the Federal Chancellery never dropped below one-third of the overall advisory staff. Interestingly, the peak number of employees under contract coincides with this period of time. When Dohnal became Minister for Women's Affairs in 1990 her staff was almost entirely female and so was the number of employees under contract. The Ministry for Labour and Social Affairs had a female minister in 1970 and there were two women among her advisers. Thereafter men served as ministers and the number of women in their *cabinets* dropped to zero. Similar developments can be observed in the ministries for Education, Science, and Research, and in the fields of Health, Family, and Environment, which were partly headed by male and female ministers.

Duration in Office and Inter-Ministerial Mobility

Those who stress the power of civil servants often refer to the common wisdom that ministers come and go but civil servants remain in office. Ministers indeed come and go. The average duration of ministers in the same portfolio is 3.3 years in the 1945–92 period (Müller *et al.*, 1997). But what is the duration of top civil servants, not in the civil service in general, but in key positions? A related question is whether leading civil servants remain bound to one specific ministry or, conversely, whether there is a relevant amount of inter-ministerial mobility among them. We have no data which allows us to answer the duration question straightforwardly. Rather we have to rely on stability indicators which we have again generated from the Austrian *Amtskalender*. This is also the source for our answers to the inter-ministerial mobility question.

We might expect duration in post and mobility to differ between heads of department and staff members. Senior civil servants usually become heads of department a few years before they retire. This regular pattern is thwarted only when a relatively young senior civil servant not up for promotion is preferred due to political reasons or on merit. Members of the *cabinets ministériels* stay in office only as long as their patron (the minister) wants. If he or she resigns or is removed, they have to leave as well, though occasionally a new minister may decide to recruit some of his staff members from the *cabinets ministériels* of his or her predecessor, provided that the portfolio remains within the hands of the same party. In the case of ministerial reshuffles, staff members are generally expected to follow their patron, although staff members with special policy expertise are more likely to stay than personal and press secretaries.

1. Stability Indicators

In order to compare the duration in office, we calculated figures for three separate periods in which the relevant officials took up their positions— 1970 to 1975, 1976 to 1985, and 1986 to 1995. Among the 117 heads of departments appointed before 1975 traced through the *Amtskalendar*, the average term of office amounted to 8.4 years. Seven bureaucrats remained in office for eighteen or more years (two of them stayed eighteen, another two twenty, and another two twenty-three years, while one even enjoyed his position for a quarter of a century). During the second period the average term of office dropped to 6.0 years. However, seventeen of these eighty-three bureaucrats remained in office in 1995. The last period cannot be compared with the earlier period since almost two-thirds of these ninety-eight bureaucrats are still in office. Consequently, the average time in the office of head of department dropped to 3.4 years.

Compared to the heads of departments' duration in office the members of the *cabinets ministériels* served much shorter periods. Those 103 staff members appointed before 1975 on average worked for 3.9 years in the *cabinets ministériels*. Since only three of the 157 appointed to *cabinets ministériels* between 1976 and 1985 remained in office in 1995, the data on this period are more conclusive than for the heads of departments. The staff members' average term of office dropped to 3.1 years. More than one-third of the 267 advisers employed between 1986 and 1995 were still in office in 1995 and so the average time of office dropped further to 2.6 years.

2. Inter-Ministerial Mobility

Austrian civil servants become specialists during their career and consequently they rarely change from one ministry to another. This is certainly true once they have reached the top, as head of departments. Only fourteen out of 298 heads of departments changed from one ministry to another during the 1970–95 period. In all cases the moves followed reorganizations when departments were shifted from one ministry to another. Of the four-teen, ten resulted from reorganization of ministerial structures in Health, Family, and Environment. Another ten heads of departments served two different ministries at the same time, directing a joint department for per-sonnel and coordination matters. This joint department was the rump of a larger ministry which previously had united the tasks of the respective ministries.

Among the members of the *cabinets ministériels* inter-ministerial mobil-ity is much more common, fifty-five of the 527 appointed between 1970 and 1995 served in more than one ministry. Seven of them changed minis-tries due to the restructuring of the areas of Health, Environment, and Family, but forty-eight of these advisers actually changed from one min-istry to another. Some eighteen of those who changed ministry stayed in the same area[2] while thirty changed to a completely different policy field. About 40 per cent of those who changed ministry followed their minister, when he or she was reshuffled. One of these advisers, Rudolf Scholten, pur-sued a political career, becoming Minister for Education, Arts, and Sports after having headed a government agency for several years.

There is a third kind of mobility, namely the one between the *cabinets ministériels* and the departments of the ministries: thirty-eight (5 per cent) of all the 825 bureaucrats and ministerial staff members observed between 1970 and 1995 experienced this kind of mobility (more may be to come); thirty-three of the thirty-eight started as advisers to the minister and be-came heads of departments afterwards. Only five of these changed to a different ministry. Only one departmental head came back as (a special) member of a *cabinet*—Willibald Pahr was departmental head in the Fed-eral Chancellery from 1973 to 1977, in the 1977–83 period he was Minister of Foreign Affairs, and after serving in an international organization he came back as a special adviser of the Minister of the Interior concerning refugee matters in 1992.

The Political Role of Senior Officials

Austrian ministries are organized in a strictly hierarchical way. In principle all decisions rest with the minister. Since it would be rather cumbersome

---

[2] We combined the various ministries into nine areas: (1) Federal Chancellery, (2) Min-istry of Foreign Affairs, (3) Ministry for Labour and Social Affairs, (4) Ministries of Interior and Justice, (5) Ministries of Finance, Economic Affairs and Public Economy, and Trans-port, (6) Ministries for Education, Arts and Sports and for Science and Research, (7) Minis-tries in the field of Health, Family and Environment, (8) Ministry of Defence, (9) Ministry for Agriculture and Forestry.

and ineffective to bring all matters to the minister's attention and wait for his or her decision, the minister is entitled to delegate specified groups of tasks to heads of departments, subdepartments, divisions, and subdivisions. In these matters civil servants decide autonomously, but they do so for the minister and sign in his name. The minister remains constitutionally responsible for all these acts, and delegation of tasks to certain civil servants does not interfere with the chain of command. Thus, the minister is entitled to issue commands to the civil servants of his or her department, can withdraw issues from the scope of those civil servants to whom these matters were delegated, or can reserve decisions for himself or herself.

As elsewhere, the Austrian bureaucracy is, in reality, much more influential than the Constitution outlines (Fischer, 1977; Kneucker, 1973 and 1981; Neisser, 1974 and 1997). Its role in the making and implementation of laws is generally viewed as very important, especially since Austria is not accustomed to the practice of providing each government minister with a group of 'temporary civil servants' appointed on the basis of political criteria for the duration of the government's term of office as a sort of 'buffer' between ministers and their departments. Likewise the *cabinets ministériels* have remained small (see above). While it is true that ministers can also draw on the personnel resources of interest groups when preparing policies (Fischer, 1977: 102), this does not apply to all ministers. Moreover this could only affect the role of civil service expertise in policy formulation but not their role in policy implementation. Finally, in recent years the relations between the government and interest groups have become more strained, even in cases where the minister was recruited from an interest group. Thus the ministry's civil servants remain the most important structure on which a minister can draw. Though the ministerial structure is monocratic, and ministers can force through every particular policy decision, in general terms they depend on the cooperation of the bureaucracy. If it does not provide its expertise readily, if it 'overinforms' or 'underinforms' the minister, or if it follows a policy of deliberately limiting his or her alternatives in decision-making to the department's conventional wisdom, the minister will have little policy impact and may run into political problems.

It is not necessarily the case, however, that the minister is faced with a single, monolithic bloc of bureaucracy. The common background of law studies of most civil servants and the socialization within the bureaucracy certainly has a unifying effect, but as elsewhere, personal rivalries and career interests constitute limiting factors. Since 1945, however, the most important division within the bureaucracy has been the political one.

Party Politics and Senior Officials

Traditionally, the Austrian bureaucracy was conservative, mainly Catholic–conservative but also German–national; social democrats were excluded. During the First Republic and in particular between 1934 and 1938, the civil service was further colonized and made more partisan by the Catholic–conservative *Lager*. In the subsequent period of Nazi rule (1938–45), the bureaucracy was purged of Jews, of the supporters of the previous regime, and of those who had remained highly loyal to the notion of an Austrian state. The remaining bureaucrats were either genuine Nazis or were forced to join the Nazi Party in order to keep their jobs (Steiner, 1972: 375–83). In 1945, denazification removed some of them and brought some of the former civil servants back. However, the new government needed experts and the Socialists suspected that, if denazification was carried out properly, the civil service would consist entirely of supporters of the Austro-fascist regime (1934–8) and ÖVP partisans. Thus, both governing parties decided to give some of the ex-Nazis among the civil servants a second chance and absorbed them. The Communists, who also initially participated in the government, had advocated a more rigorous denazification policy.

In order to recruit SPÖ members to the higher ranks of the civil service, the *Proporz* system was established. It granted each of the two governing parties a proportion of public-sector jobs roughly equal to their share of the vote in the previous general election. While this was made explicit for public-sector firms in the coalition contracts, the *Proporz* remained implicit for the civil service. Each party enjoyed personnel autonomy in the ministries under its control; the departments in turn were distributed according to electoral strength (Secher, 1958: 796–808; Steiner, 1972: 383–97). Due to the lack of qualified personnel in the socialist subculture and in view of the fact that the system of a tenured civil service does not permit large-scale adjustments of civil service personnel in the short term, *Proporz* was never fully established in the civil service (Engelmann, 1966: 274). Nevertheless, during the period of grand coalition government the bureaucracy became almost entirely party controlled. Both parties had their strongholds in those government departments which were under their respective permanent control but also had 'bridgeheads' in the other ministries. Both parties could rely on a number of top civil servants with extremely strong party ties and who were inclined instinctively to think along the same lines as politicians from the same party. This, of course, had consequences for the minister–civil servant relationship and for the civil servants' role in general. Civil servants acted as *party* experts and (if a ministry was controlled by a party other than their own) even party spies. Although all this violated the classical concept of a 'neutral' or 'non-partisan' bureaucracy, it led to a civil service and an army which, for the first time in modern Austrian history, incorporated both major political subcultures and were thus fully acceptable to both major parties (Secher, 1958: 809).

After the old grand coalition ended in 1966, the party picture became more complex. The single-party governments of the ÖVP (1966–70) and SPÖ (1970–83) felt obliged to announce a non-partisan approach in their civil service recruitment and promotion policy. However, results of elections to the staff councils reveal that during the periods in which they formed single-party governments, the ÖVP and the SPÖ increased their support in their strongholds and made inroads into the strongholds of the other party (Müller, 1989: 337). Electoral results relate to *all* civil service jobs. In this chapter, however we are interested first and foremost in senior officials. Here the governing party reserved the lion's share appointments for its own purposes, but the other major party was not totally marginalized. The SPÖ government in particular was keen to demonstrate that it was not exploiting its power and turning the civil service into an SPÖ apparatus. Therefore, ÖVP supporters were still appointed to prestigious positions, and some high positions were given to 'blood group O' people (i.e. non-party members). Since the SPÖ originally had had a weak position in the civil service compared with that of the ÖVP, it would not have had appropriate candidates available for all the vacancies, in particular not in the traditional ÖVP departments. Nevertheless, the overall effect of the SPÖ government and the subsequent SPÖ–FPÖ coalition, was a considerable shift in power in the central administration in favour of the SPÖ.

The new grand coalition (since 1987) from the very beginning faced the criticism that it would return to the old 'iron' system of patronage, simply because the spoils once again had to be shared between two parties of almost equal strength. Against the background of declining trust in the major parties the government tried to pre-empt this criticism by introducing a new Appointment Law (1989), according to which entering the civil service was to be based entirely on the basis of objective tests. Moreover, appointments to a number of leading positions in the public administration were to be made only for a fixed, limited period of time according to professional criteria. In practice, however, these reforms have not substantially reduced the capacity of the government to influence personnel decisions within public administration. And, indeed, the top layer of the civil service is almost entirely appointed on the basis of party affiliation, with the appointees belonging to or being loyal to the party in charge of the ministry in question. Going down to the middle level of the civil service this still holds true for the overwhelming majority of appointments, although at this level some positions go to supporters of the party which is not in charge of the respective portfolio in order pacify this group within the ministry; sometimes, there seems to be inter-ministerial logrolling on these 'non-mainstream' appointments. Prestigious positions, such as ambassadors to foreign countries or international organizations, are normally negotiated between the government parties, and after these negotiations a minority of positions go to the SPÖ which is not in charge of the Foreign Ministry. Altogether 'party' has been more important for appointments in the civil service since the return to grand coalition government in 1987 than under the more 'liberal' regime of single-party rule (until 1983). Having been out of government for seventeen years (from 1970 until 1987) and still having a more numerous clientele among civil servants (as the elections to personnel representation bodies reveal), it is probably more important for the ÖVP to exploit its patronage potential in the grand coalition government.

The administrative reform of the grand coalition government has taken some functions away from the civil service. They now have a private-sector organization which is assumed to be more flexible and to produce better results. In the case of the agency concerned with jobs and training (Arbeitsmarktverwaltung) this led to the appointment of two managers (rather than one as previously), one from each of the governing parties. ÖVP cabinet ministers were brave enough to state publicly that this was meant to maintain political control over this sector.

However, it would be wrong to arrive, on the basis of this evidence, at the conclusion that nothing has changed in respect of the party loyalties of civil servants. Our interviews with about fifty post-war cabinet ministers point towards a loss of importance of civil servants' party affiliation for their behaviour. In many cases, the desire for party patronage replaced the conviction of earlier generations of partisan civil servants. As one long-serving minister put it: 'In terms of predicting loyalty to the minister's policies, the party book is nowadays often not worth the paper it is written on.' Indeed, many insiders assume that civil servants' party membership now primarily works the other way round, namely, to make it easier to convince the minister of the merits of their views.

If the loyalties of civil servants can no longer be taken for granted on the basis of their party affiliation, cabinet ministers fall back on two strategies in order to get the required administrative support: the introduction of ministerial cabinets and the building up of personal loyalties of civil servants by means of motivational techniques. Some ministers have succeeded in using both strategies, even though these cannot easily be applied simultaneously.

The bureaucracy of the immediate post-war decades was characterized in many respects by structures and behaviour patterns *vis-à-vis* the public which it had managed to maintain since the time of the monarchy in 1918. Among other things, this meant little public accountability and little responsiveness. Since the mid-1960s, attempts have been made to improve civil servants' training, to change the incentive structure in which they operate and to modernize the administration. These include the setting up of a civil service training academy in 1975, the introduction in the 1980s of fixed-term appointments to a few top positions in the bureaucracy and the plan of the new grand coalition to carry out a comprehensive administrative reform. These internal reforms have been accompanied by external changes. In short, the administration is nowadays exposed to more public scrutiny and criticism than ever before. The mutually re-enforcing activities of the media, the audit office, the ombudsman's office, and, more recently, of parliamentary investigative committees and independent administrative review bodies, have made life much more troublesome for bureaucrats. Moreover, citizens are no longer the docile, subject-oriented clients which they were until about the 1970s.

Though changes in the bureaucracy occur at a notoriously slow pace and are difficult to assess, it seems clear that significant changes have taken place since the 1960s. The power of party ties to determine bureaucratic structures and behaviour has been reduced as has their general significance for Austrian society. Other principles which for many decades guided the 'servants of the state' have also been eroded, albeit as yet without having been replaced by new paradigms.

Conclusion

This chapter has provided basic information about senior officials and members of the *cabinets ministériels* in Austria. We have briefly looked back to the significant role of the bureaucracy in the Habsburg Empire and have argued that in modern times it no longer constitutes an independent force with a strong political identity and mission. The chapter has also provided a systematic account of the formal structure of the Austrian bureaucracy, locating senior officials within their environment. Recent reforms aim at increasing flexibility and accountability by introducing more effective incentive systems at the very top of the permanent bureaucracy.

Our review of the demographic background of senior officials has demonstrated the obvious lack of women in top positions, though they have marginally improved their position over the last decade. In terms of education it has turned out that law school graduates do not have a 'monopoly' in filling the top positions, as conventional wisdom has suggested. However, they still have a predominant position. Despite all the societal changes over the past twenty-five years, the share of law school graduates among top civil servants has remained stable.

However, we have confirmed another piece of conventional wisdom. At the highest rank, senior officials do indeed have a long duration and on the average outlive more than two ministers. Civil servants become specialists during their career and at the top there is no real inter-ministerial mobility. Finally, we have stressed the relevance of senior civil servants for policy-making and have discussed the role of political parties in the civil service. It is fair to conclude that politics within the civil service has become more complex over the last two decades.

REFERENCES

Ausschreibungsgesetz (1989). *Bundesgesetzblatt*, 85.
——(1991). *Bundesgesetzblatt*, 366.
Bundesministeriengesetz (1924). *Bundesgesetzblatt*, 312.
——(1930). *Bundesgesetzblatt*, 168.
——(1973). *Bundesgesetzblatt*, 389.
——(1986). *Bundesgesetzblatt*, 76.
——(1991). *Bundesgesetzblatt*, 336.
——(1994). *Bundesgesetzblatt*, 506.
——(1995*a*). *Bundesgesetzblatt*, 449.
——(1995*b*). *Bundesgesetzblatt*, 569.
——(1995*c*). *Bundesgesetzblatt*, 54.
——(1995*d*). *Bundesgesetzblatt*, 627.
——(1996). *Bundesgesetzblatt*, 721.
Engelmann, Frederick C. (1966). 'Austria: The Pooling of Opposition', in Robert A. Dahl (ed.), *Political Oppositions in Western Democracies* (New Haven, Conn.: Yale University Press), 260–83.
Engelmayer, Günther (1976). *Personalpolitik im öffentlichen Dienst 1970–1976* (Vienna: ÖAAB).
Ermacora, Felix (1977). 'Der Konflikt zwischen Politik und Verwaltung', in Günther Engelmayer (ed.), *Die Diener des Staates* (Vienna: Europaverlag), 61–92.
Fischer, Heinz (1977). 'Beamte und Politik', in Günther Engelmayer (ed.), *Die Diener des Staates* (Vienna: Europaverlag), 93–116.
Gerschenkron, Alexander (1962). *Economic Backwardness in Historical Perspective* (Cambridge, Mass.: Harvard University Press).
Heindl, Waltraud (1991). *Gehorsame Rebellen: Bürokratie und Beamte in Österreich 1780–1848* (Vienna: Böhlau).
——(1995). 'Bürokratie und Beamte', in Emmerich Tálos, Herbert Dachs, Ernst

Hanisch, and Anton Staudinger (eds.), *Handbuch des politischen Systems Österreichs: Erste Republik 1918 1933* (Vienna: Manz), 90–104.

Huemer, Peter (1975). *Sektionschef Robert Hecht und die Zerstörung der Demokratie in Östereich* (Vienna: Verlag für Geschichte und Politik).

Jabloner, Clemens (1992). 'Personnel in Public Administration', in Federal Chancellery (ed.), *Public Administration in Austria* (Vienna: Federal Chancellery), 277–301.

Kneucker, Roul F. (1973). 'Austria: An Administrative State', *Österreichische Zeitschrift für Politikwissenschaft*, 2: 95–117.

——(1977). 'Öffentliche Verwaltung 1975/76', *Österreichisches Jahrbuch für Politik*, 123–51.

——(1981). 'Public Administration: The Business of Government', in Kurt Steiner (ed.), *Modern Austria* (Palo Alto, Calif.: SPOSS), 261–78.

Megner, Karl (1986). *Beamte. Wirtschafts- und sozialgeschichtliche Aspekte des k.k. Beamtentums* (Vienna: Verlag der österreichischen Akademie der Wissenschaften).

Müller, Wolfgang C. (1989). 'Party Patronage in Austria', in Anton Pelinka and Fritz Plasser (eds.), *The Austrian Party System* (Boulder, Colo.: Westview), 327–56.

——(1994). 'Aspetti della modernizzazione dell'amministrazione centrale austriaca: Dalla disponibilità nei confronti dei cittadini alla marketizzazione', in Yves Mény and Vincent Wright (eds.), *La riforma amministrativa in Europa* (Bologna: Il Mulino), 291–316.

——(1996). 'Political Institutions', in Volkmar Lauber (ed.), *Contemporary Austrian Politics* (Boulder, Colo.: Westview), 23–58.

——(1997). 'Regierung und Kabinettsystem', in Herbert Dachs *et al.* (eds.), *Handbuch des politischen Systems Österreichs*, 3rd edn. (Vienna: Manz), 122–37.

—— Wilfried Philipp, and Barbara Steininger (1995). 'Die Regierung', in Emmerich Tálos, Herbert Dachs, Ernst Hanisch, and Anton Staudinger (eds.), *Handbuch des politischen Systems Österreichs: Erste Republik 1918–1933* (Vienna: Manz), 72–89.

—— —— and —— (1997). 'Personelle Stabilität und Verflechtung als Grundlagen der österreichischen Sozialpartnerschaft', University of Vienna, manuscript.

Neisser, Heinrich (1974). 'Die Rolle der Bürokratie', in Heinz Fischer (ed.), *Das politische System Österreichs* (Vienna: Europaverlag), 233–70.

——(1997). 'Die Verwaltung', in Herbert Dachs *et al.* (eds.), *Handbuch des politischen Systems Österreichs*, 3rd edn. (Vienna: Manz), 148–61.

Neyer, Gerda (1997). 'Frauen im österreichischen politischen System', in Herbert Dachs *et al.* (eds.), *Handbuch des politischen Systems Österreichs*, 3rd edn. (Vienna: Manz), 185–201.

Pabst, Walter, Günther Ofner, and Bernhard Moser (1986). *Sozialistische Personalpolitik 1970–1986* (Forschungsbericht, 38; Vienna, Politische Akademie der ÖVP).

Schäffer, Heinz (1988). 'Austria', in Donald C. Rowat (ed.), *Public Administration in Developed Democracies* (New York: Marcel Dekker), 205–20.

Schattovits, Helmuth A. (1987). *Aufgabenplanung: Ansätze für rationale Verwaltungsreform* (Vienna: Böhlau).

Schimetschek, Bruno (1984). *Der österreichische Beamte* (Vienna: Verlag für Geschichte und Politik).

Secher, Herbert P. (1958). 'Coalition Government: The Case of the Second Republic', *American Political Science Review*, 52: 791–809.

Steiner, Kurt (1972). *Politics in Austria* (Boston: Little, Brown & Co.).

Titscher, Stefan (1975). *Struktur eines Ministeriums* (Vienna: Österreichischer Bundesverlag).

Wandruszka, Adam, and Peter Urbanitsch (eds.) (1975). *Die Habsburgermonarchie 1848–1918*, ii. *Verwaltung und Rechtswesen* (Vienna: Verlag der österreichischen Akademie der Wissenschaften).

Wenger, Karl, Christian Brünner, and Peter Oberndorfer (eds.) (1983). *Grundriß der Verwaltungslehre* (Vienna: Böhlau).

6

The Senior Civil Service in Belgium

MARLEEN BRANS AND ANNIE HONDEGHEM

Introduction

The Belgian senior civil service is in transition. External pressures are clearly pushing the government firmly towards a reform agenda and towards improving public confidence in the administrative system, in terms of democracy and accountability and of economy and efficiency. Clear expressions of public discontent with the country's institutions have inspired the introduction of measures aimed at securing greater propriety in public life. Initiatives to reshape the relationship between political and administrative élites have also reflected the desire to improve standards in public life.

In addition, budgetary pressures have combined with political will to ensure that the operation of the administration complies with the new managerialist paradigm. Slowly, civil service reform has arrived on the agenda, albeit somewhat behind other nations, mainly due to Belgium's preoccupation with territorial devolution. There are, however, strong internal constraints on the degree to which reform proposals are likely to be implemented. These constraints are linked above all to the relatively strong position of civil service unions and the preoccupation of political actors with maintaining a balance of party-political power within the administrative system. Belgium's tradition of consociational politics makes the relationship between politics and administration a troublesome one and renders any apparently neutral managerialist technology highly political.

This chapter gives an overview of the position of senior civil servants in the Belgian federal ministries. It is consists of three main parts. The first part describes the coexistence of two opposing civil service models, a formal bureaucratic one and an informal politicized one, and assesses the implications of the clash between these models for the position and role conceptions of top civil servants. The second part addresses the issue of representativeness of the senior civil service in terms of education, language, and gender.

The final part deals with two major challenges to the Belgian senior civil service and the resulting reform agenda.

The Federal Civil Service

Due to four consecutive revisions of the Constitution, resulting in the transformation from a unitary state into a federal one in 1993, the federal civil service has been severely reduced, both in terms of its functions and in terms of numbers of civil servants. We shall not attempt a detailed account of the Belgian process of federalization. However, a short overview is appropriate to place the federal civil service in proper perspective. The piecemeal and time-consuming character of twenty-two years of state reform also helps explain the relatively laggardly response of political authorities to major challenges to the federal civil service.

The original administrative structure of the Belgian state as established by the 1831 Constitution was quite simple. It was made up of three government levels: the central level and two subnational levels, provinces and municipalities. This structure remained intact until 1970. Four revisions of the Constitution, in 1970, 1980, 1988, and 1993, brought about important changes to the unitary organization of the Belgian state, dividing it into communities and regions. The 1970 reform introduced cultural and linguistic regionalization. After the country had been divided into three monolinguistic areas—the Dutch, the French, and the German—and the bilingual Brussels area, the Constitution recognized the existence of three cultural communities, namely the German, the Dutch and the French cultural communities, with responsibility for cultural matters.

The basis for socio-economic regionalization was laid down in Article 107 of the Constitution, which recognizes the existence of three regions in Belgium: the Walloon region, the Flemish region, and the Brussels region. The institutions of the cultural communities and their responsibilities were fixed in the 1970 Constitution. Those of the regions were to be decided by the national parliament. This task was not an easy one, and it was not until 1980 that enabling legislation demarcated the Walloon and Flemish regions. The Constitution was amended to remove 'cultural' from the term 'cultural communities' because the communities had also acquired responsibility for social matters (Brans, 1992: 438–40).

In 1988, the functions of the communities and regions were extended and their financial system reformed. The 1988 reform also defined the institutions and functions of the Brussels region, the future of which had been left out of the 1980 reform. In 1993, the institutional reorganization of the unitary state reached a new phase, with Belgium becoming a federal state comprising directly elected subnational units: three regions (Brussels, Flanders, and the Walloons) and three communities (the German, the French, and the Flemish). The distinction between communities and regions lies in the sort of functions they have and the territory for which they are responsible. The communities are responsible for culture, education, and 'person related' matters such as health policy, welfare, and care education. The functions of the regions relate to territorial matters such as the environment, housing, transport and communication, public health and hygiene, energy, environment, economic policy, energy, employment, water policies, financing, and statutory control of municipalities and provinces. The dual organization of the federal state has created a rather complex institutional setting. Both the federal state and the communities and regions have their own legislative and executive bodies. This means that there are three regional councils and executives (Flemish, Walloon, and Brussels), as well as three community councils and executives (Flemish, French, and German). Each region and community has its own administration.

The 1993 reform will probably not be the last. Several more institutional arrangements will need to be altered. The ongoing and piecemeal character of the Belgian reform is definitely its most striking feature.

The federal civil service has been severely reduced as a result of these different state reforms (Table 6.1). It has lost major functions to the regions and communities. In terms of public employment, the national level now represents only 33 per cent of the personnel in the public sector (federal

TABLE 6.1. *Evolution of Employment in the Public Sector in Belgium*

	1953	1964	1970	1980	1989	1995
Ministries						
National					77,232	62,535
Regional					7,848	26,804
TOTAL	83,797	99,198	108,074	88,062	85,080	89,339
Public institutions						
National					166,098	149,575
Regional					13,634	47,888
TOTAL	131,341	126,292	115,969	198,402	179,732	197,463
Particular bodies	85,830	199,806	272,684	392,336	352,965	358,780
Local government	97,200	98,010	120,299	184,643	188,556	244,729
Legislature		1,000	969	1,232	1,773	2,282
TOTAL	398,168	524,306	617,995	864,675	808,106	892,593

Source: Depré *et al.*, 1984; Hondeghem, 1997.

government, plus police, courts, and army). In fact, only 7 per cent of civil servants are actually employed in the federal ministries. In addition, many functions have been transferred to autonomous public institutions. Contrary to experience elsewhere, the reliance on autonomous agencies is not a recent development. Belgium has long-standing experience of what is called 'functional decentralization' to (semi-)autonomous institutions. To some extent, these institutions have recently experienced new public management style changes.

Formal and Informal Civil Service Models

The current system of civil service recruitment, as well as the rules relating to the careers of civil servants and the tasks they perform dates back to 1937, following the proposals of a special government commissioner Camu. With the Camu reform, Belgium caught up with developments in other countries by creating a professional and protected civil service. The Camu Statute presented the Weberian model of a neutral, apolitical, and competent civil service, based on selection by competitive examination and promotion for length of service within the lower grades and merit within higher grades. The Camu Statute defined the rights and duties of civil servants and their careers in great detail and was applied in all ministries, harmonizing the different regulations that existed at the time. As we will see, this formal model was to conflict with political objectives. Designed as a safeguard against nepotism and patronage, its rigid regulations triggered a forceful development of ways to circumvent requirements of merit and length of service. Subsequent developments towards establishing greater political control would facilitate the emergence of a more flexible, informal system, the excesses of which account for major frustrations within the senior civil service and a pathological relationship between the political and administrative élites.

Job Definition and Classification

The civil service is divided into 'levels', 'ranks', and 'grades'. The division into levels is based on the nature of work and the educational qualifications required for them. Until recently, the civil service was divided into four levels: 1, 2, 3, and 4. However, a fifth level, level '2+' has been added, to revalue specialized functions requiring higher, non-university education.

Direct access to a certain level is possible only with the right level of education. Level 1 typically requires university education. But, since education was an important aspect of social stratification, the possibility of promotion from level 2 to level 1 was built in, explicitly to avoid the development of an élite. However, two conditions have to be met: length of service and merit. After four years of service and success in an examination, civil servants can move up to level 1. Consequently, some people at the top of the federal administration do not hold university degrees.

Top civil servants belong to level 1. Within level 1, we can further distinguish between grades and ranks. The top staff comprise: secretary general (rank 17/1), director general (rank 16/1), and counsellor general (rank 15/1). Chief civil engineers, doctors, and counsellors (rank 13/D, E, C, F, A and B), belong to the middle-ranking staff. The junior staff comprises e.g. engineers, doctors, computer experts, and assistant counsellors (rank 10/D, E, F, A, B, C). Recently, the total number of ranks has been reduced. Essentially, every rank has now two levels: an entry rank and a promotion rank. However, for level 1, five ranks have been maintained. It was intended to introduce a 'mandate' system for the top three officials (15, 16, and 17), creating top functions on a temporary basis. Until today, this system has not been implemented. Within each rank is a system of grades, associated with the importance of the particular position. Increased specialization had led to an increasing number of grades over the years and the Belgian civil service evolved from a generalist to a specialist administration, leading to an increasing number of specialized grades. Recent reforms, however, have reverted towards generalist grades and a reduction in the number of grades.

Job Security

In principle, civil servants in Belgium are appointed statutorily. Their rights and duties are fixed unilaterally by government. The principle of statutory appointment is firmly rooted in the Belgian civil service and is strongly supported by the civil service unions and any measure that challenges statutory regulations is strongly opposed by them. The statute offers civil servants several advantages, the most important of which are security of tenure, extensive social benefits and pension schemes, and defined career prospects. Historically, security of tenure was one of the first established rights of civil servants and was introduced at the end of the nineteenth century as a safeguard against political arbitrariness. Around the same time, civil servants acquired the right to paid leave, health insurance, and state pensions (other categories of employees had to wait until after the Second World War for a social security scheme to be introduced). Clear career prospects are an essential part of the Belgian civil service. All higher functions are allocated by internal promotions. Exceptions are made only for public institutions, the managers of which can be recruited from outside the civil service.

In practice, however, there are many non-statutory or contractual officials in the civil service, with fewer social benefits and career prospects. This is partly explained by the rigid requirements of the statute. Contractual personnel are recruited for reasons of flexibility. However, the growth of contractual personnel at the lower levels is also explained by unemployment policies of the past as well as by patronage. Rewarding political friends is much easier through contractual employment. Although there is a substantial number of contractual personnel in level 1 (13 per cent), the top remains predominantly statutory (87 per cent).

In public enterprises and public institutions, statute officials are increasingly being replaced by contract employees, even at the top. The principle of security of tenure has also been abandoned for top managers in some of these institutions. These are now employed through the mandate system, that is on a temporary basis, and with the prospect of continuation or demotion depending upon performance evaluation. Negative evaluations mean dismissal for incumbents recruited from the outside, while internal candidates can resume their previous positions. As mentioned above, this mandate system had also been intended for the top three ranks in federal ministries. Practical and political opposition has so far hampered its implementation.

Moving up the Career Ladder

Within level 1, moving up the career ladder formally depends upon three factors, the first of which is length of service. To be considered for promotion, civil servants must have served for a specified number of years. As a result of these requirements, it is not possible to move up the career ladder very fast. To be considered for a middle-management position (rank 13), one has to have been in service in level 1 for at least nine years; for a top position (rank 16), the minimum is fifteen years. In reality, it takes even longer for officials to reach the top. In part, this is explained by the fact that promotions can occur only if a post is made vacant. Positive performance appraisals have been required for promotion since 1939. They turned out to be no more than formalities. Recently, a new system was introduced but has yet to be put into operation. We may expect it to have some influence on promotions, but at present its value cannot be assessed.

The Belgian public career system is, indeed, very slow and very closed. Civil servants are not just promoted or parachuted into higher offices. Most of them are recruited in lower grades, climb slowly to the top, and stay there until retirement: hence the old age and long service of top officials. A 1990 study (Hondeghem, 1990; data from 1988) found that civil servants enter the administration at an average age of 25. In 1988 it took twenty-two years on average to reach a middle-management position, with top-management functions reached after twenty-six years' service. In comparison to 1970, top civil servants have to work a few years longer before they reach top offices. In 1988 the average secretary general was 57 years of age, being appointed to that position at the age of 53 after twenty-three years' service (Hondeghem, 1990: 214–31).

Apart from length of service and a positive performance appraisal, promotions may take account of the advice of the Departmental Board of Directors. The Board of Directors consists of the top two or three officials of the ministry (ranks 15, 16, and 17). Formally, the most senior officials have had a say in the promotion of officials to senior positions. In practice, however, the directors' advice was often ignored by the minister who preferred to appoint candidates with the right political affiliations. A disregard of the directors' advice was a central feature of politicization. However, since 1988, attempts to put a stop to the politicization of appointments have reinforced the role of directors. Their advice on candidates' merits and suitability for the vacant post are now increasingly followed.

From these formal criteria for promotion, it is clear that training and education requirements play a role only at the time of recruitment. There have been some proposals in the past (e.g. in 1964) to require a special certificate for moving up the ranks of level 1, but these were rejected by the unions, which feared it would decrease many members' chances for career advancement. The issue of the certificate cropped up again recently, when the mandate system was considered for the top officials of the federal ministries. Only those with a special management certificate were to be considered for promotion to rank 15, after which another selection was to lead to a mandate. Its preparation and implementation will depend upon the fate of the mandate system itself.

Salaries

The salaries of top civil servants are subject to the same regulations as those of lower civil servants. The financial position of the personnel of the national ministries was established by two royal decrees of June 1973. The combination of both decrees gives us a table with salary scales. The scales are divided in five levels: level 1, 2, 2+, 3, and 4. Each scale is indicated with three figures, of which the first two indicate the rank and the third indicates the place of the scale in comparison with other scales within the same rank.

The royal decrees of 1973 fixed the scale of each grade by taking into account the rank of the grade, on the one hand, and the relative importance of the job function on the other. This means that grades belonging to the same rank may be linked to different salary scales. A civil engineer as director is better paid than an adviser, although both belong to the same rank 13. Grades in a particular rank may even correspond to higher scales than some grades in higher ranks. This distortion of hierarchy at the top is meant to reward functions involving considerable responsibilities or skills or to cope with private-sector competition which drains specialists away from the top civil service (Depré and Hondeghem, 1987: 45–9). Specialist civil servants are better paid than generalists.

Belgian civil servants are appointed for life. Retirement age is 65. Top civil servants hardly ever leave before their retirement age. After retirement top officials may be appointed to prestigious but non-lucrative functions, often as presidents of advisory boards. Only top army officials benefit from the system of *pantouflage*, taking up lucrative jobs in private companies after retirement. The obvious explanation is to be found in the fact that they retire ten years earlier than top civil servants. Post-service rewards in the form of lucrative employment after service are thus limited. The state pension, however, is quite generous (70 per cent of the salary of the last five years before retirement). It is perceived as a delayed salary and justifies, to a certain extent, the relatively low salaries during the time in office. The cost of the pensions, however, constitutes a heavy burden on the budget, and its sustainability is under constant pressure. Any modifications to pension rights, however, are expected to meet fierce resistance from the unions.

Several public services pay their top officials better than the federal ministries. Top federal officials do not appear in the top fifteen best paid jobs in the public sector (Dejaeghere, 1992). The top managers of public enterprises and public financial institutions do, and so do top magistrates and top officials in the security forces. The federal government does not pay its top officials according to function or capability but only according to grade. It will pay more only if it is forced to, as is the case for top officials in public enterprises who are more likely to get higher rates because of the need to compete with private-sector salaries.

Otherwise, pay at the top of the public sector is well below that of the private sector. In 1992, the mean general manager of a Belgian firm earned twice as much as the minimum salary of a federal secretary general and one and half times the maximum salary for federal top officials. The 5 per cent best-paid general managers earned 2.7 to 3.6 times more than their counterparts in the federal ministries. The inclusion of variable pay would widen the gap even further, as additional management bonuses and special allowances are more beneficial in the private sector. It is not possible to confirm, however, that the gap between formal top salaries between the public and private sector has widened over the last two decades. There are few market stimuli to pay competitive salaries. At the same time, the immense public debt does not enable substantial pay rises. In principle, paying for more favourable financial conditions for the top three ranks in the federal ministries would not lead to a major increase in spending. After all, we are talking only about 250 to 300 people. However, it is unlikely that the trade unions would accept pay rises for the top and not for the civil service at large. An overall salary upgrading is out of the question for budgetary reasons.

Political Appointments

The informal civil service model clashes with the formal Weberian one. The former is characterized by the leading role of ministerial *cabinets* in policy-making and by the politicization of appointments.

In principle, both recruitment and promotions are apolitical. Recruitment is based on competitive examinations, organized by a centralized independent institution, the Permanent Recruitment Secretariat. Promotions in turn are based on objective criteria such as length of service, examinations, performance appraisal, and recommendations by the Board of Directors. In reality, political criteria have played an important role in both recruitment and promotions. In 1990, when asked to rank forty factors that play a role in promotion in level 1, the majority of civil servants indicated that having the right contacts was most important: contacts with a ministerial *cabinet*, with a political party, a union, or individual politicians. In the ideal model, these factors should not play any role whatsoever (Hondeghem, 1990).

When new departments or administrations are created, the minister can deviate from the normal regulations and avoid recruiting officials who have made their way up through the ranks, by making a number of initial appointments called 'primo-appointments'. A second exception to the general rule of apolitical recruitment applies to the appointment of people of great administrative, scientific, technical, or artistic merit.

Recent decades have witnessed a strong institutionalization of the system of political appointments, in which party-political organization and cooperation among competing parties have come to play an important role (Dewachter, 1992: 245). Before 1960, political promotions used to be the result of individual lobbying (e.g. by MPs). Most political parties have now established *ad hoc* committees in order to arrive at uniform and disciplined lobbying. Candidates are shortlisted according to their proficiency, party merits, the intra-party faction they belong to, and the preference of the minister in charge of the promotion involved (Dewachter, 1992: 245; De Winter, 1981: 68; Hondeghem, 1990: 200).

The most striking feature of the institutionalization of political appointments is a political committee, composed of representatives of the different political parties in government and presided over by a close adviser of the Prime Minister. The first such committee was established in 1973, by parties that had been excluded from previous government coalitions and members of ministerial *cabinets* in charge of negotiating the political appointments who wished to make the process more efficient (*Knack Magazine*, 26 June 1984: 15). In this committee, promotions are allocated to the parties according to the relative strength of the parties in Parliament. This quota is decided after the process of coalition formation. The committee advises the minister on all level 1 promotions in the national administration, except for those in the Ministry of Finance, managers of quasi-governmental organizations, and for the highest rank in the civil service. Here, it is the core cabinet, the Council of Ministers, that decides. These appointments are often negotiated in package-deals during the process of negotiation for the government coalition. The committee discusses candidates shortlisted by the Board of Directors of the ministry. The discretionary power of the committee and eventually of the minister, is sufficient to ignore the board's advice, and this has often occurred. In the 1980s, the committee developed procedures to routinize its work. A credit system in which promotions for higher positions obtain a higher weighting facilitates the implementation of the quota. There has even been talk of designing special software to run the system (*De Standaard*, 15 Mar. 1991). Special attention is given to balance in the lower ranks to anticipate balance in the higher ranks.

Ministerial *Cabinets*

Ministerial *cabinets*, as stepping-stones to higher office, exert strong pressures on appointments at the top of the civil service. They play a central role in the party-politicization of the administration. Close as they are to the heart of decision-making, they can manipulate the conditions for appointment and alter organizational structures without the functional need to do so. All these mechanisms led to a proliferation of higher grades (Hondeghem, 1990: 206–8).

Ministerial *cabinets* have always existed in Belgium, but their size, structure, and function have strongly evolved in the twentieth century. In 1836, three of the five national ministers had a personal collaborator. At that time, there was no formal separation between politics and administration. Between 1830 and 1840, 43 per cent of MPs were at the same time civil servants. In 1848, the Parliament of officials was brought to an end after it was no longer legal to be an MP and a civil servant at the same time. The proliferation of *cabinet* members really starts after the First World War. Thereafter a process was set in motion in which the administration was increasingly bypassed in all phases of policy-making.

In 1919 there were fifty-six level 1 *cabinet* members, by 1947 this had grown to 107. This figure had nearly doubled by 1965 (200) and by 1986 there were 530 *cabinet* members. In 1995 the total number of level 1 *cabinet* members was estimated at 720, including the *cabinet* members of the ministers in the regions and communities (Hondeghem, 1996: 55). Currently each minister has an average of fifty to a hundred people on his or her personal staff. About half of them are drawn from the administration. The rest are co-opted from the entourage of the ministers or from their political parties. People may also be recruited into ministerial *cabinets* because of their specific expertise. Ministerial *cabinets* have a number of political functions which cannot, or only with great difficulty, be carried out by the administration. As Van Hassel has put it, a ministerial *cabinet* serves as

a training school for young politicians *in spe*, as an 'ante-room' for non-elected politicians waiting for a new mandate, as a hidden form of financing party officials and electoral staff of ministers, sometimes as a means of a political party or intra-party faction to control the minister, and as the key to the secrets of the administration via selected civil servants. (1974: 385).

According to Majersdorf and Dierickx (1993), ministerial *cabinets* exert an 'irresistible charm' for ministers, who prefer to work with them instead of with regular civil servants. Ministers work with ministerial *cabinets* for reasons of political trust, policy 'friendliness', flexibility, communicational skill, and political clientelism. Moreover, ministers tend to mistrust civil servants, due to the fact that many are the political appointments of other parties or factions. In 1990, 62 per cent of the top three senior civil servants of the federal ministries belonged to the Christian-Democratic party (37 per cent Flemish, 25 per cent French-speaking); 21 per cent belonged to the Socialist party (9 per cent Flemish, 12 per cent French-speaking); and 11 per cent to the Liberals (4 per cent Flemish, 7 per cent French-speaking). Only 6 per cent were independent and 1 per cent Flemish nationalist (Majersdorf and Dierickx, 1993: 549). It can, of course, be questioned whether such political affiliations are an impediment to loyal service to the minister in charge. Research has revealed that most civil servants limit their partisan activity to paying membership dues, and have technocratic rather than political outlooks. But it does not really matter how top civil servants see their role. What matters is that ministers do not fully trust their loyalty, and prefer to work with *cabinet* members. *Cabinets* play a central role in policy-making. Flexible policy support, specific expertise, and unconditional loyalty are central assets for a ministry's short-term projects. The bureaucratic features of the formal civil service system provides constraints on the civil service capacity to meet the ministry's demands.

Ministerial *cabinets* are also at the mediating heart of government. It is to ministerial *cabinets* that interest groups turn, not to the administration. Ministerial *cabinets* often explicitly draw members from interest organizations or factions within political parties, with the aim of facilitating interest mediation. Finally, ministerial *cabinets* play an important role in providing logistic support to the minister and services to the ministers' constituents, a role which cannot possibly be assumed by the civil service.

Although ministerial *cabinets* provide important policy support to the ministers, it is clear that they suffer from several defects. The scope of their activities and their size have made them develop into parallel administrations, resulting in much apparent duplication of effort. Moreover, by draining away capable elements from the civil service, they have partly dismantled the administration. Because of the central role of *cabinets* in policy, the administration is hardly involved in policy-making and is reduced to a mere executive organization. It is clear that there is a vicious circle at work. With the administration lacking the capacity to support the ministers, the latter have been forced to extend their *cabinets* even further.

Role Perceptions of Senior Civil Servants

The excesses of party politicization of the administration and the growth of ministerial *cabinets* are clearly reflected in the role perceptions of senior civil servants. Overall, they are politically alienated and marginalized in the policy-making process (Dierickx, 1991; Majersdorf and Dierickx, 1991). Senior civil servants generally hold rather negative views of politics. They tend to dislike the political aspects of their job and feel superior to politicians both morally and technically. Overall, civil servants have a strong technocratic orientation and tend to believe in 'one best way' of dealing with a problem. They have less confidence in satisfactory solutions that spring from political bargaining and negotiation. Top civil servants have a traditional notion of their profession. They regard themselves first and foremost as 'servants of the state' and as 'experts' and not as exponents of political demands or servants of a political programme. In the terms of Aberbach, Putnam, and Rockman (1981), they see themselves as 'neutral executors'. Nor do they see themselves as protagonists of particular interests. Their isolated position in the policy process has left them without much interaction with the political world.

The marginalization of top civil servants is clearly confirmed by their limited involvement in communication with other policy-making actors. Their contacts with MPs are few. They hardly ever communicate with the secretaries general and top officials of other departments. It is rare for them to meet frequently with their own ministers. Communication between government and interest and client groups is taken care of elsewhere. It appears that members of ministerial *cabinets* communicate with all those actors that are inaccessible to higher civil servants. *Cabinet* members meet frequently with cabinet members and ministers from other departments and even have access to the Prime Minster via his ministerial *cabinet*. *Cabinet* members rather than civil servants communicate with national and local politicians, interest groups, and citizens. The maintenance of communication networks is the job of ministerial *cabinet* members. Aberbach, Putnam, and Rockman's (1981) communication triangle requires modification in the Belgian case due to the central position of ministerial *cabinets*.

Only secretary generals form a partial exception to this rule of civil servants as marginal in the policy process. Their contacts among one another are institutionalized in the college of secretaries general. They also have more contacts with their ministers, MPs, and party officials than their immediate subordinates. However, compared with the heads of ministerial *cabinets*, their outside contacts remain rather limited.

Politicians, in turn, have few expectations of civil servants. Politicians and civil servants mind their own business, resulting in strong mutual alienation. This is confirmed by a correlation between the familiarity of civil servants with the political environment and their attitude towards politics. Civil servants who have worked in a ministerial *cabinet* or who are part of political networks, show more political sensitivity than others (Dierickx, 1991).

The system of political appointments has also contributed to civil servants' aversion to politics. Being a member or activist of a political party is considered more important than capability and performance, and this leads, in turn, to demotivation. This explains the paradox of the political alienation of civil servants and their high degree of political participation. Civil servants are politically active not so much out of conviction but out of necessity. Without party membership an official runs the risk of missing out on promotion opportunities. Hence, Belgian civil servants have a schizophrenic attitude: they despise politics, but they need it.

A 1990 opinion poll investigated the hierarchy of power in Belgium (Dewachter and Das, 1991), and its results confirm the relatively marginal position of senior civil servants in decision-making. Respondents were asked to rank fifteen positions on a scale according their influence in Belgian politics (1 equals no influence; 100 equals much influence). In the public's perception, top civil servants occupy the ninth place in the hierarchy of power. They are preceded by other actors who formally are supposed to have less influence in political decision-making: presidents of political parties, leaders of employers' and employees' organizations, and journalists. A parallel study took the Belgian élite as respondents. They were asked to rank the same positions according to their actual influence (Dewachter and Das, 1991). The respondents placed top functions in the civil service at the bottom of the hierarchy. This result confirms the findings of a similar study conducted in 1967 (Dewachter, 1971). Élite perceptions of the role of top civil servants thus seem to be quite stable over time.

Representation in the Senior Civil Service: Two Opposing Doctrines

Following the formal and informal civil service model, there are two opposing doctrines of representation of the Belgian civil service (Depré and Hondeghem, 1991). According to the official doctrine, representation is a matter for Parliament, since the proportional electoral system is supposed to make Parliament reflect the social composition of society. The composition of the government is based on party strength in Parliament. In line with Weber's model, the bureaucracy is nothing other than a neutral and impartial instrument in the hands of legitimate political rulers. According to the formal doctrine, this instrument is loyal to those who are in power, and, as a result, it is responsive to the population. The composition of the civil service is based on merit and equality in the sense that every Belgian must have equal opportunity to apply for a position in it. Anyone who applies for a vacancy is invited to the selection examination—nobody can be turned away. As a result, entry examinations may involve hundreds of participants, even for only a couple of vacancies.

In practice, another concept of representation is at work. One that is closely linked with the nature of Belgian society and its tradition of consociational politics. Mirror-image representation is an essential part of conflict accommodation. Balances are sought to accommodate the three cleavages that have historically divided Belgian society: language, religion, and class. The accommodation of the first cleavage, language, has a legal basis. The two other cleavages are not covered by law. Since these cleavages are reflected in the party system, their accommodation is subject to inter-party negotiation and bargaining. Political appointments in the civil service are not designed to enhance the legitimacy and responsiveness of the administration. They are meant to consolidate the balance of power between the main political parties. This produces *passive* rather than *active* representation. Civil servants are classified into particular categories of language, religion, and political party. They themselves, however, take no active party in this process of classification or pushing themselves forward as candidates. Representation is forced upon them by political expedience.

Representation and Education

Little is known about the social origin of civil servants in Belgium. It may safely be said, though, that the Belgian core administration and particularly the senior civil service is neither élitist nor the product of a particular social class. The higher classes have historically been active in banking, the army, and diplomacy. Education is closely linked to social origin and might thus give us some clues as to the social background of senior civil servants. Despite the democratization of university education, only about 7 per cent of university students come from working-class backgrounds. In comparison with other economic sectors, the public sector has the highest percentage of university graduates. In 1984–5, half the civil servants in level 1 had a university or equivalent degree (only university graduates can enter level 1 directly, officials can move from level 2 to 1).

Law (33 per cent), economics (23 per cent), and applied sciences (17 per cent) were the most common degree held by level 1 officials. The kind of degree depended strongly on the specialization of the ministry, which confirms that in the Belgian civil service, much attention has been given to expertise. Examination of the types of degrees held by the top three ranks of senior civil servants in 1996 (rank 15, 16, and 17) shows that the largest group, 37 per cent, holds a social sciences degree (including economics), 24 per cent a natural science degree, and also 24 per cent a law degree. Only 4 per cent hold an arts degree; 5 per cent had received non-university higher education, and 6 per cent had had no university or higher education. All secretaries general, however, have university degrees.

Representation and Language

Language quotas in the Belgian federal administration have a long history, and they symbolize the outcome of an important social struggle. The ethno-linguistic cleavage has been present since the birth of the Belgian state, with a language border dividing Belgium in the Flemish north and the Walloon south. The linguistic divide was politically salient, since the early political and administrative leadership was French-speaking. It received particular economic salience in the second half of the nineteenth century, with the Walloon part of the country benefiting from rapid industrialization whilst Flanders was stuck in agrarian poverty. The Flemish population could not convert their numbers into power. 'The numerical majority was a status minority, politically and economically disadvantaged and culturally stigmatised' (Heisler, 1989: 179). At the very beginning, Flemish demands were simply ignored, if not ridiculed, by the French-speaking élite of the Belgian state. When Flemish demands grew stronger and became articulated by newly enfranchised Dutch-speakers at the local and provincial level, they were accommodated, but with the francophone élite not losing an inch of control of the political centre (Rudolph, 1989: 92). Indeed, the first language laws were no more than tactical concessions to Flemish demands, which at this stage concentrated on the introduction of Dutch into public life in Flanders.

The philosophy of the first language laws was that French was the national language, but that Dutch had also some rights; additionally, French-speakers should never encounter difficulties in using their mother tongue (Van Alboom, 1990: 115). The language laws covering justice (1873, 1889, 1891), civil administration (1878), and secondary education in state-supported schools (1883), guaranteed a number of elementary rights and staged a transition towards a bilingual status for Flanders, at least for those services which were in direct contact with the population. Nonetheless, French was preserved as the superior national language and Wallonia remained monolingually French. It was not until 1908 that an examination for a position in a ministry was held in Dutch. Gradually, the language laws expanded. In 1921, civil servants dealing with the public were to speak both languages. This principle was confirmed in 1932. At the same time, language homogeneity was introduced. The official language in Flanders was Dutch and that for the Walloons was French. The central services in Brussels were bilingual. Civil servants of the national ministries were divided into two groups: the Dutch-speakers and the French-speakers. Each central ministry was to have a language division. Most administrations chose the 50 per cent rule, which meant parity of positions.

The law of 1966, passed in the heat of the linguistic conflict in Belgium, regulated representation of language groups at the top of the administration. From rank 13 onwards, complete parity is required: 40 per cent of positions are for Dutch-speakers, 40 per cent for French-speakers, 10 per cent for bilingual Dutch-speakers (Dutch-speakers who have passed a French exam), and 10 per cent for bilingual French-speakers. When a director of a department speaks only one language, a bilingual assistant is engaged. It is interesting to note that the parity rule strongly favours the French-speakers, since Dutch-speakers represent 60 per cent of the Belgian population.

TABLE 6.2. *Representation of Language Groups in Federal Ministries* (%)

	1939	1953	1964	1970	1988
Top civil servants (rank 15, 16, 17)					
Dutch		48	48	53	53
French		52	52	47	47
Level 1					
Dutch	39	43	53	55	58
French	61	57	47	45	42
Total personnel					
Dutch	48	47	55		
French	52	53	45		

Source: Depré *et al.*, 1984; Hondeghem, 1990.

Table 6.2 reveals how the Flemish caught up. Until the 1950s, the Flemish were a minority in the departments. In the 1960s there was more or less equal representation, and from the 1970s onward, the Flemish occupied the majority of posts. The catching up was first visible at the lower levels and only gradually in the higher ones, which is, of course, linked to the slow career system.

Representation and Gender

The representation of women in the administration is similar to the general position of women in the labour market. As shown in Table 6.3, the number of women in the ministries has increased since the 1970s: 19 per cent of all civil servants were women in 1970; this increased to 45 per cent in 1995. Since 42 per cent of the working population is female, we can conclude that the federal ministries are representative of the whole of society. However, there is strong horizontal and vertical segregation of labour between men and women. Women are in the majority in some ministries (Employment, Social Affairs, Health, and the Environment), and under-represented in others (Justice, Traffic and Infrastructure, Agriculture). This horizontal segregation is also expressed by differences in duties and rights. There are more statutory male personnel than female: 43 per cent of federal civil servants are women but they make up 71 per cent of the con-tractual personnel.

There is also a strong vertical segregation. The higher we climb in the hierarchy, the fewer women we meet. In 1995, 24 per cent of level 1 civil servants were women. At the top three levels, only 9 per cent was female

Marleen Brans and Annie Hondeghem

TABLE 6.3. *Representativeness According to Sex: Federal Ministries* (%)

	1939	1953	1970	1988/89	1995
Top civil servants (rank 15, 16, 17)					
Men			98	96	91
Women			2	4	9
Level 1					
Men	99	99	96	86	76
Women	1	1	4	14	24
Total personnel					
Men	93	87	81	62	55
Women	7	13	19	38	45

Source: Depré *et al.*, 1984; Hondeghem, 1997.

and at the very top only one of the thirteen secretaries general was a woman. In the 1980s, a policy of affirmative action was introduced to improve the position of women in the administration. In 1987, a minister was charged with equal opportunities policies. According to a 1991 rule, each public service needs to appoint a civil servant responsible for affirmative action, charged with the implementation of an affirmative action plan containing measures aimed at changing male-dominated cultures and improving working conditions for women. Positive discrimination, in the form of gender quotas, however, has not been introduced. In contrast with other forms of representation, of language and ideological affiliation, that of gender has not received an impetus from within the political system itself. It is more a response to external pressures and trends, particularly at the level of the European Union. The gender cleavage is not a politicized one. There is little political support for its accommodation through quotas.

A Civil Service in Transition:
External Pressure and Internal Constraints

The Belgian civil service is facing two main challenges. The first is associated with a legitimacy crisis of political institutions as a whole. The second is related to budgetary pressures and the ascendancy of the new managerialist paradigm in the public sector.

It is no exaggeration to say that the Belgian political system is facing a governance crisis. This is not only indicated by election results and survey material but also by the perceptions of the political élite and their efforts to restore public confidence in the country's institutions. A start was made in the late 1980s to curb the excesses of political nominations and the growth of ministerial *cabinets*. These measures were accompanied by other innovations, such as the reform of the system of party financing and MPs' salaries. Matters deteriorated, however, from 1991 onwards. The 1991 electoral defeat of the traditional parties (on what is generally referred to as 'black Sunday') symbolized the legitimacy crisis. The gains of right-wing extremist parties, on the one hand, and of anti-political parties on the other, was taken as a clear sign of dissatisfaction among citizens. As a reaction to the obvious discontent of citizens with administration and politics, the government developed what they called a 'contract with the citizen', under which measures were taken to address what was perceived as having caused citizen disillusionment: day-to-day problems of poverty, inner-city deterioration, social housing, crime, and access of citizens to public services.

Since then, however, political sleaze and corruption have not left the agenda. Numerous corruption scandals involving MPs, government ministers, ministerial *cabinet* members, and magistrates followed one after the other. In 1996 came the biggest and most dramatic blunder of all: the blatant incompetence of police and judicial forces in not preventing the tragic disappearance and subsequent murder of several young girls. The revelations in the aftermath of the Dutroux case led to a huge mobilization of ordinary citizens against past political practices and have firmly placed measures to restore public trust firmly on the political agenda. 'New political culture' or NPC is the new buzz word. It involves a wide range of measures to raise standards in public life, including putting an end to political appointments, limiting the accumulation of political mandates, curbing the size of ministerial *cabinets*, and reintegrating top civil servants into policy-making.

Public trust in government in general and in the civil service in particular remains low. A survey (*La Libre Belgique*, 26 Dec. 1996), dealing with people's opinions about the functioning of the political-administrative system, provided some alarming results: 64 per cent of citizens believed that democracy was in danger, 83 per cent thought that institutions functioned very badly, badly, or rather badly, and 77 per cent had no confidence in politicians' ability to solve problems. It is likely that the timing of this poll—it was conducted in the direct aftermath of the Dutroux revelations —helps account for its alarming results.

Eurobarometer surveys have also confirmed Belgians as being cynical citizens. It is difficult to account for this characteristic beyond intuitive speculation. One commonplace hypothesis points to the historically rooted distrust of Belgian citizens in the country's authorities as a consequence of long periods of foreign occupation. A second hypothesis explains the cynical attitude from the perspective of Belgian clientelist politics: citizens experience the state and its institutions as a marketplace, rather than as a collective authority that guides society. Nepotism and patronage have a negative impact on public opinion.

In 1988, a government protocol introduced two new rules. In the first place, 15 per cent of appointments in the civil service were to be depoliticized and used for promoting neutral and opposition candidates. A second rule established that the political committee had to follow the unanimous advice of the Boards of Directors (Guy Tegenbos, *De Standaard*, 30 Aug. 1988).

In the last decade, there have been signs of a changing climate, inspired by the hostility of public opinion towards political appointments, by the rulings of the State Council (the administrative court of appeal), which in some individual cases nullified political appointments, and by a new generation of apolitical higher civil servants (*De Standaard*, 9 Sept. 1991). Most strikingly, the political committee increasingly follows the unanimous advice of the Board of Directors. In principle, political parties agree that they have gone too far in politicizing the administration. The executive is left with a largely inefficient and expensive administration, in which the political incompatibility between officials and ministers has led to a huge communication gap. The mistrust of citizens might endanger the legitimacy of the system. Ministers are faced with a frustrated civil service, in which an increasing number of discontented individuals take their grievances to the State Council. Several proposals—some more radical than others—to depoliticize the administration were put forward, all aimed at limiting the discretionary power of the appointing institution. However, depoliticizing the Belgian administration is difficult, given the desire of new coalition partners to 'catch up', often justified by referring to the idea of representative bureaucracy. Moreover, unions draw support from the system of political appointments. This form of political clientelism, defined as 'a mechanism that strikes roots in the granting of material rewards in a meaningful social context' (Deschouwer, 1989: 37) is providing the parties and the pillars they belong to, whether Catholic, socialist, or liberal, with a drawing power on top of any ideological incentives. Rewarding loyal civil servants, *cabinet* members, or other party supporters is a central tool of Belgian party management. It has also proved to be a successful instrument in interparty negotiations and bargaining and, as such, it is a central feature of conflict accommodation. Depoliticization has not gone very far yet. Although a start was made in the late 1980s, political appointments are still frequently made. This has also been the case for appointments to positions that were created in the aftermath of the structural reforms inspired by new public management. Managers and board members of semi-autonomous institutions are predominantly political appointees

(Depré and Hondeghem, 1996); so are several of the recently appointed ombudsmen.

In 1990, the Flemish government decided to put a stop to the growth of ministerial *cabinets*. The federal government pursued this initiative after the 1991 elections, the results of which they interpreted as a threat to the legitimacy of the political system. The reform was also a response to the internal expression of discontent of higher civil servants with their marginalization in the policy-making process. As a result, ministers have started to cooperate on a more regular basis with their administrations. In some ministries, rules of conduct have been established concerning the relations between the minister and his administration. One of these rules is that ministers now have to meet the top civil servants of their departments every week. It is too early to assess the extent of this change and its impact on the role conceptions of senior civil servants. Also, the Board of Secretary Generals has been strengthened. In a royal decree of 1993, the Board was charged with the coordination, for the Council of Ministers and the Minister of Civil service, of all matters concerning organization and personnel management in the federal ministries. All civil service reforms now require prior consultation of the Board. It seems that the Board of Secretary Generals has, indeed, grasped this opportunity to reinforce its role in the decision-making process.

Structural Reforms

Due to unorthodox public spending in the past, Belgium has a huge public debt. Already by 1981, the budget deficit was 12 per cent of GDP and the total public debt amounted to 93 per cent of GDP. The pressure on the federal government to meet the Maastricht criteria has been considerable. In 1996, budgetary austerity policies reduced the deficit to 3.2 per cent of GDP. Public debt, however, exceeds the 60 per cent criterion by more than half, and still stands at 134 per cent of GDP. The impact of austerity was mixed. On the one hand, budgetary austerity has helped inspire managerial reforms in the public sector. On the other hand, it puts structural constraints on the implementation of reforms aimed at developing new incentive structures for civil servants. The introduction of performance-related financial incentives is clearly hampered by budgetary constraints.

There are three kinds of structural reforms that have recently been carried through. The first such reform is external privatization: government has withdrawn from several sectors, including public financial institutions, transport, and communication services. Privatization was not only meant to comply with new public-sector developments in the direction of a smaller but improved public sector. It was also an attractive tool in the reduction of public debt.

Belgium has had a long tradition of public-service delivery through autonomous or semi-autonomous institutions. Recently, the relations between core departments and executive institutions have been revised. A major innovation at the organizational level has been the introduction of the management contract, that is a long-term agreement between the minister and the organization. In return for complying with the objectives set out in the contract, organizations obtain more discretion in deciding internal management issues, including personnel matters. At the federal level, this kind of contractualization has been implemented in four autonomous public enterprises, and it is currently being prepared for eighteen public institutions responsible for social security services. Internal devolution, too, is being experimented with, and responsibilities are increasingly delegated within the autonomous public enterprises. They are being transformed into enterprises, consisting of business units accountable for their own results.

Finally, some structural reforms have targeted federal ministries. In the aftermath of regional devolution, the functions of some central departments were so severely reduced that a merger of ministries was necessary. The Ministry of Agriculture was merged with that of the Middle Class, and the Ministry of Public Health merged with that of Social Affairs. In 1994, a new ministry was established, that of the Civil Service (*Fonction Publique*), with the aim of facilitating the coordination and integration of management of the federal civil service as a whole. This operation directly affected the Office of the Prime Minister, whose services were seriously reduced because of it. Important services, such as the Permanent Recruitment Secretariat and the Control Committee for Public Tenders, were transferred to the Ministry of the Civil Service. The Prime Minister now has direct hierarchical control only over a limited number of services, such as the Chancellery, the National Committee for Cultural Pacification, and the Federal Services for Scientific Affairs. More important as providers of support for the Prime Minister are his two ministerial *cabinets* (one for political affairs and one for social and economical affairs).

In 1993, the Minister for the Civil Service submitted an extensive action plan to the Council of Ministers, comprising a wide range of measures aimed at improving the management of the public sector. The main targets of reform were the restructuring of the federal public sector, the relations between the administration and the ministers, the pattern of cooperation among departments, the improvement of relations between the administration and citizens, and personnel management. The measures proposed included an organization to encourage greater mobility, the introduction of a new performance appraisal system, the simplification of careers, a review of the salary scales, and the introduction of a 'mandate' system for top civil servants (this is a new career system, replacing permanent with temporary appointments). Some of these measures have already been implemented. The career system was slightly altered and the salary scales have been revised. Other proposals are slow in being defined and implemented, such as the new performance appraisal system and the 'mandate' system for top civil servants.

The introduction of mandates is justified on two grounds. First, it complies with the general trend towards increasing civil servants' responsibility and accountability. Top civil servants would receive more discretion in the deployment of their departments' financial and personnel resources. In return, they would be held accountable for results. At the start of the mandate, clear management objectives would be established. At the end of the mandate, performance would be evaluated. Only if the goals have been achieved, would the mandate be renewed. Secondly, the mandate system would help break through the closed nature of the senior civil service. It would bring about greater mobility, and increase the opportunities for closer collaboration between the minister and his top administrative staff.

The introduction of the mandate system is hampered by three main factors. First, it would effect a breach in the formal career system, which was designed in part to prevent political interference. The system would give ministers more freedom to appoint top civil servants as temporary spoils. Top civil servants are afraid of being evaluated on political grounds instead of on their actual performance. They doubt the objectivity of performance appraisals and fear political favouritism. Second, the introduction of the system would have to be accompanied by substantial financial compensations and incentive improvements to make up for the greater insecurity and risks top civil servants would be facing. Budgetary constraints make substantial salary increases very unlikely. Third, there seem to be a number of technical difficulties, which on closer inspection, however, are highly political, and underscore the fact that what seem to be purely managerial reforms are not politically neutral. Who will be considered for a mandate position? Who will decide on the technical abilities of the candidates? How should objectives be set and results measured for traditional departments that are not really involved in service delivery? Who will evaluate mandated officials? What will happen to them after a negative evaluation?

Other reforms have set out to restructure the relationship between citizens and the administrative system. A 1992 Citizens' Charter included measures to improve the transparency of the administration, its accessibility, and the legal protection of citizens.

Conclusion

The federal civil service is a modest administration. This is reflected in its most senior administrative ranks, whose prestige is limited and whose role in the policy-making is marginal. Over the last decades, the federal administration has lost important functions to the new state levels of government. Faced with fewer political and budgetary constraints, and keen to prove themselves, the state civil services have presented themselves as dynamic and innovative pacesetters. In comparison, the federal level is still a laggard. Budgetary pressures, party-politicization, and civil service union scepticism have hampered the implementation of reform. To say the federal civil service is a laggard in meeting the challenges it is facing is not to deny that reform is on the way. Several structural and managerial reforms have been implemented and it appears that even the mandate system will eventually get the go-ahead. As yet, however, a balanced assessment of the impact of recent and likely modifications on the senior civil service is difficult. The impact on the career patterns, roles, and mindset of senior officials will unavoidably take time to develop.

REFERENCES

Aberbach, J., R. D. Putnam, and B. A. Rockman (1981). *Bureaucrats and Politicians in Western Democracies* (Cambridge: Cambridge University Press).

Brans, M. (1992). 'Theories of Local Government Organisation: An Empirical Evaluation', *Journal of Public Administration*, 70(3): 429–51.

——(1994). 'Public Office-Private Rewards: Rewards for High Public Office in Belgium', in C. C. Hood and B. G. Peters (eds.), *Rewards at the Top: A Comparative Study of High Public Office* (London: Sage), 106–19.

Brasz, J. P. (1986). *Études comparées sur les hautes fonctions publiques: Rapport français* (Brussels: IIAS).

Camu, L. (1937). *Le Statut des agents de l'État: Premier Rapport sur la reforme administrative* (Brussels: IMIFI).

Dejaeghere, P. (1992). 'Wegwijs in de Ambtenarenlonen', *Tijdschrift voor Bestuurswetenschappen en Publiekrecht*, 47(7): 476–91.

Depré, R. (1973). *De topambtenaren van de ministeries in België* (Louvain: K. U. Leuven).

——and A. Hondeghem (1987). 'Recruitment, Career and Training of Senior

Officials in Belgium', *The Higher Civil Service in Belgium and Industrialised Countries: Recruitment, Career and Training* (Brussels: International Institute of Administrative Sciences), 45–9.

—— and —— (1991). 'Rapport sur la représentativité de l'administration en Belgique', in V. Wright (ed.), *La Représentativité de l'administration publique* (Brussels: IIAS), 93–126.

—— and —— (1996). 'Belgium', in D. Farnham *et al.*, *New Public Managers in Europe* (London: Macmillan).

—— —— and H. van Hassel (1984). *Structuurelementen bij de motivatie van het kaderpersoneel in overheidsdienst* (Brussels: Koning Boudewijnstichting).

Deschouwer, K. (1989). 'Patterns of Participation and Competition in Belgium', *West European Politics*, 12(4): 28–41.

Dewachter, W. (1971). 'De Machtshierarchie in de Belgische politiek', *Res Publica*, 13(3–4): 533–50.

—— (1992). *Besluitvorming in Politiek België* (Louvain: Acco).

—— and Das, E. (1991). *Politiek in België: Geprofileerde Machtsverhoudingen* (Louvain: Acco).

DeWinter, L. (1981). 'De Partijpolitisering als Instrument van Particratie', *Res Publica*, 23(1): 62–74.

Dierickx, G. (1991). 'De Politieke Aliënatie van Leidinggevende Ambtenaren', *Res Publica*, 33(2): 183–204.

Heisler, O. H. (1989) 'Hyphenating Belgium: Changing State and Regime to Cope with Cultural Division', in J. V. Montville (ed.), *Conflict and Peacemaking in Multi-Ethnic Societies* (Lexington, Ky.: Lexington Books), 177–95.

Hondeghem, A. (1990). *De Loopbaan van een Ambtenaar: Tussen Droom en Werkelijkheid* (Leuven: Public Management Training Centre).

—— (1996). 'De politieke en ambtelijke component in het openbaar bestuur', in R. Maes and K. Jochmans (eds.), *Inleiding tot de bestuurskunde* (Brussels: STOHO), 44–73.

—— (1997). 'The National Civil Service in Belgium', paper presented at the international conference on civil service systems in a comparative perspective, Bloomington, Ind. (USA).

Majersdorf, P., and G. Dierickx (1991). 'De Marginalisering van Leidinggevende Ambtenaren', *Tijdschrift voor Bestuurswetenschappen en Publiek Recht*, 46: 642–52.

—— and —— (1993). 'De Onweerstaanbare Charme van Ministeriële Kabinetten', *Tijdschrift voor Bestuurswetenschappen and Publiek Recht*, 48: 546–56.

Rudolph, J., Jr. (1989). 'Belgium: Variations on the Theme of Territorial Accommodation', in J. Rudolph, Jr., and R. J. Thomspon, *Ethnoterritorial Politics, Policy and the Western World* (Boulder, Colo.: Lynn and Reiner), 91–113.

—— and R. J. Thompson (1989). 'Pathways to Accommodation and the Persistence of the Ethnoterritorial Challenge in Western Democracies', in J. Rudolph, Jr., and R. J. Thomspon *Ethnoterritorial Politics, Policy and the Western World* (Boulder, Colo.: Lynn and Reiner), 221–41.

Van Alboom, R. (1990). *De Verbeulemansing van Brussel* (Brussels: BRTN).

Van den Bulck, J. (1992). 'Pillars and Politics: Neo-corporatism and Policy Communities in Belgium', *West-European Politics*, 15(2): 35–55.

Van Hassel, H. (1974). 'Regering en Ambtenarij t.o.v. Beleidsvoering in België', *Acta Politica*, 10(3): 302–34.

——(1988). 'Het Kabinetssyndroom in Historisch Perspectief', *Gemeentekrediet van België*, 11: 503–11.

7

Senior Officials in the German Federal Administration: Institutional Change and Positional Differentiation

KLAUS H. GOETZ

I. Senior Officials and the Reassertion of Political Authority

Change in the organization and the political and administrative roles of the senior civil service in Germany's Federal ministerial bureaucracy has, first and foremost, been the consequence of shifts in the political-institutional context in which higher officials operate. Since the mid-1980s, this context has been partly transformed by the increasing party politicization, parliamentarization, and federalization of public policy-making. The unmediated influence of political parties in the Federal policy process is greater today than it has ever been in the history of the Federal Republic. Contrary to what the once influential 'decline of parties thesis' suggested, political parties have not suffered a general loss of functions. Rather, they appear to have been subject to gradual 'cartellisation' (Katz and Mair, 1995), in the course of which they have shed some of their traditional societal tasks, but at the same time strengthened their governmental capacities and their presence in the institutions of the state. In the German case, political parties do not just act through their representation in Parliament, i.e. the parliamentary parties (*Fraktionen*). The national governing parties, too, with their regional and sectoral suborganizations, are

The research on which this paper is based has been carried out in the framework of a project on 'Policy initiation and co-ordination in Western Europe: core executives in France, Germany, Italy and The Netherlands'. This project is funded by the ESRC as part of its Whitehall Programme (Grant No. L124251013), and is coordinated by Dr Vincent Wright and Professor Jack Hayward, University of Oxford. I would like to thank the many officials in Bonn who agreed to be interviewed as part of this research. I also wish to thank the head of the Press Documentation Centre of the Bundestag, Professor Keim, and his staff, for their kind assistance.

directly represented in the central bodies of executive decision-making (Schreckenberger, 1992).

Progressive parliamentarization has meant that the Bundestag has become more intimately involved in the early stages of the Federal policy process. The Bundestag has always been a working parliament and its organization and procedures are geared towards the detailed scrutiny of the government's legislative agenda (Beyme, 1997). Over the years, this essentially reactive role has been complemented by a proactive stance in policy-making that allows the majority parties, and to a lesser extent the opposition, to act as legislative agenda setters in their own right. In fact, there is growing evidence to indicate that the traditional policy-making sequence, according to which executive initiation, deliberation, formulation, and Cabinet decision-taking are followed by parliamentary scrutiny and, finally, legislation, has partly been reversed (Manow, 1996). In many instances, it seems justified to speak of a role reversal, in which the executive is reduced to providing technical-administrative assistance to the parliamentary policy-makers (Schreckenberger, 1994).

Of equal importance has been the close integration of the *Länder* in Federal policy development. Reacting to the intensifying antagonism of the Bundesrat towards the Federal government, the latter has increasingly felt compelled to try to co-opt the *Länder* into the pre-parliamentary stages of policy formulation, in an attempt to avoid seeing Federal legislative initiatives thwarted by the Bundesrat. The presence of an assertive opposition majority in the Bundesrat since the early 1990s, coupled with growing difficulties in securing approval for coalition policies from some CDU–CSU-led *Länder* governments, has made early coordination with the *Länder* more critical, but also more arduous, than for much of the postwar period.

Party politicization, parliamentarization, and federalization have had a profound impact on the senior civil service, affecting its relations to political authority, its cohesion, and the career paths, roles, and essential qualifications of higher officials. These consequences can briefly be summarized as follows:

• Party-political actors have gained in importance in public policy-making, while the scope for bureaucratic politics has narrowed. There has been a gradual, if by no means uniform, shift of initiative from the bureaucratic to the political arena. In the long-fought contest between political authority and bureaucratic power (Page, 1992), politicians appear to have gained the upper hand, at least for the moment. Federal policy-making is now considerably more politicized and less bureaucratized than two decades ago (Mayntz and Scharpf, 1975).

- Political coordination units within the Federal government have been strengthened, encouraging a dual informal positional differentiation within the civil service. The Chancellery, as the government's principal institution for political-administrative coordination, has decisively increased its hold over the ministries; departmental autonomy has been curtailed. Within the ministries, political control over the activities of line divisions and sections has been tightened through the upgrading of political support units (*Assistenzeinheiten*) that are directly attached to the political leadership. Increasingly, ministerial *Leitungsstäbe* have come to resemble French-style *cabinets ministériels*. As a corollary, informal differentiation of status and influence within the bureaucracy has been heightened. Senior Chancellery officials have tended to gain in status and influence *vis-à-vis* their colleagues in the ministries; and within the latter, line officials have had to learn to live with more assertive political-support staffs.
- The role of the successful senior official has to some extent been transformed, as bureaucrats, in particular those who work in ministerial line units, have seen their opportunities for initiating and championing policies decline. The profile of the effective senior official gradually changes from an agenda setter and policy initiator to a politically highly sensitive policy coordinator. The less autonomy the ministerial administration enjoys, both in relation to the political leadership and non-executive policy-makers, the more politically sensitive and responsive officials need to be.
- Political craft is a crucially important characteristic of the competent senior official (Goetz, 1997a). Political craft involves, in particular, the ability to assess the likely political implications and ramifications of policy proposals; to consider a specific issue within the broader context of the government's programme; to anticipate and, where necessary, influence or even manipulate the reactions of other actors in the policy-making process, notably other ministries, Parliament, subnational governments, and organized interests; and to design processes that maximize the chances for the realization of ministers' substantive objectives. Comparative research into the attitudes and role perceptions of top officials has shown that most Federal senior civil servants greatly value the political aspects of their job and recognize their importance (Aberbach *et al.*, 1981, 1990, 1994; Derlien, 1994; Mayntz and Derlien, 1989; Putnam, 1975). In a sample of Federal ministerial officials covering the top four ranks in 1987, some 86 per cent agreed with the statement that 'it is at least as important for a public manager to have a talent for politics as it is to have any special management or technical subject skills' (Aberbach *et al.*, 1994: 282). The exercise of political craft requires, amongst other things, that senior officials are able to draw on personal networks of

information and communication that extend beyond their own ministry into its constitutive institutional environment. This capacity to combine an internal with an external orientation is decisive, for '[n]ot only are top officials more involved in internal vertical communication, but the frequency of external contacts with other ministries, including the office of the head of government, with parliamentary bodies, interest group representatives and press relations increases the higher the rank of a civil servant' (Derlien, 1995*b*: 81).

It would be misleading to suggest that shifts in the national policy process have been the only major development to challenge the German senior civil service. Amongst frequently discussed catalysts of change, at least three deserve mentioning: 'modernization' initiatives inspired by New Public Management (NPM) precepts; European integration; and unification. As regards 'modernization', there are unmistakable signs that since the early 1990s Germany has begun to share much more vigorously in the international NPM reform agenda than was the case during the 1980s, when, despite much talk about administrative modernization at the Federal and *Länder* levels, the public bureaucracy paradigm was not seriously called into question (Benz and Goetz, 1996; Goetz, 1994). The climate of academic and political discussion on the public sector has altered decisively, and, for the first time, public bureaucracy has come under sustained attack, with key arguments borrowed from the Anglo-Saxon experience (Goetz, 1997*b*). At present, it is principally local government that serves as a testing ground for NPM-inspired reforms; but there is also no lack of public management reform proposals for the Federal administration (see e.g. Clasen *et al.*, 1995; Jann, 1994). The Federal Government has been unwilling to support such recommendations; yet, by 1995, the political and academic reform discourse had gained sufficient momentum to propel the Federal government into establishing an expert commission *Schlanker Staat* ('lean state'), with a broad remit to coordinate and promote all activities within the Federal bureaucracy aimed at a 'slimmed-down' state, including, for example, organizational development, budgetary regulations, and privatization and deregulation projects (Busse, 1996; Meyer-Taschendorf and Hofmann, 1997).

As regards the higher civil service, these modernization initiatives have yet to show any major impact; at the Federal level at least, the notion of the public manager has not gained currency (Becker, 1994; Röber, 1996). It is, however, worth noting the amendments to the Federal civil service laws that were adopted by the Bundestag and the Bundesrat in January 1997 and came into force on 1 July of that year. The reform law does not meet the more radical demands for the wholesale abolition of the civil service status or the redefinition of the traditional principles of the civil service, both of which would have required a constitutional amendment; such demands had been voiced by some *Länder* and Federal politicians, mostly from the SPD and the Greens, but also found the support of some Christian Democrats. For the most part, the 1997 reform package does not relate directly to senior officials, but it contained one potentially significant amendment: senior positions (*Amt mit leitender Position*) are to be filled on a probationary basis, with final confirmation of the appointment within a two-year period. The Federal Civil Service Law defines senior positions in the Federal administration as heads of divisions and subdivisions and the heads of non-ministerial offices who belong to payscale B. Proposals that would have transformed Federal 'political civil servants' (*politische Beamte*) into fixed-term appointments did not get a majority; but the Federal government was forced to concede to the *Länder* the right to adopt legislation to allow for such fixed-term appointments in their own administrations. It remains to be seen whether this modest amendment will have a significant effect on the Federal senior civil service. Probationary appointments will obviously remain without any practical consequence, unless this new instrument of personnel policy is at least occasionally used. But any attempt to remove heads of subdivision is likely to be followed by a legal challenge in an administrative court. As far as heads of division are concerned, as political civil servants they are already permanently 'on probation', as they can be sent into temporary (early) retirement at any stage (see section III).

Turning to the impact of European integration, it is important to recall that the political and institutional history of the Federal Republic has been inextricably tied up with the European project. Thus, it can occasion no surprise to find congruence in institutional practices between Germany and the European Union (Bulmer, 1995), evidence of comprehensive domestic adaptation, and even a progressively dual character—both German and European—of public institutions (Goetz, 1996). European integration has influenced the political-institutional make-up of the Bonn bureaucracy since the creation of the Federal Republic, and politicians and officials have had to grapple with the resultant challenges since the late 1940s (Hesse and Goetz, 1992). A persuasive argument can be made that European integration has led to institutional and policy 'fusion', the 'mixing and merging' of German and European Union administrations and policies in 'a system of mutual engrenage' (Wessels and Rometsch, 1996: 99; see also Rometsch, 1996). Certainly, the work of the majority of senior civil servants is now routinely affected by EU-related issues, a development which has added an important dimension to their marked external orientation noted above.

Compared with European integration, the effects of unification on the

Federal senior civil service are more visible in the short term, but also more difficult to predict in a longer term perspective. During the 1980s, the size of the top ministerial civil service (pay grades B3 to B11) only grew very modestly, with the number of budgeted posts for such officials rising from 1,163 in 1980 to 1,216 in 1989 (these figures include the Chancellery, but exclude the Ministry of Post and Telecommunications, and military personnel in the Ministry of Defence). This picture of modest expansion changed with the advent of unification. The accession of the five new *Länder* and East Berlin to the Federal Republic created a strongly expansionist dynamic throughout the Federal administration, which also extended to the upper echelons of the ministerial civil service. Between 1989 and 1992, the total number of Federal budgeted staff shot up from some 300,000 to 381,000; during the same period, the number of *Planstellen* (budgeted posts) for B grade ministerial officials rose from 1,216 to 1,400 (see Table 7.1).

It is not difficult to find functional explanations for this rapid growth in the ministerial bureaucracy. Unification confronted the Federal ministries with qualitatively new problems on a scale that could not be absorbed by existing administrative capacities. Special task forces and new sections, subdivisions, and divisions proliferated as the Federal executive grappled with the consequences of unification. At the same time, all Federal ministries established representations in Berlin, mainly staffed by personnel taken over from the East German ministries, though senior positions were invariably filled with Western officials. As *Länder* administrations in Eastern Germany had to be created from scratch (Goetz, 1993), ministerial officials initially had to take on many tasks which, in the West, would have been *Länder* responsibilities. Furthermore, beyond its immediate administrative consequences, the first years after unification saw a general loosening of the Federal purse-strings, which favoured administrative growth.

The bureaucratic unification boom did not last for long. In the face of a spiralling Federal budget deficits, the political emphasis switched from expansion to contraction, and, by the mid-1990s, all Federal ministries found themselves under strong pressure to reduce their staffing levels to pre-unification levels or below. Cutbacks hit those ministries hardest that had expanded most rapidly in the wake of unification, and several ministries were merged. The most serious long-term administrative consequence of unification is, however, the division of the Federal ministerial bureaucracy between Bonn and Berlin. As will be argued below, the partial move to Berlin provides a further impetus to some of the long-term trends remoulding the civil service that were identified earlier, notably the strengthening of political coordination units and informal positional differentiation.

The following discussion takes a closer look at the changing organiza-

TABLE 7.1. *Number of Federal Ministerial Civil Servants on the B Scale in 1980, 1989, and 1992* (Planstellen)

	1980	1989	1992
Chancellery	44	48	55
Foreign Affairs	84	88	100
Interior	122	100	130
Justice	66	65	77
Finance	134	132	155
Economics	111	115	139
Agriculture	66	65	75
Labour	78	82	89
Transport	78	78	84
Post[a]	(—)	(—)	(48)
Defence[b]	149	152	157
Health	—	—	48
Youth, Family, Health	47	52	—
Environment	—	49	68
Women and Youth	—	—	20
Family and Senior Citizens	—	—	20
Development	39	39	41
Construction	44	42	44
Inner-German Relations	23	24	—
Research and Technology	46	49	55
Education and Science	32	36	43
TOTAL	1,163	1,216	1,400

Source: Federal Budgets for 1980, 1989, and 1992.

[a] Before the privatization of the Federal post and telecommunications services, ministerial officials were not paid out of the general Federal budget.

[b] Excluding military personnel.

tion, composition, and political and administrative roles of the senior civil service. After a brief survey of the Federal senior ministerial personnel (section II), the chapter considers paths to the top, paying particular attention to the procedures for recruitment and promotion and the consequences of weak formal structures for personnel planning and development (section III). Following on from the definition of political craft as a defining attribute of effective top officials, the paper highlights the central position of political coordination units as training grounds in the Federal administration and comments on the informal positional differentiation they encourage (section IV). The discussion concludes with an assessment of the implications of the partition of the ministerial bureaucracy between Bonn and Berlin (section V).

II. The Federal Senior Civil Service: An Overview

At least three criteria need to be taken into account in defining Federal senior ministerial officials: their grade on the Federal payscale; the formal rank that they occupy in the bureaucratic hierarchy; and, more ambiguously, their centrality in the policy process. In the majority of cases, all three criteria tend to be closely correlated; but there are important exceptions. They concern, in particular, staff working in the Chancellery and political support units, who are often fairly junior in grade and formal position, but may wield considerable bureaucratic influence.

1. Pay Grade and Rank

The public service in Germany is divided into three personnel categories: civil servants (*Beamte*); salaried employees (*Angestellte*); and workers (*Arbeiter*) (Johnson, 1983: 175–9; Southern, 1979: 133–41). In 1997, the Federal budget provided a total of 318,279 posts (including part-time staff, excluding military personnel), of which 140,484 were reserved for civil servants, 89,411 for salaried employees, and 87,248 for workers (there were also 583 judges and prosecutors and 553 academics). The civil service is, in turn, subdivided into four career groups (*Laufbahnen*): the basic service (*einfacher Dienst*); the intermediate service (*mittlerer Dienst*); the executive service (*gehobener Dienst*); and the higher service (*höherer Dienst*). With the exception of a small number who are either temporarily or permanently employed as *Angestellte* on a contractual basis, top administrators invariably belong to the higher service.

The higher service comprises fifteen pay grades; there is a specific official title corresponding to each grade. Within the Federal ministerial administration, the large majority of career officials enter at the level of pay grade A13 (with the title of *Regierungsrat*). An official rising from this most junior level to the apex of the bureaucratic hierarchy—the position of an administrative state secretary (*Staatssekretär*)—would typically pass through the following grades: A14 (*Oberregierungsrat*); A15 (*Regierungsdirektor*); A16 (*Ministerialrat*); B3 (also *Ministerialrat*); B6 (*Ministerialdirigent*); B9 (*Ministerialdirektor*); to reach grade B11 (*Staatssekretär*). The remaining grades on the B scale are normally only used in the non-ministerial administration (the Ministry of Defence, which, in 1997, employed some 1,330 military personnel in the ministerial service is an exception). While payscale A operates with incremental remuneration, taking into account age and length of service, a payscale B appointment carries a fixed salary. Ministerial officials included in payscale B are usually regarded as senior officials, in particular those belonging to grades B6, B9, and B11. Table 7.2 shows the number of B scale posts in the ministerial administration, including the Federal Chancellery (which, in legal terms, is not a ministry), according to the 1997 Federal budget.

As indicated above, a small number of senior officials work on a contractual basis as salaried public employees rather than civil servants, either out of choice, or because they do not fulfil the necessary prerequisites for a lifetime appointment. In 1997, there were only nine ministerial officials on salary grade BAT I (the equivalent of A16), and another three on special contracts at a higher level.

On the B scale, an official's grade and hierarchical rank are strictly correlated. Thus, a *Ministerialrat* (A16 or B3) is legally entitled to be head of section (*Referatsleiter*), a *Ministerialdirigent* head of subdivision (*Unterabteilungsleiter*), and a *Ministerialdirektor* head of division (*Abteilungsleiter*). However, these positions in the organizational hierarchy may also be filled by lower grade officials. In all ministries, the number of senior

TABLE 7.2. *Number of Federal Ministerial Civil Servants on the B Scale in 1997* (Planstellen)

	B11	B9	B6	B3	TOTAL
Chancellery	—	6	14	32	52
Foreign	2	10	22	61	95
Interior	2	11	23[a]	94	130
Justice	1	6	15	47	69
Finance	2	10	25[b]	109	147
Economics	2	7	23	95	127
Agriculture	1	7	12	51	71
Labour	2	8	14	59	83
Transport	1	8	12	60	81
Post	1	3	4	24	32
Defence[c]	2	8	22	109	141
Health	1	4	10	33	48
Environment	1	6	13	44	64
Family	1	4	8	25	38
Development	1	3	8	28	40
Construction	1	3	9	32	45
Education	2	7	15	56	80
TOTAL	23	111	249	959	1,342

Source: 1997 Federal Budget.

[a] Of these, two are on B7 and one is on B5.
[b] Of these, one is on B5.
[c] Excludes military personnel.

positions to be occupied exceeds the number of corresponding grades authorized in the Federal budget; as a consequence, senior hierarchical positions are also regularly occupied by junior staff. This is particularly common at the level of head of section, many of whom have the rank of a *Regierungsdirektor* (A15), and some of whom are even more junior *Ober-regierungsräte* (A14).

2. Centrality

By virtue of the office they hold and their formal powers and responsibilities, both administrative state secretaries and heads of division will regularly be amongst the key figures in the executive policy process. They operate directly at the interface between politics and administration (König 1992), a position which is recognized by law in their status as political civil servants (see section III, below). Their influence is, of course, determined by many factors beside their formal status, including, in particular, their relationship with subordinate staff, on the one hand, and the political executive leadership, on the other. Examples of administrative state secretaries who in effect run a ministry, with the minister as a more or less decorative figurehead, are no more difficult to find than those of ministers who seek to bypass bureaucratic hierarchies and establish close direct working relationships with line officials. But even when both the political leadership and lower level officials share an interest in circumventing an administrative state secretary or a divisional head, the latter's hierarchical position makes it difficult for them to be side-stepped.

Moving below the two top bureaucratic tiers, any general assessment of the centrality of officials becomes more hazardous. It may, at first sight, seem paradoxical that, in general, heads of section have a stronger claim to be key players in the policy process than their immediate superiors, the *Unterabteilungsleiter*. The explanation for this lies in the fact that the section (*Referat*) still constitutes the basic working unit in the ministerial organization, with primary responsibility for policy development (Mayntz and Scharpf, 1975: 67–76). Its head is, accordingly, given a range of specific functions and accorded certain prerogatives in the Common Standing Orders of the Federal Ministries. By contrast, the profile of the subdivision, and its leader, is more ambiguous. Whereas sections and divisions are traditional features of German ministerial administration, subdivisions are a relatively recent innovation, 'a consequence of gradual organisational growth' (Mayntz and Scharpf, 1975: 78), which only became a standard feature of Federal ministries during the 1970s. Their functional value has always been in dispute. Heads of section prefer to be in direct contact with the divisional heads, instead of having to go through an intermediary, and this preference for unmediated communication is often shared by the *Abteilungsleiter*. Unless the head of subdivision is, at the same time, in charge of his own section, there is a danger of him being marginalized in the policy process.

If centrality in the policy process is employed as the decisive criterion for defining senior officials, it is clear that not all section heads would qualify. The key determinant is whether the policy issue with which they deal is central to the political mission of the ministry. In every ministry one finds what is sometimes referred to as an 'elephants' graveyard', i.e. sections or even whole divisions that are marginal to the core business of the department and rarely attract the attention of the political leadership. As such, they provide convenient resting places for officials who cannot be sent into temporary retirement, but who are considered ill-suited to deal with politically sensitive matters. On the other hand, there are certain key sections which will typically be at the heart of departmental decision-making. In addition to the core policy sections, they tend to include the sections in charge of the budget, general policy development and planning (*Grundsatz-und Planungsfragen*), and personnel.

As will be discussed below, the difference between formal grade and policy influence can be particularly pronounced in the case of staff working in political-support units directly attached to the minister and in the Chancellery. For example, the minister's personal assistant (*Persönlicher Referent*, or PR) and the head of the minister's office (*Leiter des Ministerbüros*, or LMB) often wield very considerable power, although it is rare for either to occupy a rank beyond that of a *Ministerialrat* (A16/B3, or an equivalent payscale in the case of salaried employees). It is by no means unheard of for the head of the minister's office to try and act as the minister's deputy, and line officials feel under pressure to treat him as such (Schimanke, 1982: 218); there is also always the 'latent danger that the individual assistant to the leadership mistakes himself for a political-administrative decision-maker' (König, 1991: 216; my translation). Similarly, in the Chancellery, quite junior officials can become central players whose political clout can exceed that of top officials in the line ministries.

III. Paths to the Top

1. Recruitment: Career Civil Servants and Outsiders

In examining recruitment to the Federal bureaucracy, two cases must be distinguished (Staab, 1996): the standard procedures that apply to the recruitment of career civil servants, who join the *höherer Dienst* at the entry level; and the recruitment of outsiders, *Seiteneinsteiger*, a diverse category comprising those who do not meet the standard statutory entry requirements to the civil service, who enter it at a higher level, or who stay temporarily outside the civil service as salaried employees.

Federal personnel policy in general, and recruitment for the higher civil service in particular, is marked by the disparity between a detailed and uniform legal framework, on the one hand, and a great deal of decentralization and inter-ministerial variation in the handling of personnel matters, on the other. German academic commentators on civil service law regularly emphasize that 'civil service law is (. . .) at its core constitutional law' (Lecheler, 1984; my translation). Thus, Article 33 of the Basic Law specifies the principles of access to public office, defines the duties of civil servants, and safeguards the 'traditional principles of the civil service'. These constitutional provisions are at the top of the hierarchy of legal norms relating to the civil service that encompasses both statutory and extensive secondary legislation. Laws that are of particular relevance to the Federal higher civil service include the Federal Civil Service Law (*Bundesbeamtengesetz*), which sets out the principles of the Federal civil service, and the Federal Remuneration Law (*Bundesbesoldungsgesetz*). Amongst non-statutory provisions, the Federal Career Regulations (*Bundeslaufbahnverordnung*) are of special importance, as they set out in detail the career structures of the four main civil service categories (i.e. the basic, intermediate, executive, and higher services).

There is no need here to examine in detail these legal norms. It suffices to highlight the following:

- officials are recruited to one of the four main civil service categories; in accordance with the career principle (*Laufbahnprinzip*), they usually enter the service at the lowest level in their respective category;
- formal educational entry qualifications are paramount; recruits to the higher civil service must possess a university-level qualification;
- after a probationary period, civil servants are appointed for life (*Lebenszeitprinzip*);
- promotion from the executive service to the higher civil service is only granted in exceptional cases;
- as regards the Federal ministerial administration, career civil servants are recruited for the general administrative service (with the exception of the Foreign Office); within the Federal ministerial bureaucracy, there are no specialist services (though military staff serve as administrators in the Ministry of Defence and, occasionally, in the Chancellery).

The law stipulates who may, in principle, be recruited for the higher civil service, at what level, and under which conditions; but it leaves broad discretion to the individual ministries when it comes to the important question of how the recruitment process is to be organized and how the substantive qualifications of candidates are to be assessed. The Federal ministries have always been fiercely protective of their *Personalhoheit*, i.e. their autonomy in personnel matters, and they have successfully resisted attempts at standardizing personnel policy.

In assessing staffing needs, ministerial practices differ widely. Thus, the head of the Federal Audit Office, writing in his capacity as the Federal Commissioner for Administrative Efficiency, noted in 1993 that,

federal departments and agencies often did not apply the appropriate procedures for assessing staff needs (. . .) In only a few cases were the procedures for establishing staffing levels capable of being verified (. . .) Often the assessment of manpower requirements was inadequately planned (. . .) Federal departments and agencies applied procedures and methods for assessing requirements which were unacceptable or produced inadequate results. (Präsident des Bundesrechnungshofs, 1993: 55; quotation from the English summary)

Similarly, recruitment for entry-level positions often appears a fairly haphazard affair. There is, for example, no central recruitment agency for the Federal ministerial bureaucracy; each ministry is individually responsible for organizing the recruitment and selection of candidates. Some ministries tend to advertise new positions, others rely primarily on approaches by interested individuals. In assessing applicants, methods and procedures again show a great deal of variety. In 1987, a highly critical report on personnel and organization in the Federal ministries by the Federal Commissioner for Administrative Efficiency argued that 'the selection procedures for new staff are often unsystematic and frequently lack relevant decision criteria' (Präsident des Bundesrechnungshofes, 1987: 74; my translation). No ministry possessed formalized criteria for assessing applications, and only a small number used selection techniques other than a personal interview with the candidate. Selection committees were the exception, and decisions were normally made through an informal agreement between the ministry's personnel section and the line section in which the new recruit was to be placed. There is little evidence to suggest that these findings are in need of major revision in light of developments over the last decade (Maor, 1996; Staab, 1996).

New recruits to the higher ministerial service come from a range of backgrounds. Most ministries prefer candidates with several years' working experience in the private or public sectors. Research institutes, interest groups, *Länder* and local administrations, and the Federal non-ministerial authorities provide a diversified reservoir of potential recruits. Interministerial differences are marked in this respect. The Ministry of Transport, for example, supervises a sizeable group of subordinate authorities and generally draws heavily on their personnel. In the Finance Ministry, Division III, dealing with customs and excise, likewise regularly recruits staff from subordinate authorities, whilst Division IV, dealing with taxes, has many officials who started their careers in *Land* administrations; other divisions in the ministry recruit principally 'on the open market'. The Ministry of Justice has traditionally favoured staff with experience of the *Länder* judicial administrations, many of whom first join the ministry as secondees. In the past, these secondees accounted for up to 30 per cent of the higher civil servants working in the ministry, but budgetary cuts have meant that the *Länder* are increasingly reluctant to second staff. As a result, the Ministry of Justice has become more reliant on recruits from elsewhere. Finally, the Chancellery only rarely hires staff directly, except at the level of heads of division and in the case of political support units; instead, it relies on transferees from the ministries.

Recruitment to the career civil service seems almost deliberately designed to minimize the chances for the selection of a tightly knit administrative élite. It is highly decentralized and personalized; accordingly, diverse institutional and personal preferences and priorities assume great importance in staffing decisions. Even within individual ministries, personnel sections are rarely able to impose a standard candidate profile, as the line divisions to which new appointees are to be attached are typically closely involved in the selection process. There is no single, or even favoured, route into the higher Federal service, nor is there a narrowly confined reservoir of potential recruits. In sum, Federal recruitment practices promote a pluralist civil service.

The recruitment of outsiders constitutes another facet of the pluralist composition of the senior bureaucracy. *Seiteneinsteiger* do not join the ministerial service as regular career officials at the entry level. Accordingly, their appointment as civil servants constitutes an exception to the career principle, typically because they lack the usual statutory qualifications or because they wish to join the service at a higher level. The favoured route of entry of *Seiteneinsteiger* into the Federal bureaucracy leads through the political-support units; less frequently, *Seiteneinsteiger* enter directly at the very top of the civil service, as an externally recruited administrative state secretary or head of division. As a rule, a high proportion of support staff is drawn from the ministry's career officials, but the right of ministers to bring in staff from outside is generally acknowledged. Chief recruitment reservoirs include the personnel of the national parties and their regional suborganizations, and the staff employed by the parliamentary parties. There is a fairly steady stream of outsiders into the higher Federal service, many of whom eventually reach top positions. Amongst current heads of division who initially joined the civil service as *Seiteneinsteiger* in political support units one finds, for example, a former head of office of the Chief Whip of the CDU–CSU parliamentary party; a former chief clerk of the Working Group of Transport of the CDU–CSU; a personal assistant to the Chairman the CSU Group in the Bundestag; and the former head of the office of Jörgen Mällemann, then chair of the FDP's Working Group on Foreign, Security, and European Policy.

Seiteneinsteiger often first start working in the ministerial bureaucracy as public employees rather than civil servants; such an arrangement neatly circumvents the restrictions imposed by civil service law. Problems often arise, however, when externally recruited support staff are later to be appointed as civil servants. As noted above, the career principle requires, as a rule, that members of the higher civil service, in addition to having a university degree, should join the service at entry level; following a probationary period, they may then rise through the ranks. Exceptions to these principles must be approved by the Federal Personnel Committee (*Bundespersonalausschuß*), which is responsible for the consistent application of civil service regulations throughout the Federal administration. The guidelines that the Committee has adopted are fairly restrictive. For example, the Committee will only approve the appointment of an outsider to a civil service rank at one level below that which would be justified by the function he fulfils (Bundespersonalausschuß, 1994: 19). Thus, a salaried employee who has for several years headed a minister's office will, if all other conditions are met, first be appointed as a *Regierungsdirektor*, although his function would merit the rank of *Ministerialrat*. In outlining its policy on *Seiteneinsteiger*, the Committee has highlighted the need to take into account 'the budgetary situation of the Federation, and also the resultant limited possibilities for promotion, in order to ensure the equal treatment of staff' (Bundespersonalausschuß, 1994: 16; my translation). Behind this somewhat cryptic remark lies the oft-voiced concern of line civil servants that the appointment of outsiders reduces the promotion prospects of career officials (Wagener and Rückwardt, 1982). These concerns are not unfounded, for once outsiders have become civil servants, they rarely leave the ministry with the minister who was responsible for their recruitment and a vacancy needs to be found for them in the ministerial line units.

As regards the direct appointment of outsiders to the top echelons in the bureaucratic hierarchy—heads of division and administrative state secretaries—the Committee has voiced a dual concern: first, that the number of outside appointments to such positions is growing; and, second, that many outsiders do not meet the requirements to warrant their appointment as lifetime civil servants. Already by the early 1980s, some 40 per cent of political civil servants were recruited to their position from outside the ministry in which they served (Mayntz and Derlien, 1989: 392); of these, about half were genuine external recruits, not previously employed in the Federal administration. With the number of outsider appointments increasing, the constitutional principle according to which the exercise of sovereign state tasks is to be entrusted to civil servants, rather than public employees, is in danger of being slowly undermined:

The Federal Personnel Committee notes with concern that increasingly 'outsiders' are brought into top positions (*Leitungsfunktionen*), who do not meet the criteria required to grant an exception so as to allow their appointment to an equivalent civil service post. Thus, they have to be employed as salaried employees in the longer term or permanently. (Bundespersonalausschuß, 1994: 20; my translation)

2. Promotion

The strongly decentralized character of Federal personnel policy is also evident in decision-making on promotion to senior positions. As a rule, the following applies: the more senior the position to be filled and the more directly tied to the political executive leadership, the less structured and the more politicized the promotion process (Dyson, 1977). Of the senior administrative appointments, only vacancies for the post of head of section are regularly advertised within the ministries (although this principle does not usually extend to *Assistenzeinheiten*); more senior posts are almost never publicized, whether internally or to outside candidates. There is no standard procedure to be followed after a vacancy for the post of a *Referatsleiter* has been announced. In some ministries, an informal expression of interest by a prospective candidate to the personnel section or the administrative state secretary suffices; in others, a formal application is required. In some, official selection panels (of varying membership) interview all candidates; in others the personnel section will informally sound out opinions. In some, the personnel section will provide the administrative state secretary and the minister with an open shortlist; in others, it ranks potential appointees, typically in close cooperation with the head of the division in which the vacancy has occurred. It is not unusual for ministers and state secretaries to let their preferences be known well before a position falls vacant; this is most likely in the case of sections that operate in politically sensitive areas at the centre of the minister's political attention (König, 1989: 54).

The fact that ministers are regularly involved in decisions on promotion and enjoy considerable discretion should not, in itself, be treated as conclusive evidence of party politicization. The Federal Civil Service Law and the Federal Career Regulations emphasize suitability, ability, and performance as the decisive criteria on which decisions on promotions are to be based, and length of service also has to be taken into consideration. A minister would be ill-advised to ignore these principles and conventions conspicuously and consistently in favour of party-political and personal sympathies. Not only would a personnel policy based principally on patronage diminish the quality of the ministerial staff over the longer term. Officials seeking promotion who feel that they have been passed over in favour of less qualified party loyalists can also seek redress in the courts, and ministers must then be able to present a solid defence of their decision. Arbitrariness and blatant patronage are, therefore, rare.

Undoubtedly, however, ministers possess considerable latitude in staffing matters, especially at the very top levels. As was briefly noted above, *Ministerialdirektoren* and administrative state secretaries belong to the category of political civil servants, as defined by Article 36 of the Federal Civil Service Law. As such, they form a key link between politics and administration. The law recognizes that they need to be in continuous basic agreement with the government's views and objectives in order to perform their task of assisting in transforming the government's political will into administrative action. The discretion of ministers in appointing political civil servants is matched by the ease with which they can be dropped. Ministers can at any time request that a political civil servant take (temporary) early retirement (*einstweiliger Ruhestand*), a device that is frequently used, especially in the case of administrative state secretaries (Derlien, 1984) and after a change of government (Derlien, 1988).

At the top of the administrative hierarchy, the political leadership would thus appear to face few effective constraints on appointments and promotions. There are no standard procedures to be followed and potential appointees are not limited to officials from within the ministry or even the Federal bureaucracy. The possibility of sending officials into early retirement provides a further element of flexibility. However, top administrative appointments can also become the object of intensive political bargaining within the governing coalition, restricting the discretion of ministers and even the head of government. In 1992, for example, Chancellor Kohl wanted to create the post of an administrative state secretary in the Chancellery; he intended to fill the new post with his close economic adviser, the career civil servant Johannes Ludewig, who had come to the Chancellery from the Economics Ministry in 1983. The FDP feared that with Ludewig as state secretary in the Chancellery, the role of the Liberal-led Economics Ministry might be diminished. For this reason, FDP politicians blocked the new post (see 'Der Kanzler muß ohne einen neuen Staatssekretär auskommen', *Frankfurter Allgemeine Zeitung*, 5 Nov. 1992). After the Federal elections of 1994, in which the Liberals were weakened, Chancellor Kohl exerted heavy pressure on his coalition partner and eventually succeeded in installing Ludewig as state secretary in the Economics Ministry itself, in the face of resistance by the minister.

3. Getting Noticed

Recruitment and promotion practices provide perhaps the best illustration of the low degree of institutionalization in Federal personnel policy; but other examples could be mentioned. They include, *inter alia*, the absence of prestigious élite training institutions for future top officials either within or outside the administration; the lack of technical corps; and the low priority accorded to systematic staff appraisal and development. The institutional framework is not conducive to cultivating a homogeneous, cohesive bureaucratic élite, possessed of a strong common identity and *esprit de corps*. This lack of institutions that could encourage the development of a distinct group identity might be all the more surprising given the well-documented diversity of the social backgrounds of top officials (Derlien, 1990*a*, 1990*b*, 1994, 1995*a*). It is then scarcely unexpected to find a 'lack of cohesion and homogeneity among high civil servants as a group' (Mayntz, 1984: 202). The pluralist nature of the personnel system serves to reinforce this diversity and helps to explain why 'the higher civil service, instead of sharing and jointly promoting the collective interest of any particular social class or group, reflects the full range of diverse and often conflicting interests that are organisationally represented in the departments and departmental divisions of the Federal bureaucracy' (Mayntz, 1984: 203).

Weak institutionalization promotes a pluralist civil service, but it also places a particular onus on the ambitious junior official. There are no obvious mechanisms for the early identification of potential high fliers, no formal supportive career development structures, and no clearly marked 'fast streams' to the top. Advancement is, accordingly, strongly dependent on an official's resourcefulness, his relationship with his immediate superiors, and, in particular, his skill in making his mark with the minister and the administrative state secretary, who hold the keys to senior appointments.

In order to secure advancement, younger officials, thus, ought to combine at least three qualities. First, they should have administrative-technical expertise that is not too narrowly focused. Excessive specialization tends to diminish promotion prospects, as it restricts intra-ministerial and inter-ministerial mobility. Generalists are likely to be considered for a wider range of senior positions than officials with a highly specialized technical background. Younger officials intent on improving their promotion prospects will seek to ensure that they do not stay within any one section for too long, although section heads have an incentive to discourage qualified junior staff from rotating. Secondly, they should have a good personal rapport with the ministerial leadership. Given the role played by the political executive in decisions on promotion, this aspect is clearly important, doubly so because German ministers tend to stay in office for a long time. Sympathy with the party-political views of the minister will, in general, prove helpful, although not in itself decisive. And thirdly, they require political craft. This involves the capacity to think and act politically; to be effective within the ministry; and to establish and maintain a strong network of professional contacts for information and communication throughout the ministerial bureaucracy and extending into the political parties, Parliament, the *Länder* administrations, and, where appropriate, interest groups.

IV. Political Coordination Units as Training Grounds

Wide-ranging administrative-technical expertise, access to political decision-makers, and political craft are not qualities that regular career civil servants can typically be expected to bring to the job; for the most part, they need to be nurtured after an official has joined the service. Political coordination units within the Federal government provide a particularly favourable environment in which to cultivate expertise, access, and political craft: officials in coordination units are usually exposed to a wider range of administrative-political problems than staff working in line units; they are confronted on an everyday basis with the need for political policy management; and their work at the interface of politics and administration allows them to build up an extensive range of contacts inside their own organization, the Federal executive as a whole, and amongst their interlocutors in the governing parties, Parliament, the parliamentary parties, and the *Länder* governments. Of course, the proximity of political coordination units to the executive leadership also offers ample scope for establishing a trusty relationship with the executive leadership. It is not surprising, therefore, that work experience in political coordination units has long been seen as an attractive proposition by many younger officials keen to make their mark. The progressive strengthening of coordination units noted above has increased their appeal. In short, the importance of political coordination units as informal training grounds reflects their centrality in the policy process (Goetz, 1997a).

1. The Chancellery: The Hub of Executive Coordination

The growing power of the Chancellery has arguably been single most important change in the Federal policy system during the last decade;

it reflects, to a large extent, the domination of the Chancellor over his Cabinet. In the present context, it is not necessary to consider in detail the reasons which led seasoned commentators on German politics to argue that, by the mid-1990s, Germany was again experiencing a 'Chancellor democracy' reminiscent of Adenauer's heyday (Kaltefleiter, 1996). What is important here is that during the 'third life' of Chancellor Kohl, after unification (Smith, 1994), his hold on Cabinet, coupled with the political management skills of successive Chiefs of the Chancellery, made the office into the single most influential coordinating agency in the Federal policy system.

The more pivotal the Chancellery, the more closely involved in the process of political management are its staff. This observation applies both to officials serving in the Chancellery's main policy divisions and to the personnel of the support units that are directly linked to the Chancellor, the Chief of the Chancellery, and the two parliamentary state secretaries (with the title of ministers of state) (Busse, 1994a; Müller-Rommel, 1994). These support units include the Chancellor's Office (*Kanzlerbüro*), the Working Staff for Public Relations and Media Policy, the Steering Group and Minister's Office of the Chief of the Chancellery, the Working Group on the New *Länder* that is also directly subordinate to him, and also the offices of the parliamentary state secretaries. Amongst the six line divisions of the Chancellery, Divisions 2 to 5, and Groups 12 and 13 in Division 1, focus on policy coordination, both through 'mirror sections' that shadow the work of ministerial departments and through sections whose remit deliberately cuts across departmental boundaries.

Political-support units, mirror sections, and cross-cutting sections provide younger officials with unrivalled opportunities for gaining broad policy expertise, building up extensive personal networks, and learning the art of political policy management. Mirror sections, for example, which for the most part cover the whole of a ministry's policy range, are typically staffed by no more than two or three higher civil servants, and the same applies to the cross-cutting sections. The whole of Division 2 only has a regular staff of thirteen higher civil servants (figure for 1995), yet under its successive heads Horst Teltschik, Peter Hartmann, and Joachim Bitterlich, it has come to play an often decisive role in foreign policy, in particular the formulation of EU policy (Paterson, 1994). This broad exposure to policy problems is coupled with the requirement to assess initiatives emerging from the individual departments from an administrative-technical and a political perspective before they reach Cabinet. Moreover, to operate effectively, Chancellery staff will necessarily strive to build up 'informal channels' to the individual ministries, often including the state secretaries and the minister (König, 1989: 64). The heads of mirror sections, and perhaps even their deputies, can thus gain political power and influence disproportionate to their formal position in the bureaucratic hierarchy.

Although the pressures of work in the Chancellery can be extremely high, the career opportunities afforded by working at the centre of power lead many ambitious younger officials to seize the chance of transferring there. Secondments from other ministries account for a considerable proportion of the Chancellery's total staff. By no means all officials will eventually return to their home ministries; but there is a steady rotation of personnel between the ministries and the Chancellery. The bulk of secondees are at the level of *Regierungsdirektor* (grade A15) and *Ministerialrat* (grade A16/B3). This indicates that for many secondees their time in the Chancellery is an important stepping-stone on their way to heading a section or subdivision upon leaving the Chancellery, though it is, of course, also possible to rise through the ranks within the Chancellery itself. Service in the Chancellery can even lead directly to the apex of a civil service career, i.e. the appointment to the position of administrative state secretary, as a string of appointments in recent years has shown (Goetz, 1997*a*).

2. Political Support Units: The Art of Political Management

The core staff of the ministerial *Assistenzeinheiten* is typically made up of the personal assistants (*Persönlicher Referent*) to the minister and the state secretaries and at least three offices: the Minister's Office (*Ministerbüro*); the Office for Cabinet and Parliamentary Affairs (*Kabinett- und Parlamentreferat*), which is sometimes split into two; and the Press- and Information Office, which is often divided into a Pressereferat and an office for public relations (*Öffentlichkeitsarbeit*) (Gorges, 1992; Mester-Grüner, 1987). Frequently, these units are complemented by further support offices, including, for example, special sections for medium and longer term policy planning and development, or offices for communication (often a euphemism for the speechwriters' bureau). An inter-ministerial comparison reveals considerable variation in the formal organization of support staff. In several ministries, all political support units, including the offices of the parliamentary and professional state secretaries and their personal assistants, are formally integrated in a *Leitungsstab* that is placed outside the main divisional structure; in others, even the minister's office and the office for cabinet and parliamentary matters officially belong to a line division (Mayntz, 1987: 6).

In part, such differences can be explained by ministers' preferences, and in part by differences in organizational culture. Perhaps the strongest influences on institutional choice at the level of political-support staff are, however, considerations concerning personnel, and unusual organizational solutions are sometimes adopted to accommodate a minister's particular personnel requirements. As a minister's office is equivalent to a section, it is normally headed by an official with the rank of *Ministerialrat* or even *Regierungsdirektor*. In the Ministries of Agriculture and of Labour, however, the heads of the minister's office have the rank of a *Ministerial-direktor*. The employment of a top official to head a minister's office would scarcely find favour with the Bundestag's budget committee. To circumvent possible criticism, the minister's office in the Ministry of Agriculture is part of a division for 'coordination and communication', and in the Labour Ministry, the head of the minister's office at the same time leads a very small line division.

Whilst research on political support units is sparse, their importance would appear to have grown over the years; in important respects they have come to resemble *cabinets ministériels*. Thus, Wright's description of French *cabinets* could be applied to German *Leitungsstäbe* without major qualifications. Like their French counterparts, *Leitungsstäbe* are made up of 'a small (and sometimes not so small) group of close, politically-sensitive and policy-oriented advisers which is recruited by the Minister and which expires on his or her departure'; their role is 'to act as the eyes and ears of the Minister, to define and push through his programme, and to look after his parliamentary and constituency work'; they do not 'fit into the normal departmental hierarchical structure', and sometimes they constitute a 'parallel administration designed to subvert the official ministerial hierarchy' (Wright, 1996: 306). In the German case, the tensions between line units and political coordination staffs have, so far, not been studied systematically; but it is not difficult to find impressionistic evidence to underpin the general argument. Shortly after the Federal elections of 1994, for example, the Minister of Transport decided to remove his long-serving administrative state secretary. Although no official reasons were given, it was made clear to the press that the two men differed fundamentally about the manner in which the ministry should be run. The *Frankfurter Allgemeine Zeitung* noted that the minister 'leads the ministry through a *Leitungsstab*, whose members he has brought with him (. . .) Heads of division and the administrative state secretary, thus, feel sidelined' (3 Feb. 1995).

What distinguishes officials working in the top positions of the political-support units from their colleagues in the line sections is not their formal hierarchical rank, but their proximity to, and constant close interaction with, the political leadership. Whereas the head of a line section will tend to communicate with the minister through his head of division and the administrative state secretary, his colleague of the same rank who leads the minister's office is tied to the minister in a relationship that must be founded on personal trust and loyalty. Key officials in political-support units thus differ from their colleagues in line sections in important respects: their close rapport, and often identification, with the political executive; the breadth of the subject-matters they need to deal with; their direct exposure to the diverse political pressures under which the political core executive operates; and the external orientation of much of their daily work.

In terms of personnel policy, political-support units have a dual effect: they help to bring in outsiders to the Federal bureaucracy, either on a temporary basis or permanently; and they acquaint personnel recruited from within the ministry at first hand with the political aspects of the work of the core executive. It is not surprising, therefore, that at least one-third of all current heads of division have at some stage in their career served as personal assistants or heads of support units. In some ministries, having worked directly with the executive leadership seems almost an unspoken precondition for promotion to the top. In the Ministry for Education and Research, for example, four out of seven heads of division have served as chiefs of the minister's office, and a fifth has been press spokesman. Similarly, in the Ministry of the Labour, four out of nine heads of division have previously led the minister's office. These examples would tend to support the view that officials who have worked in key positions in support units possess a better chance of reaching the top of the bureaucratic hierarchy than their colleagues in line sections (Schimanke, 1982: 226).

V. Senior Officials in the Berlin Republic

Our discussion of the reasons behind change in the German senior civil service has highlighted the impact of the Federal policy process. Party politicization, parliamentarization, and federalization of Federal policy-making have entailed a partial redefinition of the role of senior officials and have encouraged informal differentiation within the senior civil service. The strengthening of political authority over the Federal bureaucracy has provoked no dramatic upheaval in the senior ranks; yet, if considered over a longer period of time, signs of a gradual shift in the personnel system are clearly visible.

In retrospect, it may well turn out that the changes that took place during the 1980s and the first half of the 1990s were minor compared to the long-term effects of unification. Without doubt, the division of the Federal ministerial bureaucracy between Berlin, as the Federal capital (*Bundeshauptstadt*), and Bonn, which is now known as Federal city (*Bundesstadt*), raises the prospect of a potentially far-reaching reshaping of the Federal personnel system. The latest plans of the Federal government envisage that by the year 2000, the ministerial administration as whole will be considerably smaller than at present. However, this reduction in size is unlikely to lead to greater homogeneity. On the contrary, it seems certain that the partial move to Berlin will result in a much sharper and more visible distinction between senior officials who belong to a core administrative élite by virtue of their function and centrality in the policy process, and those who, while also senior in grade and rank, are consigned to the margins.

Present plans for the partition of governmental functions between Berlin and Bonn are principally based on the Resolution of the Bundestag of 20 June 1991 on the Completion of German Unity, and the so-called Berlin–Bonn Law of March 1994, which contains detailed regulations for the implementation of the 1991 Bundestag Resolution (BT-Drs. 13/5371; Busse, 1994*b*). According to these provisions, the Federal government, as a constitutional organ, is to take its residence in Berlin by the year 2000, alongside the Bundestag. The Bundesrat, which had initially decided to remain in Bonn, will also move. However, rather than transfer the entire Federal ministerial administration to Berlin, a complex 'combination model' has been adopted, which bears the imprint of the strong Bonn lobby in the main parliamentary parties.

According to the 'combination model' there will be two categories of ministries: those whose principal residence (*erster Dienstsitz*) is in Berlin and those that remain in Bonn. The former include the Foreign Office and the Ministries of the Interior; Justice; Finance; Economics; Labour and Social Affairs; Family, Senior Citizens, Women, and Youth; Transport; Territorial Planning, Construction, and Cities. The Chancellery and the Federal Press and Information Office will also move to the capital. The other seven ministries will retain their principal residence in Bonn. However, ministries with their principal residence in the capital will have a secondary office in Bonn (*zweiter Dienstsitz*), and vice versa. There is, however, a further complication. The Ministries of Family, Senior Citizens, Women, and Youth; Labour and Social Affairs; and Transport will have their principal residence in Berlin, but most of their staff are to remain in Bonn. The following list shows the expected number of staff for each ministry in Berlin in 2000 (Nawrocki, 1997).

(*a*) Ministries with principal residence in Berlin:

Chancellery	400
Foreign Affairs	1,580
Interior	870
Justice	560
Finance	1,200
Economics	1,110
Construction	400
Press and Information Office	500

(*b*) Ministries with principal residence in Berlin
but majority of staff in Bonn:

Labour	120
Family	230
Transport	280

(*c*) Ministries with principal residence in Bonn:

Defence	500
Agriculture, Health, Environment, Education	450

(*d*) Total staff in Berlin: 8,200

Overall, it is expected that some 8,200 staff, i.e. one-third of all Federal ministerial personnel, will be located in Berlin. Moreover, to compensate the Bonn region for the loss of jobs in the Federal ministries, a host of Federal administrative authorities currently in Berlin will be transferred to the Rhine, including, for example, the Federal Anti-Monopoly Office, the Federal Insurance Office, and the Federal Audit Office.

Most academic commentators are extremely doubtful whether the combination model or, rather more accurately, division model can be made to work (Derlien, 1995*c*; Müller, 1994). Their reservations are shared by the heads of *Zentralabteilungen* in the Federal ministries, in charge of organization and personnel, and other high-ranking officials. The head of the Federal government's task force for the implementation of the Bundestag's 1991 Resolution has remarked that,

Those who have been responsible for implementing the resolution for the Federal Government have almost despaired of it (. . .) The 'combination model' was a political, a politically initiated decision. It is important to stress this point. Sometimes the recent discussion has created the impression that, judged on the basis of organizational and other criteria, this 'combination model' is so absurd that it could only have sprung from a 'confused bureaucrat's mind'. (Westkamp, 1997: 7–8; my translation)

The major criticism levied against the model is that it ignores the need for face-to-face communication within the ministries and the Federal core executive as a whole and, in particular, the close interlocking between the executive and Parliament. With the Federal government as a collegiate body, the Federal Chancellor, the heads of some of the most important ministries, and, in particular, Parliament all moving to Berlin, all ministers will, inevitably, need to spend most of their time in the capital. For a minister to work effectively, direct and immediate access to all parts of his department is imperative. Moreover, members of the Bundestag, in particular, are not only reliant on continuous cooperation with the ministerial bureaucracy, but also expect officials to answer directly, at very short notice, and in person to any requests they may have (Zeh, 1995, 1997). As Zeh notes, it is, for example, not unusual, in meetings of parliamentary committees, for ministerial officials to outnumber members of Parliament by a factor of two, and they tend to take an active part in the committees' deliberations. The ministries resident in Bonn will find it very difficult to satisfy parliamentarians' demands.

Despite the objections that have been raised against the combination model, the Federal government remains committed to its implementation along the lines outlined above. It thus appears likely that politically sensitive administrative matters will, as far as possible, be dealt with in the capital. The Bonn representation will focus on administrative routine issues with lower political salience and ministers will spend most of their time in Berlin. They will seek to transfer key policy-related staff, on whom they rely most, to the capital.

The consequences that flow from such a scenario are evident: as Berlin evolves into the centre of political power, civil servants in Bonn will be increasingly removed from direct and regular contact with the ministerial leadership. Over time, they will come to be regarded as less influential players. Thus, the territorial division of the ministerial administration is likely to lead to a sharper and more visible split between top civil servants who are central to the political process and those whose role is primarily administrative. As Derlien (1995c: 178; my translation) predicts:

The more technical expertise will be transferred to the secondary offices in Berlin, on a case by case basis or in the form of units for principal policy matters and planning, the more these offices will come to resemble French ministerial *cabinets* in their function and the more the department in Bonn will be downgraded. More-over, cross-sectoral functions from the Zentralabteilung of the Bonn ministries, including the sections for budget, organization, and personnel, will migrate to Berlin. There will be a snowball effect from the self-recruitment of candidates, who will be increasingly attracted to the more prestigious positions in Berlin that are close to the minister.

Of course, there are qualifications to this general prediction of a growing duality between a functional élite of senior civil servants with immediate access to the political executive in Berlin, on the one hand, and a more remote higher civil service in the administrative backwaters of Bonn, on the other. For example, much will depend on the division of labour and political influence between the minister and the administrative state secretary. In ministries resident in Bonn, the minister's orientation towards events in Berlin may well bolster the influence of the administrative state secretary remaining in Bonn. Where the administrative state secretary or, in rare instances, the parliamentary state secretary acts as the focus of real political power in the ministry, the pull of Berlin may be weaker.

Nonetheless, a growing differentiation between civil servants with very close links to the political executive and those without seems unavoidable.

Such a development would provide further impetus to the already existing trends towards growing positional differentiation in the senior civil service that were noted earlier. Political coordination units, in particular the *Leitungsstäbe*, are set to increase in power and prestige, whereas the discretion of line units, especially in the Bonn ministries, is in danger of being further curtailed. Opportunities for working directly with the political leadership will, accordingly, gain in attractiveness. At the same time, political craft will become an even more important quality in civil servants, as the territorial division of governmental-administrative responsibilities raises novel qualitative challenges of intra-ministerial and inter-ministerial coordination.

REFERENCES

Aberbach, Joel D., Hans-Ulrich Derlien, Renate Mayntz, and Bert A. Rockman (1990). 'American and German Federal Executives: Technocratic and Political Attitudes', *International Social Science Journal*, 123: 3–18.

—— Hans-Ulrich Derlien, and Bert A. Rockman (1994). 'Unity and Fragmentation: Themes in German and American Public Administration', in Hans-Ulrich Derlien *et al.* (eds.), *Systemrationalität und Partialinteresse: Festschrift für Renate Mayntz* (Baden-Baden: Nomos), 271–89.

—— Robert D. Putnam, and Bert A. Rockman (1981). *Bureaucrats and Politicians in Western Democracies* (Cambridge, Mass.: Harvard University Press).

Becker, Maria (1994). 'Germania: Le politiche del personale', in Yves Mény and Vincent Wright (eds.), *La riforma amministrativa in Europa* (Bologna: Il Mulino), 647–84.

Benz, Arthur, and Klaus H. Goetz (1996). 'The German Public Sector: National Priorities and the International Reform Agenda', in Arthur Benz and Klaus H. Goetz (eds.), *A New German Public Sector?* (Aldershot: Dartmouth), 1–26.

Beyme, Klaus von (1997). *Der Gesetzgeber: Der Bundestag als Entscheidungszentrum* (Opladen: Westdeutscher).

BT-Drs. 13/5371: Bundestags-Drucksache (1996) *Bericht zum Stand der Maßnahmen der Bundesregierung zum Umzug nach Berlin und zum Ausgleich für die Region Bonn* (30 July)

Bulmer, Simon (1995). 'European Integration and Germany: The Constitutive Politics of the EU and the Institutional Mediation of German Power', paper for the Annual Conference of the Association for the Study of German Politics, University of Birmingham, 7–8 Apr.

Bundespersonalausschuß (1994). 'Geschäftsbericht 1993' 21, Geschäftsbericht für den Berichtszeitraum 1.1.1991 bis 20.10.1993, no publisher.

Busse, Volker (1994*a*). *Bundeskanzleramt und Bundesregierung* (Heidelberg: Hüthig).

—— (1994*b*). 'Umzugsplanung Bonn-Berlin', *Die Öffentliche Verwaltung*, 47(12): 497–504.

—— (1996). 'Verfahrenswege zu einem schlankeren Staat', *Die Öffentliche Verwaltung*, 49(10): 389–96.

Clasen, Ralf, Eckhard Schröter, Helmut Wiesenthal, and Hellmut Wollman (1995). 'Effizienz und Verantwortlichkiet'. Reformempfehlungen für eine effiziente, aufgabengerechte und bürgerkontrollierte Verwaltung. Gutachten im Auftrag der Bundestagsfraktion Bündnis 90/Die Grünen. Berlin.

Derlien, Hans-Ulrich (1984). 'Einstweiliger Ruhestand politischer Beamter des Bundes 1949 bis 1983', *Die Öffentliche Verwaltung*, 37(17): 689–99.

—— (1988). 'Repercussions of Government Change on the Career Civil Service in West Germany', *Governance*, 1(1): 50–78.

—— (1990*a*). 'Continuity and Change in the West German Federal Executive Elite 1949–1984', *European Journal of Political Research*, 18: 349–72.

—— (1990*b*). 'Wer macht in Bonn Karriere? Spitzenbeamte und ihr beruflicher Werdegang', *Die Öffentliche Verwaltung*, 43(8): 311–19.

—— (1994). 'Karrieren, Tätigkeitsprofil und Rollenverständnis der Spitzenbeamten des Bundes: Konstanz und Wandel', *Verwaltung und Fortbildung*, 22(4): 255–74.

—— (1995*a*). 'Compétence bureaucratique et allégeances politiques en Allemagne', in Ezra Suleiman and Henri Mendras (eds.), *Le Récrutement des élites en Europe* (Paris: La Découverte), 64–90.

—— (1995*b*). 'Public Administration in Germany: Political and Societal Relations', in Jon Pierre (ed.), *Bureaucracy in the Modern State* (Aldershot: Elgar), 64–91.

—— (1995*c*). 'Regierung und Verwaltung in der räumlichen Zweiteilung', in Werner Süß (ed.), *Hauptstadt Berlin*, ii. *Berlin im vereinten Deutschland* (Berlin: Berlin Verlag), 159–80.

Dyson, Kenneth (1977). *Party, State and Bureaucracy in Western Germany* (Beverly Hills, Calif.: Sage).

Goetz, Klaus H. (1993). 'Rebuilding Public Administration in the New German Länder: Transfer and Differentiation', *West European Politics*, 16(4): 447–69.

—— (1994). 'La modernizzazione dell'amministrazione tedesca: Cambiamenti organizzativi ai livelli Federale e statale', in Yves Mény and Vincent Wright (eds.), *La riforma amministrativa in Europa* (Bologna: Il Mulino), 137–71.

—— (1996). 'Integration Policy in a Europeanized State: Germany and the Intergovernmental Conference', *Journal of European Public Policy*, 3(1): 23–44.

—— (1997*a*). 'Acquiring Political Craft: Training Grounds for Top Officials in the German Core Executive', *Public Administration*, 75(4): 753–75.

—— (1997*b*). *Challenges to the Public Bureaucracy State: Six Propositions on Administrative Development in Germany* (LSE Public Policy Group Paper, 2/1; London: LSE).

Gorges, Renate (1992). *So arbeiten Regierung und Parlament: Organisation, Zusammenarbeit und Kontrolle im parlamentarischen Regierungssystem* (Rheinbreitenbach: Neue Darmstädter Verlagsanstalt).

Hesse, Joachim Jens, and Klaus H. Goetz (1992). 'Early Administrative Adjustment to the European Communities: The Case of the Federal Republic of Germany', *Yearbook of European Administrative History*, 4: 181–205.

Jann, Werner (1994). *Moderner Staat und effiziente Verwaltung: Zur Reform des öffentlichen Sektors in Deutschland* (Bonn: Friedrich Ebert Stiftung).

Jekewitz, Jürgen (1989). 'Politische Bedeutung, Rechtsstellung und Verfahren der Bundestagsfraktion', in Hans-Peter Schneider and Wolfgang Zeh (eds.), *Parlamentsrecht und Parlamentspraxis in der Bundesrepublik Deutschland* (Berlin: de Gruyter), 1021–53.

Johnson, Nevil (1979). 'Committees in the West German Bundestag', in John D. Lees and Malcolm Shaw (eds.), *Committees in Legislatures: A Comparative Analysis* (Oxford: Martin Robinson), 102–47.

——(1983). *State and Government in the Federal Republic of Germany: The Executive at Work*, 2nd edn. (Oxford: Pergamon).

Kaltefleiter, Werner (1996). 'Die Kanzlerdemokratie des Helmut Kohl', *Zeitschrift für Parlamentsfragen*, 27(1): 27–37.

Katz, R., and Mair, P. (1995). 'Changing Models of Party Organization and Party Democracy: The Emergence of the Cartel Party', *Party Politics*, 1(1): 5–27.

König, Klaus (1989). 'Vom Umgang mit Komplexität in Organisationen: Das Bundeskanzleramt', *Der Staat*, 28(1): 49–70.

——(1991). 'Formalisierung und Informalisierung im Regierungszentrum', in Hans-Hermann Hartwich and Güttrik Wever (eds.), *Regieren in der Bundesrepublik II* (Opladen: Leske & Budrich), 203–20.

——(1992). 'Politiker und Beamte: Zur personellen Differenzierung im Regierungsbereich', in Karl-Dieter Bracher (ed.), *Staat und Parteien: Festschrift für Rudolf Morsey zum 65. Geburtstag* (Berlin: Duncker & Humblot), 107–32.

Lecheler, Helmut (1984). 'Das Recht des öffentlichen Dienstes', in Karl Heinrich Friauf (ed.), *Handbuch für die Öffentliche Verwaltung*, ii. *Besonderes Verwaltungsrecht* (Neuwied and Darmstadt: Luchterhand), 489–529.

Manow, Philip (1996). 'Informalisierung und Parteipolitisierung: Zum Wandel exekutiver Entscheidungsprozesse in der Bundesrepublik', *Zeitschrift für Parlamentsfragen*, 27(1): 96–107.

Maor, Moshe (1996). *Changes in Recruitment and Training of Senior Public Officials in Britain and Germany, 1970–1995: Rhetorics or Realitities?* (LSE European Institute, Working Paper, Series: Converging Administrative Systems; London: LSE).

Mayntz, Renate (1984). 'German Federal Bureaucrats: A Functional Elite between Politics and Administration', in Ezra N. Suleiman (ed.), *Bureaucrats and Policy Making: A Comparative Overview* (New York: Holmes & Meier), 174–205.

——(1987). 'West Germany', in William Plowden (ed.), *Advising the Rulers* (Oxford: Blackwell), 3–18.

——and Hans-Ulrich Derlien (1989). 'Party Patronage and Politicization of the West German Administrative Elite 1970–1987: Toward Hybridization?', *Governance*, 2(4): 384–404.

——and Fritz W. Scharpf (1975). *Policy-Making in the German Federal Bureaucracy* (Amsterdam: Elsevier).

Mester-Grüner, Maria (1987). 'Ministergehilfen als Filter am Flaschenhals der Regierungspartei: Zur Transparenz politischer Assistenz', *Zeitschrift für Parlamentsfragen*, 18(3): 361–8.

Meyer-Taschendorf, Klaus G., and Hans Hofmann (1997). 'Zwischenergebnisse des Sachverständigenrats "Schlanker Staat" ', *Die Öffentliche Verwaltung*, 50(7): 268–77.

Müller, Edda (1994). 'Das Bundesumweltministerium—Randbereich der Bundesregierung? Organisationsreform mit dem Taschenrechner', *Zeitschrift für Parlamentsfragen*, 25(4): 611–19.

Müller-Rommel, Ferdinand (1994). 'The Chancellor and his Staff', in Stephen Padgett (ed.), *Adenauer to Kohl: The Development of the German Chancellorship* (London: Hurst), 106–26.

Nawrocki, Joachim (1997). 'Große Politik kehrt in große Stadt zürück', *Das Parlament*, 10 (28 Feb.).

Page, Edward C. (1992). *Political Authority and Bureaucratic Power: A Comparative Analysis*, 2nd edn. (Hemel Hempstead: Harvester Wheatsheaf).

Paterson, William E. (1994). 'The Chancellor and Foreign Policy', in Stephen Padgett (ed.), *Adenauer to Kohl: The Development of the German Chancellorship* (London: Hurst), 127–56.

Präsident des Bundesrechnungshof als Bundesbeauftragter für Wirtschaftlichkeit in der Verwaltung (1987). *Personal- und Organisationsaufgaben in der Öffentlichen Verwaltung am Beispiel oberster Bundesbehörden* (Stuttgart: Kohlhammer).

——— (1993). *Typische Mängel bei der Ermittlung des Personalbedarfs in der Bundesverwaltung*, 2nd edn. (Stuttgart: Kohlhammer).

Putnam, Robert D. (1975). 'The Political Attitudes of Senior Civil Servants in Britain, Germany, and Italy', in Mattei Dogan (ed.), *The Mandarins of Western Europe: The Political Role of Top Civil Servants* (New York: John Wiley & Sons), 87–127.

Röber, Manfred (1996). 'Germany', in David Farnham, Sylvia Horton, John Barlow, and Annie Hondeghem (eds.), *New Public Managers in Europe: Public Servants in Transition* (Basingstoke: Macmillan), 169–93.

Rometsch, Dietrich (1996). 'The Federal Republic of Germany', in Dietrich Rometsch and Wolfgang Wessels (eds.), *The European Union and Member States: Towards Institutional Fusion?* (Manchester: Manchester University Press), 61–104.

Schimanke, Dieter (1982). 'Assistenzeinheiten der politischen Leitung in Ministerien', *Verwaltungsarchiv*, 73(2): 216–29.

Schreckenberger, Waldemar (1992). 'Veränderungen im parlamentarischen Regierungssystem: Zur Oligarchie der Spitzenpolitiker der Parteien', in Karl-Dietrich Bracher (ed.), *Staat und Parteien: Festschrift für Rudolf Morsey zum 65. Geburtstag* (Berlin: Duncker & Humblot), 133–57.

——— (1994). 'Informelle Verfahren der Entscheidungsvorbereitung zwischen Bundesregierung und den Mehrheitsfraktionen: Koalitionsgespräche und Koalitionsrunden', *Zeitschrift für Parlamentsfragen*, 25(3): 329–46.

Smith, Gordon (1994). 'The Changing Parameters of the Chancellorship', in

Stephen Padgett (ed.), *Adenauer to Kohl: The Development of the German Chancellorship* (London: Hurst), 178–97.

Southern, David (1979) 'Germany', in F. F. Ridley (ed.), *Government and Administration in Western Europe* (Oxford: Martin Robertson), 107–55.

Staab, Andreas (1996). *Recruitment and Training in the Federal Republic of Germany* (LSE European Institute; Working Paper, Series: Converging Administrative Systems; London: LSE).

Wagener, Frido, and Bernd Rückwardt (1982). *Führungshilfskräfte in Ministerien: Stellenbesetzung und spätere Verwendung von Persönlichen Referenten und Leitern von Ministerbüros in Bundesministerien* (Baden-Baden: Nomos).

Wessels, Wolfgang, and Dietrich Rometsch (1996). 'German Administrative Interaction and European Union: The Fusion of Public Policies', in Yves Mény, Jean Louis Quermonne, and Pierre Muller (eds.), *Adjusting to Europe: The Impact of the European Union on National Institutions and Policies* (London: Routledge), 72–109.

Westkamp, Klaus (1997). 'Das Kombinationsmodell als Kompromiß', in Klaus König (ed.), *Ministerialorganisation zwischen Berlin und Bonn* (Speyerer Forschungsberichte, 173; Speyer: Forschungsinstitut für Öffentliche Verwaltung), 5–11.

Wright, Vincent (1996). 'The Development of Public Administration in Britain and France: Fundamental Similarities Masking Basic Differences', *Yearbook of European Administrative History*, 8: 305–19.

Zeh, Wolfgang (1995). 'Das Parlament zwischen Berlin und Bonn', in Werner Süß (ed.), *Hauptstadt Berlin*, ii. (Berlin: Berlin Verlag), 141–58.

—— (1997). 'Wirkungen des Berlin-Umzugs auf das parlamentarische Regierungssystem', in Klaus König (ed.), *Ministerialorganisation zwischen Berlin und Bonn* (Speyerer Forschungsberichte, 173; Speyer: Forschungsinstitut für Öffentliche Verwaltung), 12–27.

8

The British Senior Civil Service

CHARLOTTE DARGIE AND RACHEL LOCKE

Introduction

Tracing the origins of the modern civil service, Parris (1969: 22) defines a service as 'a body of full-time, salaried officers, systematically recruited, with clear lines of authority, and uniform rules on such questions as super-annuation'. The British civil service exhibits the following characteristics: it is civil, permanent, unified, non-political, and anonymous. As a *civil* service it is 'distinct from the political, or parliamentary, service of the crown' (Parris, 1969: 23–4). Secure tenure ensures its *permanence*: 'the retention of that job during a change of government' (Parris, 1969: 27). Being perman-ent has facilitated the separation of administration from politics. The civil service is *non-political*; it does not rely on patronage. Finally, the accept-ance of ministerial responsibility means that civil servants are *anonymous*; it is the minister who answers in Parliament with respect to government policy.

The civil service developed as a respected profession in Britain, with mobility, lifetime service, and standardized recruitment through open competition. It is important to understand the professional values and ethics of the service in addition to its founding characteristics of perman-ence, non-partisanship, and anonymity. Like many British institutions, the civil service has evolved in its current form over time. Generally comment-ators trace the origins of the present service to the Northcote–Trevelyan Report of 1854. However, the modern civil service was the subject of many commissions and reports in the nineteenth century. It was only in the twentieth century that the civil service developed as a fully unified service with a sense of cohesion and set of common values.

Importantly, civil service ethics and high standards of public service have developed through civil servants themselves. As Chapman notes, the civil service has developed through a process of socialization; the 'variable combination of education, unstructured learning, observation, and experi-ence of life' (1996: 1–2). Individual civil servants also learnt from highly influential civil service leaders, like Sir Warren Fisher in the 1930s and Lord Edward Bridges in the post-war period, who published a pamphlet entitled *Portrait of a Profession* (Bridges, 1950); both imposed their standards on the service. An understanding of the socialization of common civil service norms and values is important for evaluating the response of the senior civil service to the reforms of the 1980s. The set of common values and expectations made the civil service, and in particular the senior civil service, a cohesive group.

Many argue that the civil service was revolutionized during the reforms of the Conservative government in office from 1979 to 1997. Permanence, non-partisanship, and anonymity were each under threat. Some senior civil servants are now employed on short-term contracts, posts are opened up to competition from outside, civil servants are now appearing personally before select committees, and senior civil servants have found themselves in the spotlight, boosted by high-profile appointments and political rows.

The aim of this chapter is to describe the current senior civil service in Britain. In order to do this, recent changes instigated by the Thatcher and Major governments have to be addressed. To explain the developments, we use four analytical themes that run through the different reforms of the senior civil service. They are: managerialism (private-sector management styles in the civil service), marketization (introducing markets into civil service operations), agencification ('hiving off' civil service functions to separate agencies), and politicization (breaking down the barriers between political and non-partisan tasks in government). We provide an introduction to these four themes, followed by an assessment of change through various aspects of the senior civil service.

1. Managerialism

'More of a Manager than a Mandarin' described a retiring permanent secretary at the Department of Social Security (*The Times*, 5 Oct. 1995). Traditionally, the civil service was responsible for administering services and advising ministers on policy matters. Within the senior civil service it is the latter that carries more prestige and power. However, the managerialist movement of the 1980s questioned both *what* civil servants did and *how* they did it. Management in the civil service was by no means introduced only in the 1980s. Nor was it invented by the Thatcher government. It is significant here because of the range of policies that the Conservative government introduced as part of improving management in government and because they were comprehensive enough to reach the top of the civil service.

'Managerialism' is a set of practices based on the belief that 'private sector is best'. Under the umbrella term 'The New Public Management', private-sector practices have been introduced into the British civil service. Key features of managerialism are 'hands on' professional management; explicit standards and measures of performance; discipline in resource use; stress on private-sector styles of management practice; and a greater emphasis on output controls (Hood, 1991: 4–5). They are similar to the principles of scientific management: set clear targets; measure using performance indicators, and reward individuals by results (Pollitt, 1993: 56). Throughout the Thatcher period various efficiency scrutinies of civil service work have been conducted, including the Financial Management Initiative, MINIS, the '3Es' of economy, efficiency, and effectiveness, and the Next Steps. The scrutinies looked at the work of the whole civil service and required the cooperation of the senior civil service. However, now the focus of change has worked its way to the top of the civil service.

2. Marketization

The introduction of markets into the public sector has been one of the most significant changes made by the last Conservative government. The move to market-based exchange and provision represents a fundamental shift away from traditional bureaucracy and hierarchical control. Based on ideas of the institutional economics school (see for example, Williamson 1975), it is accepted that there is a choice in organization between markets and hierarchies and that both work well in different circumstances. The ideas of economics say that efficiency is a way of deciding between markets and hierarchies. In some circumstances introducing the internal (agent acts in the interests of the principal) and allocative (via the price mechanism) efficiencies of the market system *may* provide overall gains. The important factors are competition, information, and prices. These have consequences for the associated transaction costs of contracts in market exchange. In the public sector these factors sometimes make the efficiency gains of market exchange relatively small and possibly negative. Nevertheless, the government has adopted marketization wholeheartedly throughout the public sector.

3. Agencification

With the publication of the Ibbs report, *Improving Management in Government: The Next Steps* (Efficiency Unit, 1988), the civil service has been largely divided along policy and operational lines. Operational functions of the civil service are the responsibility of Next Steps agencies, headed up by an agency chief executive who reports, with the permanent secretary, to

House of Commons select committees. As accounting officers, chief executives appear before the Public Accounts Committee. The principles extend the philosophy of managerialism outlined above; operational management functions could be overseen at a distance by the department, using performance indicators and targets. Policy functions are kept within the department. There was now a clear separation of policy-making and operational management. It would seem that the senior civil service has suffered a dramatic loss of function with the creation of agencies. Some say the reverse is true; with the transparency of agencies and targets for their achievement, responsibility for management has taken on a more important role.

4. Politicization

The politicization thesis suggests that the senior civil service is no longer impartial. Dowding (1995: 124) argues, amongst others, that impartiality is better described as 'objectivity'. It means the civil service is able to serve equally any incoming government, whatever the political party—hence, the ability of the civil service to be permanent. The senior civil service is politicized, or it is no longer objective, because of the effects of the last Conservative government. Commentators cited both the political will of the government and the length it had been in power. The government was alleged to have driven through policies, rewarding senior civil servants for being 'can do' managers rather than 'wait a minute' advisers. Ministers of the Thatcher period frequently describe themselves retrospectively as policy initiators; they knew what they wanted and they needed senior policy advisers to implement policy rather than help them decide which was the appropriate route to follow. The balance of power between the amateur politician and the career civil servant shifted between 1979 and 1997. Ministers were described as bullying or macho in the press. The government was headed, under Margaret Thatcher, by a leader who was openly hostile to the senior civil service. Mrs Thatcher had a specific policy programme to implement. Ministers were part of that programme. They thought up the policy ideas. They mistrusted civil servants who were trying to interfere and therefore rejected any advice that went contrary to their plans. Experience was seen to cloud the clarity with which ministers saw the political issues.

We have established that the tradition of the British civil service was civil, permanent, unified, non-political, and anonymous. The 1980s and 1990s apparently revolutionized the whole of the civil service. Our aim is to assess how far change has affected the *senior* civil service. We assess change in the areas of recruitment and promotion; mobility; sociological characteristics; interdepartmental and external relations; and relationships with the political machinery of government. First, we have to establish what we mean by the 'senior civil service'.

The Senior Civil Service

1. Definition

The senior civil service has recently been redefined. Moving away from describing civil servants by their grade, there is now a broad Senior Civil Service which includes the previously defined Senior Open Structure (SOS; grades 1–3) and also grades 4 and 5. The new Senior Civil Service has among its responsibilities the provision of policy advice to ministers, representing and implementing policies, and managing public services (Cm 2627, 1994).

It includes the managerial grades of 4 and 5 and is intended to produce a senior civil service that reflects the new structures and responsibilities of senior civil servants. The new Senior Civil Service was established on 1 April 1996 to uphold the values that underpin the civil service as a whole: 'One of the key aims in establishing a new, wider, cohesive Senior Civil Service is to provide clear leadership in sustaining core values' (Cm 2748, 1995: 6). Cohesion is expected to filter down the system: 'It would strengthen the cohesion not only of the senior management of departments, but also of the wider civil service' (Cm 2627, 1994: 37). The values of the civil service are integrity, political impartiality, objectivity, selection and promotion on merit, and accountability through ministers to Parliament (Cm 2748, 1995: 3). It is believed that they will be as important in the next century as they were in the last; they represent 'continuity' in the title of the 1994 White Paper on the civil service, *Continuity and Change*. The creation of the Senior Civil Service is designed to achieve this continuity whilst being itself one of the changes. Mountfield makes the point about the newly created Senior Civil Service: as one of the changes, it is at the same time an important instrument of continuity (1997: 309).

The new Senior Civil Service is also a managerialist tool for leading the civil service. Mountfield (1997: 308–9) describes it a 'corporate resource'; its aim is to 'adopt a more strategic focus: to co-ordinate the work of others across a wider canvas; to assume greater management, leadership and representational responsibilities and to begin to look more widely across government'. The new group of senior civil servants is expected to guide other areas of the service through change. The description could apply to the senior management of any large, private corporation. We begin with change in the current senior civil service.

2. Numbers

In 1996 there were 590 civil servants in the top three grades (Cabinet Office, 1996). Of those, 447 are grade 3, 110 grade 2, and just 33 grade 1, the top grade in the civil service. The total number of staff in post in the civil service (excluding staff in the diplomatic service) is 474,876 (*Civil Service Yearbook*, 1996: p. cxxii), a reduction from nearly three-quarters of a million in 1979. The senior officials account for about 0.1 per cent of the total civil service. The reductions in civil service numbers were part of the Conservative government's fundamental review of public expenditure. Public-sector workers were used as an example to private firms on how to curb unionization and pay demands. Recently, as a result of departmental senior management reviews, numbers of staff were reduced by 23 per cent (Mountfield, 1997: 310).

Now the top grades of the civil service include the heads of the Next Steps agencies as well as civil servants in central government departments. The Efficiency Unit Report (1988), *Improving Management in Government: The Next Steps* (the Ibbs Report), proposed that service and policy delivery be improved with the creation of agencies to carry out the administrative functions of government, leaving core departments responsible for policy-making. After a slow start now more than 75 per cent of the civil service has been hived-off in this way. Areas of departmental work continue to be hived off and the Oughton Report predicts that, if trends continue, just over 10 per cent of the total of the top three grades of the civil service will be in agencies.

Recruitment and Promotion

There have been visible policy changes in the recruitment and promotion of senior civil servants which several commentators focus on. Plowden (1994: 46–87) describes the development of open competitions for senior appointment as a 'quantum leap' compared with past practice. Chapman (1994: 607) says flexible performance pay arrangements and written contracts for senior civil servants are 'landmark' changes. The Efficiency Unit commissioned a study on career management and succession planning which resulted (1993) in the Oughton Report. It made recommendations in three areas: internal training and development; selection and appointment; and terms of employment. Oughton was followed a year later by a review of fast stream recruitment which devolved more responsibilities for recruitment to departments. The two reports signalled change for the senior civil service. These developments are now assessed.

1. The Fast Stream Generalist

Traditionally in the civil service the generalist, career civil servant domin-
ates; specialists (for example, scientists, lawyers, accountants, and economists) play a supportive and subordinate role. The term 'generalist' refers
to an individual who has received a general education. Generalists still
dominant the top tier of the civil service. Nearly two-thirds of the SOS are
generalists, fast or main stream (Efficiency Unit, 1993). There are only small
groups of economists, statisticians, and scientists. The only really significant group of specialists is lawyers, who make up about 12 per cent of the
SOS. A significant number of the SOS were recruited through the fast stream.
This recruitment scheme supplies many of the senior civil service. Oughton
reports that nearly 50 per cent of the SOS are fast stream generalists.

The fast stream refers to the process of recruitment of graduates to the
civil service, with opportunities for fast-track training and promotion.
Graduates are centrally recruited through the Recruitment and Assessment Service Agency (RAS). They undergo a rigorous process of aptitude
tests followed by interviews and finally a panel of the Civil Service
Selection Board (CSSB). The new pool of generalist, graduate administrators are then picked by the various departments. Fast-streamers are the
backbone of the senior civil service; they stay in the civil service throughout their career.

2. Senior Appointments

The top of the civil service differs from the rest of the service where recruitment and promotion are now done departmentally. Appointments at
permanent secretary and deputy secretary level are made centrally by the
Prime Minister on the advice of the Head of the Home Civil Service. In
this task they are supported by the Senior Appointments Selection Committee (SASC) that sifts through proposals from departments. Richards
(1996) describes a personalized system of senior civil service appointments
where the crucial element is the relationship between the Prime Minister
and the Cabinet Secretary. In particular, the system relies on the nature of
the Prime Minister. There are passive and proactive Prime Ministers, with
the former rubber-stamping what the Cabinet Secretary has proposed and
the latter being involved in choosing the final shortlist, even scrapping all
existing names (Richards, 1996: 666–70). Margaret Thatcher was famously
proactive in the process: 'I was told that she [Mrs Thatcher] had said that
she was not prepared to see me made a full Permanent Secretary and therefore I just took it for granted that SASC could not put my name forward'
(William Ryrie, Treasury official, quoted in Richards, 1996: 667).

It was Mrs Thatcher who removed Sir Ian Bancroft and combined the posts of Cabinet Secretary and Head of the Civil Service, which Sir Richard Wilson now holds. So, the Prime Minister plays an integral part in the appointment of the combined post itself. As a single post the new Head of the Civil Service is 'in the contradictory position of being the agent for his organisation, whilst also acting as the role of the government's spokesman in Whitehall' (Richards, 1996: 667). It is a position of weakness: 'The work of SASC, the CSC, the Senior and Public Appointments Group and all the strategic planning that has gone before it, can potentially be nullified, by an over-bearing Prime Minister and a deferential Cabinet Secretary' (Richards, 1996: 672).

Appointments procedures for senior posts have changed little since the early 1980s, except for the Senior Appointments Selection Committee which is being opened up in line with other market changes. Now the First Civil Service Commissioner sits on the selection committee, which is also required to include a woman and an outsider (Cm 2748, 1995). The First Civil Service Commissioner is responsible for advising on the choice between open competition and internal appointment, as well as being responsible for approving all appointments from outside the civil service to senior posts. The post of Civil Service Commissioner itself is being advertised (Cm 2748, 1995). These changes reflect an attempt to broaden selection on appointment and promotion, as traditionally posts have gone to male civil service careerists. The outsider appointed to the Senior Appointments Selection Committee is Sir Michael Angus, Chairman of Whitbread plc.

There are still few women in the senior civil service. In 1996, 9 per cent of grade 1 civil servants, 7 per cent of grade 2, and 12 per cent of grade 3, were women (Cabinet Office, 1996). The position for a woman on the Senior Appointments Selection Committee has not yet been filled, although the Cabinet Office claims that more females will be in post in the millennium and that the service is doing well:

A benchmark figure of at least 15% of SOS posts to be held by women by the year 2000 has been set. This will require adaptation to the new Senior Civil Service. The Civil Service record compares well with other sectors e.g. the proportion of women directors of private companies was quoted as 2.5% in a recent Institute of Management/Remuneration Economics Survey (1994). (Cabinet Office, 1996).

3. Recruitment and Pay

Recent change in senior recruitment and promotion is part of managerialism applied to the senior civil service. The Oughton Report (Efficiency Unit, 1993: 5) which looked at planning and succession specifically for senior posts drew on the practice of foreign government and private-sector firms. Oughton describes the current civil service context as follows:

Work to determine core criteria for Senior Open Structure posts suggests that some skills—for example leadership, team building, contract management—are being given greater emphasis than before alongside 'traditional' Civil Service qualities. The report concludes that the Civil Service requires the range of skills needed in any large organisation; and in particular adaptability and long-term corporate knowledge are as important to effectiveness in the Civil Service as elsewhere. (Efficiency Unit, 1993: 1–2)

Since 1979 various managerialist practices have been applied to the senior civil service. Changes have been seen in the area of recruitment, contracts, pay, and incentives. Some of the changes to the senior civil service have been introduced via the new agency chief executives. The Conservative government used the recruitment, reward, and retention of chief executives as an example of new policies for the broader senior civil service. Chief executive posts were advertised through open competition, they were recruited on a fixed contract, they had performance targets set, and they were rewarded partly through performance bonuses. The aim was to attract and recruit chief executives from outside the civil service. Therefore, private-sector packages, including comparable levels of pay were required. After the recruitment of many chief executives, including several high-profile cases from outside the civil service—Derek Lewis (Prison Service), Ross Hepplewhite (Child Support Agency), and Michael Bichard (Benefits Agency) are examples—policies have been extended across the senior civil service. In several departments the agency chief executive was earning more than the permanent secretary.

The Oughton Report's (Efficiency Unit, 1993) recommendations for the senior civil service were the culmination of a number of wide-ranging policies affecting senior civil servants. Accepted recommendations included leaner, flatter management structures; movement quickly through the service for outstanding individuals; explicit written contracts for senior civil servants (not fixed contracts but indefinite, with a fixed period of notice); and flexible pay arrangements to reward and retain high performers.

4. Open Competition

Traditionally top posts were filled by people from inside the service with few positions being filled through open competition. Today 'departments and agencies will always consider advertising openly posts at these levels when a vacancy occurs, and then will use open competition wherever it is necessary and justifiable in the interest of providing a strong field or of introducing new blood' (Cm 2627, 1994: 3). As Oughton (Efficiency Unit, 1993: 55) reports, there remains a desire to 'grow its own timber' in the senior civil service. *Continuity and Change* also 'expects that most of the top Civil Service posts will continue to be filled by those with substantial previous experience within the Service' (Cm 2627, 1994: 3). Today, although more posts are now being externally advertised *less* are actually being appointed from outside.

Currently, the evidence suggests that recruitment is still mainly internal. The Civil Service Commissioners reported in 1996 that approximately one-third of senior vacancies were open to external candidates in 1995 compared with one-sixth in 1992. Those actually being recruited from outside constituted a *falling* proportion of that figure. Eight of the thirteen posts open to outside competition were filled by external appointments in 1992; in 1995 this was seven out of sixteen (Cabinet Office, 1996). The report comments that: 'it is worth considering the reasons why good quality external candidates are not always attracted to apply for Senior Civil Service posts, or if they apply, are unable to compete successfully against the internal candidates' (1996: 6). The report cites a number of possible reasons including: pay (still not comparable with the private sector); some positions were not easy for an outsider to take on; formality of the selection process; some external candidates were not sufficiently strong. Also, looking more closely at the make-up of external recruits reveals that most are actually specialist appointments: lawyers, statisticians, and economists, rather than officials in general managerial posts (Efficiency Unit, 1993: 95).

So, although open competition is trumpeted as an important development in the senior civil service and a reflection of modern, managerial practice, it is neither automatic nor the preferred option. In practice, the White Paper proposes that departments be required to address a series of questions to justify open competition: 'is there a sufficient field of candidates already within the department, or in order to get a strong field is it necessary to extend the search to the wider Civil Service or to full open competition?' (Cm 2627, 1994: 41). Open competition is expensive and such an exercise can be demotivating as it means the post cannot be filled using internal resources. The government's expectation continues to be that most posts will be filled by those with experience within the service.

5. Contracts

Traditionally civil servants have enjoyed security of tenure. Once appointed they cannot be easily removed. It gives the civil service its permanent characteristic in contrast with the position of ministers who spend much less time in the department before they are moved on. *Continuity and*

Change proposed changes to contractual arrangements (Cm 2627, 1994). It took the Efficiency Unit's (1993) recommendations about contracts based on the experience of the private sector (i.e. the rejection of fixed-term contracts which are demotivating and do not emphasize career development) and proposed, 'that members of the new Senior Civil Service should be on explicit, written employment contracts. One form of contract should cover the great majority of circumstances—employment for an indefinite term, but with specified periods of notice. Fixed term and rolling contracts would be used in appropriate circumstances' (Cm 2627, 1994: 3). Senior civil servants have now moved to 'individually-determined pay' and 'a written contract of service' (Cm 2627, 1994: 37). There has been an explicit policy to bring the public sector into line with private-sector practice. Senior civil servants are now appraised on their managerial skills and part of their pay is performance based. However, the government, in rejecting fixed-term contracts has maintained the distinction between departmental senior civil servants and the heads of the executive agencies; many of the latter were recruited on fixed-term contracts with strict performance targets.

Also, current findings on performance-related pay in the senior civil service are mixed. The Review Body on Senior Salaries (Cm 2464, 1994; 2465, 1994) surveyed senior civil servants on performance-related pay. They came up with the following points. First, bonuses were regarded as a reward for good performance rather than an incentive or motivator. Partly this resulted from the rewards not being a sufficiently large proportion of salaries and partly because senior civil servants felt rewarded by the recognition rather than money. Second, there was insufficient range in the scheme. Individuals were marked on a scale of 1–5, but nobody performed in boxes 4 and 5. Not surprisingly, given a highly competitive and rigorous entry and promotion scheme in the civil service, the poor performers are weeded out at a much earlier stage than at grade 3 or above. Third, senior civil servants wanted performance pay to constitute a greater proportion of their salary and a refinement of the awards (Cm 2464, 1994: 14–27; Cm 2465, 1994). In short, performance-pay schemes seem a rather clumsy tool to assess and reward a group of people who are quite often motivated by factors other than the financial and who set themselves high standards of performance and conduct.

Our overall assessment of the changes in recruitment and promotion is pragmatic; the senior civil service remains today a careerist, centrally re-cruited, and internally sustained system; outsiders and women are still marginal recruits. This section has also illustrated continuity in the form of little change to the fast stream process, open competition showing a declin-ing influence (although the figures are extremely small), most senior civil servants doing well in performance schemes, and civil servants remaining on indefinite, rather than fixed-term contracts.

Mobility

Mobility forms part of the generalist, professional administrator which provides the model for the modern senior civil servant. The policy skills which were required for senior civil servants could be learnt best by experiencing different policy arenas. The training for the senior civil service was traditionally training by doing. So, fast stream civil servants were moved from position to position in order to develop skills in a range of policy areas. The ethos of the mobile policy expert is summed up by Edward Bridges:

The first time a man is told to change from work which he has mastered to a new job, he may feel that the special knowledge he has acquired is being wasted. He may grudge the labour of mastering a new subject and may wonder whether he will be equally successful at it. But when a man has done five jobs in fifteen years and has done them all with a measure of success, he is afraid of nothing and welcomes change. He has learned the art of spotting what points are crucial for forming a judgement on a disputed question even when he has the most cursory knowledge of the subject as a whole. (1950: 15)

Mobility amongst senior civil servants helps to create common values and practices; those values are associated with the civil service as a whole rather than a particular department or policy area. We distinguish between three types of mobility for review purposes. First, horizontal mobility across different ministries; second, vertical mobility between central departments and Next Steps agencies; and third, external mobility between the civil service and private organizations.

1. Inter-ministerial Mobility

The senior civil servant is encouraged to move between departments. *Continuity and Change* states that: 'The Government attaches particular importance to ... [amongst other things] greater interchange of staff between departments and between the centres of departments and agencies' (Cm 2627, 1994: 39). Such interchange *between departments* supports the notion of the generalist civil servant. It is not without critics. Richards (1996: 674–5) points to several weaknesses. First, the mobility system favours the generalist over the specialist. Second, there is not perfect competition between departments; candidates will still be protected by their own departments. Third, the system is self-perpetuating; existing systems and practices are maintained by mobile civil servants learning about the status quo. Barberis (1996*b*: 169) identifies the following two criticisms: 'one is that civil servants are moved too frequently between too many departments. The other is that movements have been capricious rather than carefully directed; that they have had little apparent regard to the nature of the work.'

The Fulton Committee in the late 1960s recommended that moves should be less frequent and between related areas of activity, which had long been a concern. Barberis (1996*b*: 167–71) traces the history of concern about mobility. Over fifty years ago Warren Fisher advocated unrelated moves, a type of mobility referred to as 'musical chairs'. This approach is still thought too prevalent (Plowden, 1994; Pollard, 1984). More recently, *Continuity and Change* advocates that civil servants are moved within a few discrete areas of related work. This reiterates the Northcote–Trevelyan Report's recommendation last century for the movement between 'cognate areas' of work for civil servants. Now such movement is to be centrally directed and the Cabinet Office 'will also continue to play a role in promoting movements between departments in the context of the annual succession planning bilaterals' (Cm 2627, 1994: 39).

Current statistical data on interdepartmental movement is not available, other than the percentage of civil servants currently 'on loan' to other departments which was approximately 17 per cent of grades 1 to 3 in 1993 (Efficiency Unit, 1993: 95). The figures illustrate how long individuals in the senior civil service have been in their current post, but do not say where posts are located, or where they came from. Recent data from Oughton (Efficiency Unit, 1993: 96) show that mobility levels are high in the senior civil service and similar throughout the senior grades: 34 per cent of all the Senior Open Structure (grades 1–3) have been in the same post for less than or equal to one year. Three-quarters of all the SOS have been in their posts for three years or less. Senior civil servants do not stay in their posts long. Mobility is a recurring feature of the senior civil service.

2. Department-Agency Mobility

The White Paper, *Continuity and Change* (Cm 2627, 1994), encourages interchange between centres of departments and Next Steps agencies. The Trosa Report on managing agencies encourages such interchange as 'the only way to show that the same value is attributed to both levels of management' (Cabinet Office, 1994: 5). The assumption is that agencies are not to become completely separated from their related departments. Rather, a common culture is to be created by facilitating staff mobility, although such mobility is not happening at present. According to chief executives of agencies interviewed for the purposes of the Trosa Report, 'people coming from Agencies and able to successfully return to the Department are *exceptions*' (Cabinet Office, 1994: 48, emphasis added). The reason is 'probably because having worked in an Agency is still not considered as advantageous for a successful career' (Cabinet Office, 1994: 49). It will be interesting to see how a new requirement for senior civil servants to have had experience in agency management is actually implemented (Cm 3321, 1996, cited in Horton and Jones, 1996: 32).

Agency chief executives represent a new class of senior civil servant: externally recruited, on short-term contracts, with direct management responsibilities based on explicit objectives and performance targets and at a distance, both physically and managerially, from policy-making functions. Chief executives threaten the cohesion and uniformity of top civil servants. However, the 'model' agency chief executive as just described does not represent the majority; most agency chief executives have been appointed from *within* the civil service. Of 175 chief executives sampled since 1988, only 13 per cent came from the private sector (Horton and Jones, 1996: 23). Management skills are viewed as necessary but not sufficient criteria for policy jobs. The appointment in 1995 of the externally recruited chief executive of the Benefits Agency, Michael Bichard, to the permanent secretary position at the merged Department for Education and Employment was an exception to prevailing practice.

3. External Mobility

Few senior civil servants have any outside experience. Oughton (Efficiency Unit, 1993: 96) reports on a survey of the senior civil service in 1992 which found that most experience was gained *before* entering the civil service. Most experience is gained in industry and commerce, and education. Having entered the civil service, civil servants do not move back and forth. Oughton reports that the percentage of the SOS on loan and secondment, as at 1993, was 19 per cent. However, the proportion of the 19 per cent on secondment, outside the civil service, is small. As noted above, about 17 per cent are on loan; gaining experience in other departments within the civil service. The Conservative government planned to increase the number of secondments between public and private sectors, setting a target of 500 (Horton and Jones, 1996: 32). Horton and Jones argue that recent narrowing of salary differentials between the sector's top managers was designed to facilitate this. However, open competition has not led to large-scale private-sector recruitment as discussed above, and salary levels, when private-sector bonuses and share options are included, fall far short of parity.

An exception to the low levels of external mobility amongst senior civil servants is the Treasury, which has a greater than average number of specialists in its ranks, mostly economists. Here, economists recruited externally have moved further up the civil service hierarchy (for example, Sir Terence Burns, permanent secretary between 1991 and 1998) and the make-up of the department is consequently more heterogeneous. In addition, the specialist nature of the Treasury's work means more external advisers are recruited. Most notably the current Chancellor, Gordon Brown, has established his own team of specialist economic advisers, a practice started by his predecessor Kenneth Clarke whose advisers were known as the seven 'wise men'. The group are external experts from business and academia brought in to advise on economic policy. Gordon Brown's new team, with different personnel from Clarke's, promises to have a more integral role in policy-making, providing advice and reports for the Chancellor.

Sociological Characteristics of Senior Officials

With a managerial revolution in government in the 1980s and 1990s, it is feasible to anticipate a change in characteristics of those at the top of the senior civil service. The traditional administrator was described back in the 1950s as follows: 'he must be a practical person, yet have some of the qualities of the academic theorist; his work encourages the longest views and yet his day-to-day responsibilities are limited; he is a student of public opinion, but no party politician' (Bridges, 1950: 18). Whether these characteristics survive is considered through the education and social background of senior civil servants. We also consider their personal values and their role orientation as well as departmental values.

1. Education

Top officials today tend to be male, white, and middle class; 60 per cent of grade 1 officials, 63 per cent of grade 2, and 45 per cent of grade 3 officials graduated from Oxford or Cambridge University (figures taken from a 1994 survey—see Cabinet Office, 1996). They are, educationally and socially, the élite. Somewhat under one-half (42 per cent) of grade 1–3 officials are educated in private schools. Research shows that recruitment procedures, cognitive tests, and face-to-face interviews, favour some candidates (Chapman 1984, 1993; Kellner and Crowther-Hunt, 1980). Critics on the left, politicians and academics, argue that the élite nature of the senior civil service makes the officials unable to understand the problems of ordinary people. *The Review of Fast Stream Recruitment* (OPSS, 1994*b*: 1) described the scheme as 'bedevilled by public perceptions of bias'. It acknowledged perceptions of bias in two key areas: first, in recruiting Oxbridge graduates, and second, within the civil service towards people on the fast stream against civil servants recruited outside the scheme.

The Review considered 'whether the fast stream entry should continue and if so whether it delivers the right kind of people' (OPSS, 1994*b*: 1). It found in favour of continuing the scheme but made a number of recommendations 'designed to increase public confidence in the scheme's fairness and to make it more responsive to change' (OPSS, 1994*b*: 1). Essentially the report recommends better marketing of the scheme and suggests a change of name to incorporate internal candidates. The other main changes focus on the scheme as an internal market. The report recommends greater input from departments on what graduates they want and when. There is a desire for improved fit between departmental need and the central pool of newly qualified fast streamers. In addition, there is a greater emphasis on equipping graduates with transferable skills.

Against the recommendations of the report, however, there is evidence that departments are moving *away* from central recruitment which is a threat to cohesion. The Treasury, the Department for Education and Employment, and the Department of Social Security currently have in-house recruitment schemes to attract non-fast stream civil servants which run in addition to fast stream programmes. Given the devolution of many administrative responsibilities from the centre to individual departments it is logical that departments want to take more control of their own recruitment, particularly as pay is devolved to departments. Second, the problem with *specialist* fast streamers (economists, statisticians, lawyers) is being able to retain graduates with transferable skills who can double their salary with city firms.

2. Social Background

It is difficult to obtain statistics on the social background and attitudes of the senior civil service today. In the 1950s most members of the administrative class described themselves as middle class (Chapman, 1970: 126); 8 per cent were women, although they were concentrated in the lower grades. Chapman summarises the higher civil service group in the following way:

One has the impression, for example, that Principals are the sort of people who would be popular holiday companions. They tend to have a keen, though somewhat cynical, sense of humour, wide interests, and could easily be conceded positions of leadership. They could make their mark in society, but this is often denied them by overwork, long hours, and the fatigue that results from it, all of which is largely unnecessary. Most higher civil servants work in central London, but outside office hours they may be separated from their work colleagues by sixty miles of metropolitan maze. Many feel themselves part of a classless sub-society, involved in a social process and identified with it; they have easy relations with all classes of people outside the service. (Chapman, 1970: 152).

Barberis describes a 'decline in connections' (1996*b*: 108) to social élites. He sees more cultural change than the statistics depict: 'The picture that will emerge is one of gradual but steadily increasing heterogeneity—more so during the present century than is immediately apparent from the patterns of education' (Barberis, 1996*b*: 108). However, from the account presented by Barberis, constancy is perhaps the more remarkable feature. In the press and academic literature the caricature of the senior civil servant, Sir Humphrey, from the BBC television series, *Yes Minister* is remarkably enduring. Sir Humphrey is: 'upper middle class, public school and "Oxbridge" educated; cultured, clubbable, articulate and full of subtlety; a font of knowledge and wisdom; incorruptible yet capable of deception, manipulation and disingenuity when the moves of Whitehall are challenged by wayward ministerial initiative. And all within the cloak of anonymity, the skein of constitutional propriety' (Barberis, 1996*b*: xvi). Commentators question the extent to which change is 'de-Sir Humphreyfying' the service (Hood, 1990). Certainly, patterns of education and centralized recruitment are likely to maintain a cohesive outlook.

3. Civil Service Values

Civil service values include: 'honesty, personal disinterestedness, a respect for intelligence, an enormous capacity for hard and often rapid work, loyalty to colleagues. They also include conservatism, caution, scepticism, élitism, a touch of arrogance and, too often, a deeply-held belief that the business of government can be fully understood only by government professionals' (Plowden, 1994: 74). It is argued that values such as integrity, impartiality, objectivity, selection and promotion on merit, and accountability through ministers to Parliament (Cm 2748, 1995: 3) are under threat in the current system. Managerialism has eroded the traditional ethics and values of the senior civil service. There is a new civil service code in the Civil Service Handbook. The White Paper, *Taking Forward Continuity and Change*, comments on the code recommended by the Treasury and Civil Service Committee (1994). The paper discusses 'maintaining civil service values' and argues there has been no decline in values and no politicization. It cites the conclusion of the committee that there is 'little doubt that civil servants would be able to demonstrate the same level of commitment to any incoming Government' and its belief that 'the commitment of the overwhelming majority of civil servants to the principle and practice of a politically impartial Civil Service is undiminished' (Cm 2748, 1995: 4).

However, *Taking Forward Continuity and Change* does acknowledge that a new cohesive senior civil service is not yet achieved. One of its aims is to provide 'clear leadership in sustaining core values' and it mentions *specifically* the new agency heads, stating that they will be issued with a new handbook to 'ensure that Service-wide rules on conduct and financial propriety are always available to them in a readily accessible form' (Cm 2748, 1995: 4). It is difficult to measure a decline in civil service values. New members of the senior civil service and new measures of performance and promotion represent change. However, most commentators agree there remains a public service ethos amongst civil servants.

Senior civil servants are traditionally policy advisers to ministers and as such have secured a monopoly on policy advice. Along with managerial changes to the senior civil service role, it is argued that their policy role also shifted during the Thatcher government. Dowding (1995: 108) says, with reference to the *Continuity and Change* document:

Senior mandarins have recently felt under greater pressures from their political masters as their policy-making role is increasingly threatened with suggestions of outside political advisers taking on a much more major role (Cm 2627, 1994). Civil servants have also complained that ministers are ignoring their advice and findings if they do not fit in with predetermined plans and that the way to get on is to become 'yes men'.

There is support for a decline in the policy role of senior civil servants. Commentators cite the rise of 'think tanks' during recent years and the increasing use of external and political advisers. Such temporary advisers include Professor Sir Alan Walters (economics) and Sir Anthony Parsons (foreign affairs) who advised Mrs Thatcher and her ministers. Campbell and Wilson (1995) assess the Thatcher period:

Even more worrying for the civil service was erosion of its near monopoly on supplying policy analysis and advice to ministers. The era of conviction politics in Britain created suspicion of the civil service among politicians of both the left and right. That most central and prized role of the higher civil service in Britain, advising ministers, was called into question. (Campbell and Wilson, 1995: 59)

Campbell and Wilson (1995: 60) and also Barberis (1994) present the view that senior civil servants became policy implementers rather than policy initiators or advisers in the 1980s: 'it seems clear that a rather different role has been handed down from the '80s. This is the role of broker, synthesiser, perhaps umpire, of the policy contributions made by others within the department, rather than that of initiator or proselytiser' (Barberis, 1994: 46).

4. Departmental Values

Senior officials work departmentally. The structure relates to policy-making which is departmental under the remit of the secretary of state and junior ministers. The exception to the above rule is the Treasury which has a unique function in interacting informally with all other departments through its responsibility for government expenditure. Spending departments meet Treasury officials in the annual bilaterals. The special inter-departmental role of the Treasury, and the specialist nature of its work generally, impacts on its senior officials.

Dowding (1995: 121) found more change in the Treasury than in other departments with professional economists from a wider social-class background reaching the top. More generally, the Treasury is singled out from other departments (Heclo and Wildavsky, 1977; Jenkins, 1975; Thain and Wright, 1995). Richards (1996: 673–5) describes high-fliers spending time at 'the centre': the Cabinet Office, Prime Minister's Office, and the Treasury. The particular ethos of the Treasury results from its focus on the purse-strings of government: 'The great responsibility felt by Treasury officials for the economic well-being of the nation, and the secret nature of their business and the feeling that they are an élite group create community spirit and an insular attitude' (Dowding, 1995: 121).

Other than Heclo and Wildavsky (1977), there are few insider accounts of government departments. Ministers rather than officials are able to write about their time in departments (although there are exceptions). Departments of Housing, Transport, and Social Services have been examined (see Castle, 1980, 1984; Crossman, 1975, 1976, 1977). A comparative perspective of the Treasury and the Home Office is provided by Roy Jenkins (1975), who served as both Chancellor and Home Secretary. Jenkins highlights the contrasts between the two departments.

The nature of Home Office activities results in less 'cross fertilisation' than in departments such as health and education: 'Home Office men had a strong tendency to end where they began, with perhaps a very brief period outside in the middle' (1975: 211). Jenkins (1975: 210) characterizes the Home Office as: uncertain about its place, always on the defensive, dealing with case work and the piecemeal formation of policy. It is highly centralized and formalized although the nature of the department is a mixture of policy orientation and a style that has developed through people who themselves maintain a 'deliberate policy of exclusivity'.

Conversely, the Treasury is self-confident, less centralized, and more relaxed. It supports the idea of being more receptive to less traditional senior civil servants. Christian names are used, which contrasts with the norm in the Home Office: 'I never heard anyone, including myself, call the Permanent Secretary anything but Sir Charles' (Jenkins, 1975: 211). The Treasury is described as a 'melting pot', taking on people not originally recruited by the Treasury, and officials are described as highly disparate, in background, appearance, and manner (1975: 213). Policy is also significant here with economic policy-making being more 'grand design' and also based on the 'opinions' of individuals (1975: 214). Policy is removed from the general public, unlike the glare of publicity to which prisons, miscarriages of justice, and race issues are prone. Consequently, Jenkins witnessed decisions being taken at a lower level in Treasury and the open expression of opinion by officials encouraged at meetings.

More recently, in his memoirs of being Chancellor, Nigel Lawson notes the power of the Treasury. The then Prime Minister, Margaret Thatcher, went against previous governments and attempted to strengthen the role of the Treasury. As Lawson (1992: 586) notes, '[the Treasury is] both in name and in reality, the central Department, with a finger in pretty well every pie that the Government bakes'. Lawson (1992: 397) also makes a reference to the nature of the Home Office as part of an inter-ministerial group on fraud that concurs with Roy Jenkins: 'the Home Office, with responsibility for the police in general and the fraud squad in particular, and a strong sense of its high place in the Whitehall pecking order, was adamant that not an inch of its departmental turf should be surrendered'. He describes the inter-ministerial group as a failure, with departments like the Home Office and Department of Trade and Industry unwilling to cooperate and subordinate 'departmental *amour propre* to the common cause' (1992: 397; italics in original).

Relationship with the Political Machinery of Government

In other countries civil servants become members of the legislature without resigning from official posts and may be given leave of absence for the discharge of their parliamentary duties. British civil servants are disqualified from being elected to either the House of Commons or the European Assembly. Set down by the House of Commons Disqualification Action 1975 and European Assembly Elections Act 1978, these rules ensure that civil servants should be politically neutral in order to be able to serve ministers from any political party.

The civil service is distinct from the political service of the Crown; it retains its position through changes in political leadership and, being non-political, it does not rely on patronage. Several features of the present political climate and recent changes to the civil service threaten the traditional characteristics. It is alleged that the processes of managerialism, marketization, agencification, and politicization have eroded the impartiality of the current senior civil service. Several of these features are explored.

1. Permanent Party in Government

The senior civil service is alleged to have lost its objectivity because of the commitment and perseverance of the Conservative government in office for eighteen years. One of the consequences of a permanent party in government is illustrated by the position of chief executives in the political debate over the creation of agencies. Senior civil servants variously described as 'non political', 'impartial', or 'objective' keep their distance from policy implementation. However, the chief executives of agencies *themselves* represent the policies of the government who created them:

If they are to speak at all, one cannot but expect chief executives of the new agencies to defend the Next Steps process: that is part of their responsibility. Given the role of senior mandarins in shaping Next Steps, one cannot but expect them to defend it, no matter what the political consequences. Senior civil servants have also been closely associated with privatisation policies, again a highly politicised area. (Dowding, 1995: 110)

Because the Conservative government was in power so long and because changes were so significant during that period, it is argued that the senior officials have lost their 'institutionalised scepticism' (Plowden, 1994: 104). There have been changes in language—contracting out, market testing, Citizen's Charter, league tables, agencies, grant-maintained schools—and what was once Conservative policy has now become part of the machinery of government. Before the general election in May 1997, Sir Robin Butler, then Head of the Civil Service, reassured opposition politicians and commentators that the civil service was equipped to serve a new government. At the same time newspapers reported that Michael Heseltine, Deputy Prime Minister, was pushing civil servants to undertake party-political tasks (*Observer*, 10 Nov. 1996).

It will be interesting to see how the senior civil service develops under the Blair government. Robin Butler stayed on for a year as Head of the Civil Service and Cabinet Secretary with the new Labour government. However, he was nearing retirement age and a successor, Sir Richard Wilson, was appointed in 1998. A possibility is that over the longer term the two posts, combined under Thatcher, will be split up once again, so that there is a strategic head of the civil service and another senior civil servant who advises the Cabinet. Terence Burns, permanent secretary to the Treasury, left the civil service. He was appointed and promoted under Thatcher and was closely identified with Conservative policies.

2. Politicization

The Royal Institute of Public Administration conducted research in 1985 but found no evidence of politicization. Commentators such as Drewry and Butcher (1993), Hennessy (1995), Barberis (1996*b*), and Kemp (1994) reject politicization but agree that there was an impact in increasing the ratio of 'can do' to 'wait a minute' mandarins. Between 1979 and 1985, forty-three permanent secretaries and 138 deputies left the civil service (Rhodes, 1997: 90). There are also several 'instances' or reported cases of political pressure being exerted. For example early on in the Thatcher government the head and the deputy head of the civil service were unceremoniously 'retired' before their time. They were not 'one of us'; they did not think like Thatcher. Other examples of political appointments and dismissals include the action of Home Secretary Kenneth Clarke, who in 1993 by-passed the selectors to appoint the Granada boss, Derek Lewis, as head of the Prison Service. The appointment was unsuccessful as Mr Lewis was later sacked by the Home Secretary Michael Howard over security lapses in several prisons, which were allegedly operational rather than policy matters. Sir Peter Kemp, project manager of Next Steps, a career civil servant, was removed from his post and 'retired' at the behest of the then Minister of Public Service and Science, William Waldegrave in 1992.

3. Accountability

The principle of ministerial accountability is that ministers are answerable in Parliament for activities within their department and that civil servants report to ministers. So, it is the ministers who take responsibility for government policy; civil servants remain anonymous. Events in the last Conservative government such as the Belgrano affair, Spycatcher, and the Whitemoor and Parkhurst Prison outbreaks challenged ministerial responsibility and the anonymity of senior civil servants. In particular, the creation of the Next Steps agencies has blurred the lines of accountability, with chief executives of agencies taking responsibility for management within their agency. Permanent secretaries and chief executives of agencies appear before select committees. The sacking of Derek Lewis as Director General of the Prison Service illustrated the difficulties of distinguishing policy and management. What Derek Lewis interpreted as policy, Michael Howard interpreted as operations. Derek Lewis went and Michael Howard stayed. Other cases such as Ross Hepplewhite, chief executive of the Child Support Agency, who was also removed from her job, heightened the profile of the senior civil service and, in particular, unsuccessful external appointments.

In response, a House of Commons Select Committee examined accountability and the responsibility of ministers in the light of Next Steps agencies (Public Service Committee, 1996*b*). Two of the report's recommendations call for a re-examination of the respective roles of ministers and agency chief executives. In particular, framework documents should set down more precisely their respective roles (Public Service Committee, 1996*b*: paragraph 122). The weight of evidence presented to the committee suggested there is confusion about what responsibility and accountability mean for ministers and civil servants in the late 1990s. The government's reply to the above recommendations was to take no further action; roles are set out in agency framework documents and reviewed in each agencies' five-yearly review (Public Service Committee, 1996*a*: pp. xi, xii).

Debate about ministerial accountability is not new. Ministers argue that they cannot be personally responsible for all the decisions taken in their departments. However, there are fears that as ministers distance themselves from agencies, the link between responsibility and accountability becomes weaker: the 'accountability gap'. In the case of the Child Support Agency and the Prison Service it was the senior civil servant who was forced to take responsibility for agency failures.

Conclusion

We finish with themes of continuity and change to describe the current senior civil service in Britain. The nature of change in the British civil service is gradual; it is an evolving service. However, the eighteen years from 1979 to 1997 have amounted to a revolution in government. Fittingly, it is an 'evolutionary revolution' (Greer, 1994: 132). For some, 'modernising the mandarins' (*Independent*, 7 Apr. 1994) has changed the senior civil service completely and irreversibly. Change has been comprehensive and backed by strong political will from a permanent government. Its consequences are ethical, political, cultural, and managerial for the senior civil service. There is now a heterogeneous group called the 'senior civil service' following eighteen years of change. Sir Robin Butler talked of a senior civil service that is 'unified but not uniform'. Private-sector methods of reward and retention are now in place. The senior civil service is made up of both departmental managers and agency chief executives who deliver services. Changes are ongoing. Numbers in the top three grades of the civil service fell by 20 per cent during the Conservative government. The Conservative government believed that 'it will be in the national interest to have over a period a somewhat smaller but better paid Senior Civil Service' (Cm 2627, 1994: 44).

However, there are also elements of continuity and permanence in the current senior civil service. It is important to distinguish the senior positions from the bulk of the civil service. Change which has so far affected the majority of service-delivery areas in the civil service are only now reaching the top ranks. The central characteristics of an élite, permanent, impartial, or objective senior civil service which is selected and promoted on merit currently remain. In each of the areas of recruitment, mobility, departmental contacts, and relation to the political machinery of government, we found strains in the cohesion of the senior civil service; new values and practices were successfully implemented. The current senior civil service is characterized by heterogeneity. There are tensions. However, the senior civil service has survived the changes. As yet, the agency principle has not been extended to policy functions and the senior civil service has not yet been contracted out.

REFERENCES

Barberis, P. (1994). 'Permanent Secretaries and Policy-Making in the 1980s', *Public Policy and Administration*, 9(1): 35–48.

—— (ed.) (1996a). *The Whitehall Reader* (Buckingham: Open University Press).

—— (1996b). *The Elite of the Elite: Permanent Secretaries in the British Higher Civil Service* (Aldershot: Dartmouth).

Bridges, Sir Edward (1950). *Portrait of a Profession* (London: Cambridge University Press).

Butler, R. (1993). 'Evolution of the Civil Service: A Progress Report', *Public Administration*, 71(3): 395–406.

Cabinet Office (1994). (Trosa Report) *Next Steps: Moving On* (London: Cabinet Office).

—— (1996). Data from Office of Public Service, Senior Civil Service Group (unpublished). Written Communication to the authors, Dec. 1996.

Campbell, C. (1994). 'Reconciling Central Guidance and Managerialism: Conflicts between Coherence and Discretion, the Case of Whitehall', Conference paper. 'XVth World Congress of the International Political Science Association', Berlin 21–5 Aug.

—— and G. K. Wilson (1995). *The End of Whitehall: Death of a Paradigm?* (Oxford: Blackwell).

Castle, B. (1980). *The Castle Diaries 1974–1976* (London: Weidenfeld and Nicolson).

—— (1984). *The Castle Diaries 1964–1970* (London: Weidenfeld and Nicolson).

Chapman, R. A. (1970). *The Higher Civil Service in Britain* (London: Constable).

—— (1984). *Leadership in the British Civil Service: A Study of Sir Percival*

Waterfield and the Creation of the Civil Service Selection Board (London: Croom Helm).

Chapman, R. A. (1991). 'New Arrangements for Recruitment to the British Civil Service: Cause for Concern', *Public Policy and Administration*, 6(3): 1–6.

——(1993). 'Civil Service Recruitment: Fairness or Preferential Advantage', *Public Policy and Administration*, 8: 68–73.

——(1994). 'Change in the Civil Service', *Public Administration*, 72: 599–610.

——(1996). 'Standards in Public Life: A Valediction', *Teaching Public Administration*, 16(1): 1–19.

Civil Service Year Book (1996) (London: HMSO).

Cm 1730 (1991). *Competing for Quality: Buying Better Public Services* (London: HMSO).

Cm 2464 (1994). *Review Body on Senior Salaries, Report 34: Sixteenth Report on Senior Salaries* (London: HMSO).

Cm 2465 (1994). *Review Body on Senior Salaries, Report 34: Annex to the Sixteenth Report on Senior Salaries* (London: HMSO).

Cm 2627 (1994). *The Civil Service: Continuity and Change* (London: HMSO).

Cm 2748 (1995). *The Civil Service: Taking Forward Continuity and Change* (London: HMSO).

Cmnd 3638 (1968). (Fulton Report) *The Civil Service*, i. *Report of the Committee* (London: HMSO).

Crossman, R. H. S. (1975). *The Diaries of a Cabinet Minister*, i. *Minister for Housing 1964–66* (London: Hamilton and Cape).

——(1976). *The Diaries of a Cabinet Minister*, ii. *Lord President of the Council and Leader of the House of Commons 1966–68* (London: Weidenfeld and Nicolson).

——(1977). *The Diaries of a Cabinet Minister*, iii. *Secretary of State for Social Services 1968–70* (London: Weidenfeld and Nicolson).

Davies, A., and J. Willman (1991). *What Next? Agencies, Departments and the Civil Service* (London: IPPR).

Dowding, K. (1995). *The Civil Service* (London: Routledge).

Drewry, G. (1994). 'The Civil Service: From the 1940s to "Next Steps" and Beyond', *Parliamentary Affairs*, 47(4): 583–97.

——and T. Butcher (1993). *The Civil Service Today*, 2nd edn. (Oxford: Blackwell).

Efficiency Unit (1988). *Improving Management in Government: The Next Steps* (London: HMSO).

——(1991) (Fraser Report). *Making the Most of Next Steps: the Management of Ministers' Departments and their Executive Agencies* (London: HMSO).

——(1993) (Oughton Report). *Career Management and Succession Planning Study* (London: HMSO).

Fry, G. K. (1985). *The Changing Civil Service* (London: Allen and Unwin).

Greenwood, J. R., and D. J. Wilson (1989). *Public Administration in Britain Today*, 2nd edn. (London: Unwin Hyman).

Greer, Patricia (1994). *Transforming Central Government: The Next Steps Initiative* (Buckingham: Open University Press).

Heclo, H., and A. Wildavsky (1977). *The Private Government of Public Money: Community and Policy Inside British Politics* (London: Macmillan).

Hennessy, P. (1988). *Whitehall* (London: Secker and Warburg).

—— (1995). *The Hidden Wiring: Unearthing the British Constitution* (London: Gollancz).

Hood, C. (1990). 'De-Sir Humphreyfying the Westminster Model of Bureaucracy: A New Style of Governance?', *Governance*, 3(2): 205–14.

—— (1991). 'A Public Management for All Seasons?', *Public Administration*, 69(1): 3–19.

Horton, S., and J. Jones (1996). 'Who are the New Public Managers? An Initial Analysis of "Next Steps" Chief Executives and their Managerial Role', *Public Policy and Administration*, 11(4): 18–44.

Jenkins, R. (1975). 'On Being a Minister', in V. Herman and J. E. Alt (eds.), *Cabinet Studies: A Reader* (London: Macmillan), 210–20.

Kellner, P., and Lord Crowther-Hunt (1980). *The Civil Servants: An Inquiry into Britain's Ruling Class* (London: MacDonald).

Kemp, P. (1994). 'The Civil Service White Paper: A Job Half Finished?', *Public Administration*, 72(4): 591–8.

Lawson, N. (1992). *The View from No. 11: Memoirs of a Tory Radical* (London: Bantam).

Mellon, E. (1993). 'Executive Agencies: Leading Change from the Outside', *Public Money and Management*, 13(2): 25–31.

Mountfield, R (1997). 'The New Senior Civil Service: Managing the Paradox', *Public Administration*, 75(2): 307–12.

Office of Public Service and Science (1994*a*). *Responsibilities for Recruitment to the Civil Service* (London: HMSO).

—— (1994*b*). *Review of Fast Stream Recruitment* (London: HMSO).

Office of the Civil Service Commissioners (1996). *Civil Service Commissioners' Annual Report '95–'96* (London: HMSO).

Parris, H. (1969). *Constitutional Bureaucracy* (London: Allen and Unwin).

Plowden, W. (1994). *Ministers and Mandarins* (London: Institute for Public Policy Research).

Pollard, S. (1984). *The Wasting of the British Economy*, 2nd edn. (London: Croom Helm).

Pollitt, C. (1993). *Managerialism and the Public Services*, 2nd edn. (Oxford: Blackwell).

Public Service Committee (1996*a*). *Government Response to the Second Report from the Committee (session 1995–6) on Ministerial Accountability and Responsibility: First Special Report. Report with an Appendix. Session 96–97* (London: HMSO).

—— (1996*b*). *Ministerial Accountability and Responsibility. Second Report, Session 95–96* (London: HMSO).

Rhodes, R. A. W. (1997). *Understanding Governance* (Buckingham: Open University Press).

Richards, D. (1996). 'Appointments to the Highest Grades in the Civil Service—Drawing the Curtain Open', *Public Administration,* 74(4): 657–77.

Royal Institute of Public Administration (1987). *Top Jobs in Whitehall: Appointments and Promotions in the Senior Civil Service*, Report of an RIPA Working Group (London: RIPA).

Smith, M. J., D. Marsh, and D. Richards (1993). 'Central Government Departments and the Policy Process', *Public Administration*, 71: 567–94.

Thain, C., and M. Wright (1995). *The Treasury and Whitehall: The Planning and Control of Public Expenditure, 1976–1993* (Oxford: Clarendon Press).

Treasury and Civil Service Committee (TCSC) (1986). *Civil Servants and Ministers: Duties and Responsibilities. HC 92. Seventh Report.* (London: HMSO).

—— (1993). *The Role of the Civil Service: Interim Report. HC 390-1 and II. Sixth Report.* (London: HMSO).

—— (1994). *The Role of the Civil Service. HC 27-1, II and III. Fifth Report.* (London: HMSO).

Williamson, O. E. (1975). *Markets and Hierarchies: Analysis and Antitrust Implications* (New York: Free Press).

9

The Senior Civil Service in the Netherlands: A Quest for Unity

FRITS M. VAN DER MEER AND JOS C. N. RAADSCHELDERS

I. Introduction

Perhaps because of their geographical condition those who live in the Low Countries are averse to any heights, whether physical or social. In a society that takes pride in its egalitarian character, political and administrative officeholders are not placed on a pedestal. Government officials are neither separated from the rest of society nor enshrined in state grandeur. This general attitude originates in the predominantly middle-class nature of Dutch society as it became manifest especially after the Second World War. Furthermore, the formal incorporation of top civil servants in a separate class of administrative personnel, and thus distinct from the rest of public personnel, has long been foreign to the Dutch administrative system. Rather, senior civil servants in Dutch government tended to identify themselves with a particular department. In the 1970s some observers even spoke about the '14 law-families' in reference to the fourteen central government departments at the time. However, at the same time a striving for unity characterized national administration, as is illustrated by various government reports since the early nineteenth century and by the proliferation of interdepartmental committees after the Second World War.

The issue of the tension between unity and fragmentation forces us to assess current developments in the higher civil service in comparison to the situation as it existed from the Second World War up to the early 1990s. The emphasis, however, will be on developments in the past two decades. The most important event is the formation of a Senior Public Service (*Algemene Bestuursdienst*, ABD) after 1 July 1995.

First we will examine what is meant by a 'senior civil service' in the Dutch context. Even the creation of the ABD is not conclusive in this respect as there are many senior civil servants outside the ABD. In order to address this issue the characteristics of the Dutch personnel system will be examined (section II). In this section the ABD will be briefly outlined, and then the number of top civil servants working at central government level in the period 1976–95 will be presented. In section III we turn to the political-administrative organization and the consultative structures at the top of the central government departments. In this section we will discuss the structure of the ABD. Important for a proper understanding of the role, position, and status of the senior civil servant is the degree to which its incumbents have been subject to politicization (section IV). Hence, in this section we will pay attention to the political affiliation of top civil servants. Section IV provides the foundation upon which we can discuss functional mobility at the top, with special attention to the functional motives for creating the ABD (section V). Finally, the social political structure of the civil service will be reviewed. Relevant for our purposes is attention to the social background (section VI) and the educational background (section VII). Sections II, IV, V, and VII present new data, compiled for this chapter, concerning the highest civil servants in 1995 and 1996.

II. Senior Civil Servants and the Dutch System of Personnel Management

Under the Civil Servants Act of 1929 a civil servant is a person who is appointed to be employed in the public service. The public service includes all agencies and (public) enterprises administered by the state and public authorities. The 1929 Act only provides a very general framework for regulating the legal position of civil servants (although only the general provisions of some of its articles remain in force). For a real understanding of the Dutch public sector we need to look at the civil service regulations. In the case of central government departments, the General Civil Service Regulations (ARAR issued under the CSA) have to be mentioned. In addition to the ARAR there is a Civil Servants' Pay Decree (BBRA), which governs salaries, holiday pay, and allowances. This pay decree constitutes the base for our definition of the senior civil service. Besides the government departments there are separate regulations for the judiciary (law on legal organization), for military defence personnel (AMAR), and for the civilian defence personnel (BARD). Both the defence personnel systems are roughly the same as the ARAR. To complicate matters, the independent public agencies have their own regulations.

The ARAR and the BBRA can help us in defining the senior civil service. Before the revision of the BBRA in 1984 the rank structure could have been used, that for the higher departmental grades included the secretary general, the director general, the councillor (*raadadviseur*), the director, and the chief administrative officer (*hoofd administrateur*), and so on. Most of these rank structures in central government were abolished in 1984. Only the military rank structure is unchanged to date. The names of the positions of secretary general, director general, and councillor have survived.

Even before 1984 the number of higher departmental ranks was quite sizeable. It amounted to more than 10 per cent in 1976 or 10,000 people (van der Meer and Roborgh, 1993: 229). A position was considered high if occupants had to have a university degree. Nowadays more factors are included, such as the responsibility involved and the complexity of a task. What is interesting is that 'high' in the Netherlands does not always imply 'senior'. This problem of demarcation still exists. Instead of looking at the rank structure we nowadays have to use the functional and salary systems. The basis of these systems is to be found in the ARAR and BBRA. Most departmental officials are paid according to BBRA. The pay levels rank from grade 1 (the lowest) to grade 18 (the highest). Besides these regular eighteen grades there is a so-called 'Annex A'. People in this annex are paid a fixed sum. Functionaries in this category include the directors general, the secretaries general, and functionaries of comparable importance. Their salary is sometimes referred to, strangely enough, as grade 19. The ministers and under-ministers are also paid a fixed salary (grades 20/21) on basis of the Act on the Legal Position of Ministers and Under-Ministers (Ministerie van Binnenlandse Zaken, 1996).

This pay structure is based on a system of job (or function) classification. Central government uses a job comparison system called *Functie Waarderings Systeem* (FuWaSys or Function Assessment System). To establish the importance of a particular position six 'levels of expertise and workload' are used. Each function level is subdivided into a number of grades. These function levels are placed in a ranking order from one reserved for mainly unskilled work and six for top civil servants. The weight of a function is decided by fourteen criteria such as the required level of education, responsibility, independence, and the risk involved. By comparing a new to an already classified job ('normative' function) this new function is located in one of the six groups.

For our purposes it is important to notice that officials in function groups IV, V, and VI and in Annex A are considered to be higher civil servants. In practice this is equivalent to grade 10 and higher in the salary system. 'Higher' in the old ranking structure included grade 11 and above. A further distinction within this rather large group can be made. First, there are the civil servants with a salary in categories V and VI of the BBRA (Civil Servants' Pay Decree) who are appointed to the general service of the state. Second, there are the other civil servants who are appointed in a particular government department. Even these groups are quite substantial as we will show below.

Civil servants from grade 1 to 14 are appointed by the minister. From grade 15 (groups VI) onwards a civil servant is appointed by royal decree on the recommendation of the minister. From the level of director general upwards (Annex A) appointments are made by the Council of Ministers. Group VI and the persons mentioned in Annex A are considered to be top civil servants. This group includes the secretaries general, the directors general, and directors. As material concerning some of the topics we have to discuss refers to the wider group of higher civil servants, including also senior policy advisors (*beleidsambtenaren*), groups IV, V, and VI, it is necessary to set out the size of the group involved (Table 9.1).

As mentioned in our introduction, the first steps have only recently been taken to create a general civil service at central government level. In future top civil servants will not be employed by an individual department but collectively. They are supposed to alternate between the different departments. If this initiative is successful, it would mean a step towards a British-style civil service. At present this ABD comprises functionaries in grade 17 and higher. It is the intention to widen the ABD gradually to functionaries at lower levels. Top civil servants include personnel in grades 15 and higher. Senior civil servants also consist of functionaries in grades 13 and 14. Higher civil servants are all employees in grade 10 and higher. Technical and administrative police personnel from 1992 are omitted (grade VI consists of seven officials). Civil personnel in the military are included. From 1987 all personnel in the foreign service, the diplomats, are included in these figures (grades V and VIa; the total of all those from IV–VIa is 425 functionaries). All figures from 1976 onwards include personnel employed at the High Councils of State.

The rapid increase in the number of top civil servants (VIa) after 1985

TABLE 9.1. *The Overall Number of Civil Servants in Central Government and in the Categories High, Senior, and Top, 1976–1994*

	VIa (top)		V and VIa (senior)		IV–VIa (high)		All	
	N	index	*N*	index	*N*	index	*N*	index
1976	699	100.0	3,106	100.0	16,630	100.0	135,210	100.0
1987	2,193	313.7	5,340	171.9	27,370	164.6	156,598	115.9
1994	2,323	332.3	7,974	256.7	34,726	208.8	142,429	105.4

Source: *Kerngegevens bezoldiging burgerlijk overheidspersoneel* (1976–).

as compared to the 'high' group (V and VIa) is partly technical since group VIa was enlarged (with the addition of grade 15) in that particular period. We can correct the 1976 figures to take account of this (in which case the comparable number of VIa officials in 1976 was 1,180). Thus the level of growth from 1976 to 1994 among top civil servants (index figure of 196.9) was below that of the senior or the higher civil servants. The stabilization of the size of the civil service in general has to do with privatization and decentralization. As a result the civil service tends to look like an army of generals. This is part of a strategy according to which central government is not burdened with responsibility for policy implementation but concerns itself with strategy and long-term development. The number of the highest civil servants in group VIa (level 17 and higher) who are part of the ABD stood at 458 in 1994 (Ministerie van Binnenlandse Zaken, 1994). In 1987 the size of the same group amounted to 496 (Ministerie van Binnenlandse Zaken, 1988). The size of the real summit of the civil service has therefore declined.

III. Organizational and Consultative Structures at the Top

A brief outline of the organizational and consultative structures at the top of government bureaucracy, including the relations with political office-holders, is necessary, since it indicates that the top civil service since the Second World War has operated on a basis of establishing both vertical (intradepartmental) and horizontal (interdepartmental) coordination and was fashioned along functional lines. Hence, at various levels of responsibility the officials immediately involved in a particular policy area were brought together.

The Cabinet, or Council of Ministers, is the highest executive decision-making body in the Netherlands and only includes the ministers. In general, issues that require decision-making at the collegial ministerial level have been prepared in a number of stages. We have to distinguish between the interdepartmental and the intradepartmental level. The main outlines and political ramifications of decisions brought to attention of the Cabinet have been discussed in the relevant subcouncil of the Cabinet (*onderraad van de ministerraad*). This body includes the relevant ministers as well as the relevant under-ministers. They act upon what has been presented by the so-called 'bureaucratic anti-chamber' (*ambtelijk voorportaal*), which consists of the highest civil servants of the various departments (usually directors general and secretaries general) involved in policy-making for a particular area. In turn, they review the proposals prepared by the inter-departmental committees, again involving high civil servants (directors general, sometimes secretaries general, directors, and specialists) from various departments who contribute their particular expertise to a policy area. Those participating in the bureaucratic anti-chamber and the interdepartmental committees operate on the basis of a mandate from the government department to which they are appointed. Thus, this structure, while intended to overcome interdepartmental differences, in practice encourages compartmentalization.

Within a government department the highest coordinative structure in the traditional SG–DG model is the ministerial staff (*ministersstaf*), meeting weekly and including the secretary general (SG), the directors general (DG), and the directors. Working procedures in this model emphasize unity of command and a clear chain of command, but also generate compartmentalization of responsibilities between the various directorates general. A variant upon this model is the 'civil service staff-model' where the top level coordinates and discusses issues that concern the department as a whole, thus reducing the risk of compartmentalization (Bekke *et al.*, 1996: 41–3). Since they are based on distinct organizational units and/or hierarchies, these rather traditional systems have in some departments (Department of Justice; Department of Education, Culture, and Sciences; Department of Social Affairs and Employment; Department of Agriculture and Fisheries; Department of Traffic and Water Management) been replaced by a management council (*bestuursraad*). Members of this council are the secretary general and—in two cases—his deputy, the directors general, and other officials in comparable position. The interesting feature of this management council is that the directors general used to head directorates general but their tasks have now been brought under directorates. The 'disjointed' DG in a management council has certain directorates and/or issues in his portfolio, but is no longer hierarchically or operationally responsible for them. For information the directors general are completely dependent upon minister and directors. The management council develops a framework for the annual contracts within which the directors, responsible for a particular policy, operate. 'Integral management' is the key concept that characterizes the management council model.

It will be clear that compartmentalization is a prime concern in the interdepartmental as well as the intradepartmental coordination structures. In a sense one could say that the creation of a general civil service (ABD) is a strategy that affects both intradepartmental and interdepartmental coordination. After all, in a general civil service it is the generalist whose management experience can be deployed in any department. Ideally, the generalist does not identify him/herself with a particular department, but rather with a particular group of officeholders. What is more, they will only serve in any one department for a finite period of time, to be transferred to another department after, say, five years when their particular management expertise (reformer, consolidator, peacemaker, etc.) is needed there. The ABD has to meet five different but related goals: enhancing interdepartmental mobility of top civil servants; strengthening skills (negotiation, presentation) and knowledge (seminars, study trips); development of career instruments (management profiles, assessments); administrative and management development; and developing procedures, regulations, and IT systems necessary for the ABD to function properly.

The major priority and emphasis of the ABD so far has been on horizontal mobility and recruitment patterns. The ABD comprises all top civil servants at central government level, and as such functions both in the more traditional top structures and in the departments that adopted a management council model. Policy with respect to the ABD is coordinated by the Bureau for the ABD, located in the Department of Home Affairs. The Bureau operates as a management development agency and as a headhunter for top positions.

IV. Senior Civil Servants and Politicization

The discussion on politicization has a long pedigree in Dutch administrative thinking. It was raised by Thorbecke, the nineteenth-century builder of the modern Dutch state, who made political appointments—controversial to some—both in his Ministry of Home Affairs as well as in top positions in subnational government. At least two elements have to be distinguished in any discussion on politicization: the politicization of recruitment; and the politicization of behaviour after appointment.

Politicization of recruitment implies that increasingly political criteria are involved in the selection of candidates for particular top positions in the civil service. Different explanations can be given for the importance of political criteria, widely assumed to be on the increase, in recruitment procedures. First, there is the desire by politicians to be served by officials who agree broadly with their policies (this was the reasoning associated with Thorbeke). Second, political sensitivity is a vital quality for a candidate in a key agency or departmental unit. Third, in order to avoid a politically homogeneous culture within the administration, some distribution of position according to political affiliation is informally pursued. This attempt to achieve a wider spectrum of opinion among civil servants working in key functions is put forward, for instance, in the case of the Prime Minister's Office (*De Volkskrant*, 12 Dec. 1987). Last but not least, political patronage can be another motive. With the development of a mature party system in the Netherlands, political appointments are party-political appointments.

A second perspective on politicization emerges when we look at the political behaviour of senior civil servants. The fact that civil servants play an active role alongside politicians in the policy-making process may indicate several things at the same time. First it can signify that senior civil servants are open to societal demands and aware of the democratic and political nature of their job. Furthermore it can include the perception that the top civil service constitutes an important actor on the political scene in its own right. Finally, apart from the political power of bureaucracy, senior civil servants can operate as party politicians serving and promoting their own ideas and interests.

Both the recruitment and the behavioural dimensions can be observed in contemporary discussions about the level of politicization of the senior civil service. Starting with the issue of political nominations, it is remarkable how little is actually known about this. The issue of the political recruitment of senior civil servants appears mainly as a recurring theme in national daily newspaper coverage of Dutch administration. Newspapers are in effect one of the most important sources on the political background of the senior civil servants—possibly because many political comment-ators and journalists have a political science background. When a new sec-retary general is appointed his/her political affiliation is mentioned. This is taken as an opportunity for the papers to publish an up-to-date tally of the number of positions each party 'holds'. When comments are solicited from the political parties involved, the issue is put back on the political agenda again. So questions are asked in Parliament by those political parties who feel that they have been unfairly treated or have not got their proper share of the pie. The same applies to the nomination of mayors and Queen's commissioners.

The official position of the Cabinet in power is to deny the practice of politically motivated nominations. In the words of former Prime Minister Lubbers: 'In the appointment of top civil servants in government depart-ments only the suitability for a position is considered.' The political profile of the candidate does not play a role in the selection. A possible over- or underrepresentation of a particular political colour is not matter of policy (Lubbers, quoted in van der Meer and Roborgh, 1993: 377). This view was reiterated in comments by members of the new social-democratic and liberal coalition about the results of a survey among top civil servants by De Vries and Rosenthal. It was also reinforced by the present liberal (VVD) minister of Home Affairs who stated in an interview that since he was in office he had not nominated an individual on party-political grounds. He observed that in the past this practice had existed.

TABLE 9.2. *Party-Political Affiliation of Secretaries General,*
1988 and 1996

	1988		1996	
	N	%	N	%
PVDA (socialist, labour)	1	7.7	5	38.5
CDA (Christian Democrats)	9	69.2	3	23.1
VVD (orthodox liberals)	2	7.7	1	7.7
D'66 (social liberals)	1	15.4	2	15.4
Green party	—	—	1	7.7
None	—	—	1	7.7
TOTAL	13	100.0	13	100.1

Source: NRC-Handelsblad (19 Oct. 1988); NRC-Handelsblad (2 Dec. 1996).

Instead of presenting official government statements we should first look at some material concerning the political membership of secretaries general. For instance, in 1988 J. M. Bik, a leading columnist of a national daily (*NRC-Handelsblad*) remarked that it is quite useful for an ambitious top civil servant to become a member of the Christian Democratic Party (CDA) in order to promote his (or less frequently her) career. At that point nine out of thirteen secretaries general were CDA members. According to this journalist, 'Ministers, under-ministers and secretaries-general are coming and going but the CDA will remain' (*NRC-Handelsblad*, 19 Oct. 1988). After the May 1994 elections, the number of CDA secretaries general dropped dramatically (Table 9.2). It is tempting to suggest that the explanation is to be found in the declining qualities of senior civil servants belonging to the CDA. An alternative explanation could be that for the first time in almost seventy-five years the Christian Democrats are not members of the governing coalition.

Two decades ago a large proportion of top civil servants considered it not done to ask questions about their political preference let alone their membership of a political party (see for instance the many indignant re-actions Rosenthal (1979) received in his survey of secretaries general). Nowadays the secrecy surrounding this issue has decreased substantially. Widening the group of officials to include directors general and directors, a recent survey by De Vries and Rosenthal (published in a number of articles in *NRC-Handelsblad* between September and November 1995) indicated that almost half of the top civil servants were members of a political party. Although some questioned the validity of the survey be-cause of the level of non-response (39 per cent) and its possible distorting effects (the Ministries of Agriculture and General Affairs, both regarded as CDA fortresses, were underrepresented, see *NRC Handelsblad* (6 Jan. 1995), 2), it led to two different kinds of reaction. The first was that the top of the Dutch civil service was very politicized, while a second, completely different, reaction was that 'it was much less than we expected'. De Vries and Rosenthal found that some 22 per cent of top civil servants were members of the Labour Party (PVDA). The number of top civil servants who were members of the other main political parties was found to be substantially lower: the Social Liberal Party (D'66) and the orthodox Liberal Party (VVD) (both 7 per cent) and the Christian Democratic Party (9 per cent; see *NRC-Handelsblad* (30 Sept. 1995), 2).

The inclusion of the directors' level may in part explain the low percentages of Christian Democrats among top officials. As we can see in Table 9.2, all secretaries general except one are members of a political party. The same broadly applies to the directors general, but to a lesser extent. The generic figures of De Vries and Rosenthal refer to a larger group. From Table 9.2 it is clear that among secretaries general Christian-Democrats are very well represented. The same can be assumed for directors general. One possible reason could be that the appointment of secretaries general and directors general has to be approved in the Council of Ministers. The room for political manœuvre is, or was, larger here (see for instance the remarks on the 'political recruitment machines' of the Labour Party and the Christian Democrats in *NRC-Handelsblad* (6 Oct. 1995), 2). The appointment of a director was the sole prerogative of the minister. This has changed with the introduction of the ABD. It has been suggested that the ABD could limit the scope for political nominations (T. H. Korthals Altes (VVD) in *NRC-Handelsblad* (6 Oct. 1995), 2).

Apart from the membership of political parties, material is available on the voting preferences of senior civil servants. In Table 9.3 the figures concerning the political preference of senior civil servants in 1988 (13 and higher) are compared to top civil servants (17 and higher) in 1995 (see van der Meer and Roborgh, 1993: 49). For better comparison, the figures for the parliamentary election in 1994 in general and voters with university degrees are given.

The main difference between the 1988 and 1995 survey is the discrepancy between the Labour Party and the CDA. In the 1994 elections the CDA suffered severe defeat. This is one possible explanation for the difference.

From the viewpoint of administrative culture, purely political nominations are considered not done. According to the system of merit the best candidate is supposed to win. Senior ministers constantly reassert this principle. However, it is argued that in very special parts of the top of administration political criteria are relevant. This can be seen in the overall distribution of positions and has been confirmed by some off-hand remarks

TABLE 9.3. *Political Preference of Civil Servants in 1988 Compared to Top Civil Servants in 1995*

	All civil servants 1988	High (V–VI) civil servants 1988	Top civil servants 1995	Election 1994, total population	Election 1994, university-educated voters
PVDA	31.9	22.0	37.9	24.0	27.0
CDA	27.5	30.7	15.4	22.2	23.0
VVD	18.3	27.1	25.8	20.0	20.0
D'66	13.3	17.2	17.5	15.5	17.0
Others	9.0	3.0	3.3	18.4	13.0
TOTAL	100.0	100.0	99.9	100.0	100.0

Source: Van der Meer and Roborgh, 1993: 383–7; Roborgh and Rosenthal, 1989: 12–17; De Vries and Rosenthal, *NRC-Handelsblad* (6 Oct. 1995). The figures relating to the elections for the Second Chamber in 1994 are taken from CBS, 1994: 402 and 404.

made by politicians to the effect that political preference and affiliation play at least a part in the selection. It should be added that there are indications that the extent to which this is relevant may vary over time.

Some ambitious top civil servants join a political party because they have a declared interest in administration and politics by virtue of their chosen profession and because they want to increase their career opportunities by active membership (see van der Meer *et al.*, 1997; for the political profile of junior civil servants see Daalder, 1993). However, in practice, top civil servants normally do not act in a party-political way. The explanation for this can be found in the character of the political system. The coalition nature of Dutch politics prevents a one-sided composition within a particular government department. Appointment to top-level positions is subject to a Cabinet decision. It is not solely in the gift or purview of a particular minister, although, of course, s/he has an important say. This means that in a department it is not necessary for a minister, under-minister, and the top civil servants to share the same broad political outlook, particularly since Cabinet ministers come and go at a faster rate than top civil servants. Most secretaries general at present have different political leanings to those of the minister. At the same time we also need to realize that minister and under-ministers usually do not share the same party affiliation.

There is one feature we have not yet addressed: the appointment of political advisers. Political advisers have been appointed in the past and there are still some around. The phenomenon of appointing political advisers was introduced by the first post-war Cabinet (Schermerhorn) and was vehemently opposed by the senior civil service who saw this as questioning their loyalty. Parliament, too, opposed this construction. In the 1970s the issue of political advisers was reopened by the centre-left Cabinet of Den Uyl—the most left-wing Cabinet of the post-war era. This period was characterized by a strong polarization between the parties of the left and right. The left-wing parties were more in favour of political advisers than the centre and right-wing parties. Although it is not a general practice, and one cannot speak of an organized system of political advisers or *cabinets*, even in the current Cabinet political advisers have been appointed. While the motive of having a countervailing power *vis-à-vis* bureaucracy plays a role, the main emphasis is on advising ministers on party and public relations matters. Political advisers can be appointed on a short-term basis from outside the permanent bureaucracy. The other procedure is the selection of a permanent official to serve as an adviser for the duration of the government. It rarely happens, but officials with high political profiles can be appointed to a permanent civil service job. Party-political neutrality is here even more important than in other cases, otherwise the career will be short-lived.

V. Functional Mobility at the Top

In this section we will concentrate on the functional mobility of secretaries general and their deputies (including those termed 'loco-' and 'assistant secretary general') and the directors general. How are these officials recruited? Are they recruited from within their organizational unit? Does seniority play a role in the selection decisions for the top positions? To what degree is a top official recruited out of his or her own department or is s/he recruited from central government at large? Looking at these questions we can see whether there really is one civil service in a sociological sense or whether it is compartmentalized among groups of independent departments. From an organizational point of view the mobility issue concerns the open or closed nature of central government bureaucracy. Other matters need to be addressed as well. What is the mobility between the different levels of government and, more specifically, between central and local government. We will briefly mention mobility between the public and private sector in section VII below. Is there an open border between top-level administration and private enterprise or are they clearly different worlds? These questions are highly relevant given the aim of the ABD to promote mobility of top-rank civil servants by seeking to make them change positions each five years or so. We have to see whether this goal is really

TABLE 9.4. *Secretaries General, Deputy Secretaries General, Directors General in 1996 who were Recruited from a Government Organization Position (in Central, Provincial, or Local Government) Compared to the Rosenthal Findings for 1961, 1971, and 1981* (%)

	Yes	No	Unknown
Secretaries general	92	8	—
Dep. secretaries general	86	7	7
Directors general	91	9	—
Total	90	8	1
Rosenthal, 1961	87	9	4
Rosenthal, 1971	86	12	2
Rosenthal, 1981	86	14	—

Source: 1996, authors; Rosenthal, 1983.

necessary, considering the level of mobility within central government bureaucracy and the length of the time these officials stay in office.

As can be seen in Table 9.4, approximately 90 per cent of top officials are recruited from a government organization (the data for 1996 were compiled from the *Staatsalmanak*). Compared to the results Rosenthal (1983) has compiled for 1961, 1971, and 1981 for the directors general and (most important) directors there is virtually no change at all. From the 10 per cent who are not recruited from a government position, the majority had previous experience in government bureaucracy. As can be seen from Table 9.4, and comparing these results with Table 9.5, it is clear that intergovernmental mobility is really low. Very rarely is there a change of positions

TABLE 9.5. *Secretaries General, Deputy Secretaries General, Directors General in 1996 who were Recruited from a Central Government Position, Compared to the Rosenthal Findings for 1961, 1971, and 1981* (%)

	Yes	No	Unknown
Secretaries general	85	15	—
Dep. secretaries general	86	7	7
Directors general	91	9	—
Total	89	10	1
Rosenthal, 1961	78	18	4
Rosenthal, 1971	83	15	2
Rosenthal, 1981	83	17	—

Source: 1996, authors; Rosenthal, 1983.

TABLE 9.6. *Secretaries General, Deputy Secretaries General, Directors General in 1996 who were Recruited from the Same Government Department, Compared to the Rosenthal Findings for 1961, 1971, and 1981* (%)

	Yes	No	Unknown
Secretaries general	54	46	—
Dep. secretaries general	64	29	7
Directors general	63	37	—
Total	61	38	1
Rosenthal, 1961	71	26	4
Rosenthal, 1971	82	17	2
Rosenthal, 1981	75	25	—

Source: 1996, authors; Rosenthal, 1983.

between the levels of government. It was proposed to enlarge the ABD by including top local government officials in order to increase inter-governmental mobility.

The only marked change has been the increase of interdepartmental mobility (see Table 9.6) since the 1980s. Although not apparent in these tables the level of recruitment from within the specific departmental unit through seniority (i.e. length of service) has decreased substantially. Rosenthal (1983) found that around 50 per cent of top civil servants in 1981 were recruited from within the departmental unit. Our findings for 1996 shows a figure of 22 per cent, although it should be noted that the Rosenthal research also included directors and deputy directors generals. These functionaries could in the recent past were more often recruited from their 'own' unit. The creation of the ABD could be one of the explanations for this decline in internal nominations.

A final point is the rate of mobility. Certainly many secretaries general and directors general have been appointed in recent years (since 1994). But the average rate of mobility has been high in the recent past (see Table 9.7). Rosenthal and van Schendelen (1977: 389) concluded in 1977 that 70 per cent of top civil servants were recruited within a period of five and a half years up to the end of 1975. For 1996 and using a comparable period of nominations, in the last five and a half years 74 per cent of directors general and 85 per cent of secretaries general were appointed.

The average age of secretaries general and directors general at the moment of their appointment was 48.3 and 44.1 years respectively. In 1996, according to the biographical material we collected, their average ages were 51.6 and 48.3 years respectively. This implies that the current secretaries

TABLE 9.7. *The Period in which the Secretaries General and Directors General in Office in 1996 were Recruited*

Period	Secretaries general	Directors general
1980–1985	—	8.7
1985–1990	7.7	13.0
1990–1994	46.2	41.3
1994–1996	46.2	37.0

Source: Authors.

general are in office on average 3.3 years and the directors general on average 4.2 years. Of course most incumbents had a long (departmental) career before arriving at their present position. Comparatively few top civil servants have had experience in the private sector. More top civil servants are leaving government to go to the private sector than the other way around. The ABD will presumably reinforce the closed nature of the civil service.

VI. Social Background

The social background of senior civil servants as such has not received a lot of attention. A debate about their middle-class nature has never been engaged in to the extent found in some other Western countries. Relevant perhaps is the fact that Dutch society and culture have always been more middle-class. As a consequence the social background of civil servants has not attracted the attention of politicians, scholars, or the general public. Related issues, such as political, religious, and other affiliations in which a class element could come forward, have been discussed, but not class itself. Social background is operationalized here in terms of father's occupation.

As compared to the situation in 1951, there has been a shift by 1988/9 from the old middle class to the working class, with the new middle class remaining about the same. It is clear that the middle-class orientation of the civil service in the post-war era has remained unchanged. We need to add, though, that the middle classes have penetrated the top positions more than ever before. While a fair number of top civil servants belonged to the aristocracy and the upper class, both these groups have lost ground in the traditional government departments.

TABLE 9.8. *Social Background of Civil Servants in 1951 and 1988* (%)

Group	Low	Old middle	New middle
High civil servants, central government, 1951	6	27	68
High civil servants, central government, 1988	15	21	64
High civil servants, local government, 1988	18	23	58
Civil servants total, 1988	29	22	49
Labour force (intellectuals), 1988	26	25	49
Labour force (all), 1988	46	25	27

Source: van der Meer and Roborgh, 1993; van Braam, 1957.

VII. Education

The relative importance of pre-entry training for the higher civil service can be assessed on the basis of an examination of the work experience of officials before joining the civil service. The material used in this section is drawn from research on the composition of the Dutch civil service in 1988 (van der Meer and Roborgh, 1993: 326–7). We can conclude from this that the higher civil service in the Netherlands is relatively closed. Other material indicates that mobility between the private and public sectors is very limited. For central government departments it has become more routine practice to select graduates from the universities and the higher professional colleges with a bachelors degree. The pre-entry educational background of higher civil servants is shown by the following percentages:

primary education	0.7
primary/middle-level education	12.7
middle-level education	19.0
high vocational education	24.4
university education	42.7
other	0.4

Of all higher civil servants 67 per cent have had some training in higher education.

At present the number of people with a higher educational background is much larger than in the past. Formerly people could join a government department and rise in the hierarchy on the basis of experience or additional post-entry training. The result can still be seen in the present composition of the higher civil service. Now, however, the emphasis has shifted, especially in the higher levels of the civil service, to pre-entry education at

TABLE 9.9. *University Education of the Top Civil Servants in 1996* (%)

University	Secretaries general	Adjunct secretaries general	Directors general	TOTAL
Yes	92	100	93	94
No	8	0	7	6

Source: Authors.

the higher professional schools and the universities. It almost impossible to join the higher civil service without a university education.

By way of conclusion, standard university or higher professional education is indispensable for entering the senior civil service. As the occupational structure of the senior civil service is very diverse this also implies that a wide variety of training is in demand. The material presented in Tables 9.10–12 provides an impression of the variation in university background of these higher government officials.

TABLE 9.10. *University-Trained Personnel by Subject, 1930–1988* (%)

	1930	1947	1988
Law	75	56	27
Economics and social sciences	1	9	35
Natural sciences and engineering	16	23	21
Other (including humanities)	8	12	17
TOTAL	100	100	100

Source: van der Meer and Roborgh, 1993: 326.

TABLE 9.11. *Disciplinary Background of Secretaries General (SG) and Directors General (DG) in 1996* (%)

	SG	DG
Law	31	28
Economics and social sciences	38	36
Natural sciences and engineering	8	23
Other (including humanities)	8	2
None	8	6
Unknown	8	4
TOTAL	101	99

Source: Authors.

TABLE 9.12. *University Affiliation of Secretaries General (SG) and Directors General (DG) in 1996* (%)

University	SG	DG
VU Amsterdam	18	8
University of Amsterdam	18	13
Delft	9	13
Groningen	27	13
Leiden	9	18
Rotterdam	—	13
Tilburg	—	5
Utrecht	18	13
Wageningen	—	3

Source: Authors.

The findings in Table 9.12 are relevant since they clearly show that the assumed dominance of Leiden (and Utrecht) trained jurists is no longer correct. This was the case in a more distant past, before the Second World War. Given that the mobility of people in general has increased in the past four or five decades, we suggest that personnel are no longer recruited exclusively from the western part of the country. Another explanation is that experts were needed with backgrounds different to those that legal study could provide. Hence the pool from which top officials were recruited expanded to other universities as well. Furthermore, the enormous demand for experts in government in the post-war era could not simply have been supplied by Leiden alumni alone. Previously the senior civil service was dominated by legal trainees. The monopoly of legal experts has eroded over the years. Besides academically trained personnel in general it is also visible at the top level. Rosenthal (1983: 311) points to a decline in the proportion of directors general with a law degree from 64 per cent in 1961 to 26 per cent in 1981. It is somewhat higher now, but there is still a clear decline from the earlier period.

An explanation is found in the changing nature of government tasks. The extension of the scope of government to economic, social, and welfare tasks in this century has broadened the expertise demanded from senior civil servants. As a result personnel has been increasingly recruited from among those with training in the social, economic, and natural sciences. The significance of the natural sciences is somewhat less among officials involved in policy formulation. At the same time the legal monopoly has been eroded in the area of policy formulation and implementation. Not only has this been caused by a growing demand for specialist skills and knowledge but also by an increasing popularity of a generalist approach

TABLE 9.13. *Legal or Other Background of Academically Trained Top Civil Servants—(Adj.) Secretaries General and Directors General—in 1996* (%)

	SG	Adj. SG	DG	TOTAL
Legal	33.3	53.3	29.5	35.7
Other	67.7	46.7	70.5	64.3

Source: Authors.

to public management issues. Law used to be regarded as the broadest training for the civil service. Particularly since the Second World War the social sciences have been competing with the legal studies in this field. Public administration departments were created at the universities of Twente (1976) and Rotterdam and Leiden (1984). Their curricula were aimed at students who wanted to study government from an interdisciplinary perspective combining legal, economic, and social science perspectives.

Training higher civil servants does not depend solely on pre-entry education. Looking at the way post-entry training for higher civil servants is organized in the Netherlands, four different training methods can be distinguished that all seek to transmit both knowledge and skills: formal instruction by providing long-term courses; training in and on the job; supporting and encouraging secondments and internships; and the commissioning of research and seminars.

The first method mentioned is the best-known. Training often suggests a formal and structured method of transfer of knowledge and skills. Courses provided or commissioned by various government departments and other public organizations are obvious examples. Nevertheless it is a mistake to limit post-entry training to formal training. A far more simple training style is to be found in training in and on the job. Starting a new job often means slowly becoming more competent in meeting the job requirements. This often follows a path of trial and error. Training on the job can also be more institutionalized, for instance by assigning a more experienced colleague to a new official. Coaching is a method of training. Transfer of practical knowledge is crucial to this training system. Connected to training on the job is the secondment of higher personnel to relevant institutions. This method is increasingly attracting more attention. The same applies to the much shorter internships. The extent to which this instrument is being used by Dutch government departments and the problems associated with its implementation will be discussed below. Finally, a transfer of knowledge and experience also lies at the heart of the strategy of commissioning research and organizing seminars.

What is done in the Dutch civil service with respect to post-entry courses? There is a close relationship between the recruitment system and the organization of post-entry education. Earlier we remarked that a division can be made between recruitment for a specific position and recruitment for a career. Recruitment for a specific position is most common. Recruitment for a career is mainly found in the military, the police, the judiciary, and the diplomatic service. In these latter instances a formal career path has been defined that a selected official is expected to pursue. Designing these career paths and arranging the necessary training programmes are central tasks for personnel management within these organizations. An individual recruited for a specific post of course also pursues a particular career path, but these routes are not formally laid down at the moment of entry. They only become manifest as a person changes from position to position.

We have discussed this rather extensively because the implications for the organization of civil service training for our subject are very significant. For the higher ranks both in the job and in the career recruitment systems a high level of pre-entry training is required. We need to add, though, that in the career system people are sometimes recruited from grammar schools instead of from universities. The important difference lies in the fact that individuals recruited under the career system have to attend extensive post-entry education before continuing in their career. In some cases, for instance with respect to the military and the police, this internal professional instruction is given at a government academy and takes two to four years.

Under the job recruitment system the emphasis is placed on the right kind of instruction *before* entering government. A person is supposed to start right away performing his or her tasks. The relevance of post-entry training for this group of higher civil servants is not to be belittled. Although a person may be qualified for a major part of his job there still may be gaps. This is the reason why almost every government department has an introductory course (very often on public administration) for new higher officials.

Career-oriented education is not so much intended to improve actual job performance but to prepare a civil servant for his line of career in a particular branch of government. Two different categories of career programmes are to be distinguished. The first are the courses given to, for instance, future diplomats and other higher foreign office officials, judges, public prosecutors, officers in the army, and higher police officers. These career programmes can be considered as in-service professional training. For instance in the case of the Foreign Office, future diplomats and officials receive a nine-month training course after their selection. This programme is provided by the department itself in cooperation with the International Institute. This institute also provides short courses on international relations, for instance to the Defence Department, and international relations and European affairs form a substantial part of the training programme. A second type of career-oriented education is provided to higher civil servants in the context of the management development programmes. Management development programmes involve developing the personal qualities and skills of the higher civil servant in order to improve performance. Management development (MD) presupposes a systematic approach to career development of higher civil servants and the existence of appropriate training facilities. It involves selected groups of personnel who have shown some promise or are considered to have ample opportunities to make a substantial career step. These MD programmes are developed by each department individually. This initiative is fairly new and some of these programmes are still in the their infancy. In the context of these MD programmes a higher civil servant is offered a combination of formal education, job-rotation, sometimes secondments and internships. A wide range of courses is used although the emphasis here is more on management-related issues. Some candidates selected for the MD programme are sent to, for instance, the master of public administration programmes of the Netherlands School of Government (NSOG) in the Hague or the Master of Business Administration programme of the Erasmus University Rotterdam. The MBA programme is roughly comparable in this respect. This post-doctoral programme is meant for higher civil servants with extensive experience in government. Its aim is to prepare them for top positions in the civil service at all levels of government. Internationalization of government has acquired a prominent and integral place in this programme. Courses have been developed on internationalization and Europeanization and the consequences for central, regional, and local government. Students are also trained in skills of international negotiation.

Besides the formal training courses a less structured method of training was mentioned in the introduction to this section on post-entry training. The term 'learning-by-doing' is sometimes used to describe this particular training method. The word 'method' may perhaps sound too presumptuous. Nevertheless learning-by-doing is one of the fundamentals in the improvement of individual performance in an organization. On entering a government organization a person possesses a certain level of expertise and a number of skills. Doing the job and trial and error are methods of gaining experience. There is also a more formalized way of training on the job. Secondments and internships are sometimes seen as a part of training on the job.

VIII. Conclusion

Attention to the senior civil service is not something recent. Indeed, ever since the Kingdom of the Netherlands was constituted (1815) the fragmented departmental and political system heralded discussions about compartmentalization. Little mobility existed among top civil servants. In many cases they started and ended their career in one department, or went to another department when sections of the department of Home Affairs were organized into a new department (1877, 1905, 1917, 1921, 1932). A variety of reorganizations have been attempted since the early nineteenth century. In order to break through this compartmentalization, experiments with interdepartmental mobility have been attempted since the end of the Second World War. Thus a Central Personnel Service was envisaged (1950s) and coordinated by the department of Home Affairs, but was short-lived, meeting with resistance from the other departments and ministers. The Committee on the Main Structure of Central Government, known in the Netherlands by the name of its chairman, the Vonhoff-Committee (1979–81), started a process of change that is still in motion. Attempts to enhance interdepartmental and intergovernmental mobility at the top acquired new momentum in the social-democratic and liberal Cabinet of Prime Minister Kok (1994–8). It was under this Cabinet that a Senior Public Service (ABD) was created. It is too early to tell whether the ABD has a chance of success, but some tentative remarks can be made about its potential for success.

In general the civil service became a white-collar administrative organization during the post-war era, mainly because of the decline of the number of blue-collar workers in central government through privatization. Among the top civil servants in the past decade or so we find more with a working-class background than forty years ago. Since the 1980s the rate of interdepartmental mobility has increased. However, positions at the top in central government have in the 1961–96 period been predominantly filled by civil servants already working centrally. Intergovernmental mobility is as low as it always has been. The ABD is not implemented yet to the degree that intergovernmental mobility is increased. The chances of intergovernmental mobility could be limited, given that the experience in top positions at local level may not be considered relevant for what is perceived as a requirement for central civil service top positions. Furthermore, if the ABD were also to develop to include top positions in local government, this could well result in a centralization of recruitment and would be contrary to contemporary notions of local autonomy since it denies the separate status that local government is supposed to have. So far it appears that the ABD will only reinforce the closed nature of the top civil service in central government. At the same time it may well limit politicization of top appointments.

What is very interesting is that our findings about the current composition of the top civil service in the Netherlands indicate that the average rate of mobility has been fairly high in the past seven years. Hence, mobility was high before the ABD was created. The ABD was pursued in the conviction that higher mobility will strengthen generalist attitudes at the top and create an *esprit de corps* that transcends compartmentalization. It appears, though, that—at least in terms of mobility—the ABD is not really necessary. Instead, the Bureau for the ABD could focus more on the other four goals mentioned in section III (strengthening skills, administrative and management development, and developing procedures). After all, neither in private business nor in government will top officials perceive their position as the final one in their career. Rather, top civil servants seek new challenges after a number of years, maybe at the same level (within another department), or in private business, or a higher level (political office, international public positions). This is all the more the case since they are on average relatively young, and probably younger than those in their posts used to be.

The ABD seeks to establish a unified administrative structure, based on recruitment and mobility, for the top civil servants, while at the same time these top officials will have to operate in a fragmented political system. First, there is the ministerial system (the members of the Cabinet) in which each minister is responsible for his/her own department, while at the same time sharing Cabinet responsibility for the general policies of government. Second, Cabinets in the Netherlands are always coalitions, so in that sense too one could speak of fragmentation. It will be interesting to see how the ABD operates within this arena of unified administration and fragmented politics.

REFERENCES

Bekke, A. J. G. M., R. Bekker, and A. D. J. Verhoeven (1996). *Haagse bazen: Een verkenning van de topstructuur van de ministeries* (Alphen aan den Rijn: Samsom H. D. Tjeenk Willink).

Daalder, Hans (1993). 'Van oude en nieuwe regenten. Of: politiek als beroep', farewell lecture upon his retirement as professor of political science, University of Leiden.

Ministerie van Binnenlandse Zaken (1988). *Overheid en arbeidsmarkt 1988.*

Ministerie van Binnenlandse Zaken (1994). *Mensen en management in de rijksdienst 1994* (The Hague: Ministerie van Binnenlandse Zaken).

—— (1995). *Mensen en management in de rijksdienst 1995*, situation on 31 Dec. 1994 (The Hague: Ministerie van Binnenlandse Zaken).

—— (1996). *Benoeming, beloning topambtenaren* (The Hague: Ministerie van Binnenlandse Zaken).

Roborgh, L. J., and U. Rosenthal (1989). 'Van rechts naar links: de politieke voorkeuren van rijksambtenaren', *Namens*, 6/4: 12–17.

Rosenthal, U. (1979). 'De secretaris-generaal: politisering of verambtelijking', *Acta Politica*, 4(3): 343–77.

—— (1983). 'De mandarijnen van de Rijksdienst: Modieuze stellingen en harde feiten over de Nederlandse topambtenarij', *Bestuurswetenschappen*, 5 (June/July): 302–16.

—— and M. C. P. M. van Schendelen (1977). 'Ambtelijke top in Nederland', *Bestuurswetenschappen*, 6: 389.

van Braam, A. (1957). 'Ambtenaren en bureaukratie', *Nederland Zeist* (Gravenhage: Excelcior).

van der Meer, F. M., and L. J. Roborgh (1993). *Ambtenaren in Nederland: Omvang, bureaucratisering en representativiteit van het ambtelijk apparaat* (Alphen a/d Rijn: Samsom H. D. Tjeenk Willink).

van der Meer, Frits M., Gerrit S. A. Dijkstra, and Renk J. Roborgh (1997). 'The Dutch Civil Service System', paper for the conference on Civil Service Systems in Comparative Perspective, 5–8 Apr. 1997, Indiana University.

10

Senior Officials in the Danish Central Administration: From Bureaucrats to Policy Professionals and Managers

HANNE NEXØ JENSEN AND TIM KNUDSEN

Introduction

The buildings housing Danish ministries and agencies are a mixture of older and postmodern architecture, though the former remains predominant. Likewise, their interiors are also a blend of antiques (the majority being of Danish design) and some postmodern pieces of furniture. The role of top civil servants in the Danish public administration happens to mirror this architecture. One finds a mixture of older and newer traditions in the senior civil service, but something very Danish to be sure—both in their norms and values as well as in the degree to which they have been shaped by influences from abroad. Since history and tradition are very important to the Danish context, we will briefly summarize the historical role of the civil servants. In addition the common organizational principles governing the central public administration will be introduced.

Historical Background

The Danish central public administration has long held a reputation for loyalty, discipline, political neutrality, and a lack of corruption. In the age of absolutism in Denmark from 1660 to 1848, lawyers gradually monopolized positions within the civil service. This monopoly was formally confirmed in 1821. In comparison to other European countries, Denmark had an extraordinarily high rate of non-nobles among its civil servants. Hence, the bureaucracy swelled with men of bourgeois origin. Loyalty to the monarchy ran high. One of the preconditions for this was the comparatively effective system of taxation which made it possible for the Danish king to pay acceptable wages to his servants. Another precondition was the conscious effort made by a number of kings in building a loyal bureaucracy as independent of aristocratic elements and connections as possible.

In 1848–9 absolutism was suddenly replaced with a democratic constitution. The state administration was reformed into seven ministries and each minister became formally responsible for every detail in his ministry. In the late nineteenth century a constitutional struggle over parliamentarism between governments of the 'right' and liberal 'left' (supported especially by farmers) took place. Though government demanded obedience from its civil servants, this was irrelevant because most civil servants belonged to the right. Half of the ministers from 1848 to 1901 were in fact recruited from the ranks of top civil servants.

In 1901 parliamentarism was introduced and the left came into power. For several decades afterwards, Denmark had a most unusual situation. Governments led by liberal, social-liberal, or social-democratic prime ministers cooperated with relatively loyal, modest, and withdrawn bureaucrats, who were mostly conservatives at heart. A kind of tacit 'historical compromise' involving a tradition for extreme separation between the political and administrative élite developed between politicians and bureaucrats, underlining their different roles: the hesitating, reserved style among bureaucrats versus the limited involvement of politicians in administrative politics (Knudsen, 1995).

Egalitarian values run strong throughout Denmark. Like Sweden, the concept of 'élite' is not often used—not even in the social sciences. Until recently the concept of 'top' civil servant had not been used either. Present-day use of the term probably derives from foreign influence. When the word 'élite' is used in connection with Danish top civil servants, it does not connotate one single élite, but several élites. Until the most recent decades, each ministry was a closed system with little recruitment of outside personnel. In fact cultures and traditions vary so greatly between the ministries that the system would generally be better characterized as segmented.

During recent years the government has consisted of twenty ministries. Basically, these can be further broken down into two types of organization: departments and agencies (or directorates). Departments (*departementer*) are considered the top organizations of the ministries, always responsible for international collaboration, policy preparation, and for the evaluation, planning, and budgeting of the department itself as well as its attached agencies. On occasion it is also responsible for casework. Due to the principle of 'personal responsibility of the ministers' (Hansen, 1996: 73), the entire department can be viewed as the minister's secretariat—although the minister also has at his disposal a smaller private secretariat *within* the department. The departments are headed by permanent secretaries (*departementschefer*).

An agency—*styrelse* or *direktorat* being the most common Danish names in this group (though a number of other names are found)—is subordinate to a department on the basis of the specific decision-making powers delegated to it (Hansen, 1996: 73). Typically the head of an agency will be called 'director' and, on average, there are three to four agencies for each department.

From 1960 to 1980, the ideal model of ministerial organization, for administrative policy, was based on small departments and relatively large agencies. 'The purpose was to take away case work, routine decisions and decisions demanding highly specialised knowledge', in order to give the minister and the department time to concentrate on principles of policy and planning (Hansen, 1996: 73). Thus, several ministries in the 1960s and the 1970s were reorganized broadly in accordance with this ideal model. In the 1980s, however, new trends emerged to influence the reorganization of some ministries in different ways. For example, in some cases the rather independent agencies were transformed into divisions within the departments, as with agencies in the Ministry of Education, while in other cases agencies were maintained but with an increased autonomy (Beck Jørgensen and Hansen, 1995; Hansen, 1996: 73–4).

In 1994 the total number of staff with academic qualifications (signifying a degree of seniority or participation in a senior civil service career path) in departments stood at 2,380, of whom 36 per cent were women. In 1995 of the approximately 780,000 public employees in Denmark, 600,000 were employees of local governments (Danmarks Statistik, 1997: 23). To this figure one can add 136,000 employees in organizations and institutions partly financed by public funds.

Since 1982 there have been waves of attempts to modernize the Danish public sector. The Ministry of Finance has been the most important actor in this regard (Ministry of Finance, 1995; see also Greve, 1998). Reforms have mainly been heavily influenced by Anglo-American experiences. These trends have not had the same impact, however, as in the UK (Jensen, 1991). This is probably due to the conflict between egalitarian norms and the New Public Management (NPM) imperatives including budget reforms, outsourcing of contracts, improved efficiency, development of flexible and locally negotiated wages, development of managerial skills, simplification of rules, debureaucratization, privatization, improved service, decentralization, and self-administration (Eldrup, 1995: 105; Hansen, 1996: 75). One of the by-products of this conflict has been vacillation in some ministries over the introduction of NPM changes (Greve, 1997*a*). Sharply

diverging ministerial cultures have meant that some government departments are more adaptive to reforms than others (Antonsen and Hansen,
1992).

Ranks and Numbers of Senior Civil Servants at the Top Levels

The career ladder in the Danish civil service is relatively short. There are
basically four levels: *fuldmægtig* (principal), *kontorchef* (assistant secretary), *afdelingschef* (head of division), and *departementschef* (permanent
secretary). The head of division was introduced in the Ministry of Foreign
Affairs in 1921. As the years have passed, this category has spread to
almost all ministries. In agencies, on the other hand, the top civil servant
normally has the title of director, while other titles are generally identical
to those in ministries.

The permanent secretaries, heads of division, and directors are, for
purposes of this chapter, considered senior officials. In 1996 there were
twenty ministers and twenty permanent secretaries in Denmark (see Table
10.1) and forty-six the heads of divisions. There are, however, some problems with the exact delineation of the number of agencies (Stjernquist,
1948: 145). The reason for this can be found in the lack of general principles in naming individual agencies. The resulting plethora of different
names make it difficult to determine whether an organization deserves to
be considered an agency or a smaller institution. We have considered larger
organizations with authority functions as agencies. In 1996 the number of
agencies was estimated at seventy-four. This number has declined during
the last few years due to certain organizational changes including mergers,
the withdrawal of agencies into departments proper, and privatizations.

TABLE 10.1. *Absolute Numbers of Senior Civil Servants in Ministries and*
Agencies, 1935–1996

	1935	1950	1960	1970	1977	1990	% of women	1996	% of women
Permanent secretary	13	25	27	26	26	22	1	20	1
Head of division	3	26	28	47	54	47	3	46	9
Director	29	61	70	79	87	76	2	74	5
TOTAL	45	112	125	152	167	145	6	140	15

Sources: Christensen, 1984, and annual issues of *Hof & Statskalenderen* and *Kraks blå bog*.

Therefore, the number of top civil servants selected for our analysis was 145 in 1990 and 140 in 1996.

The Methods of Recruitment, Promotion, and Inter-ministerial Mobility

Since Denmark has a form of ministerial government (*Ministerstyre*), a minister is at once a political leader and a top manager (*forvaltningschef*) of a ministry. Each individual minister—within certain general rules and in regards to the size of the management group (civil servants grades 37–42)—is entitled to recruit, promote, and dismiss officials without interference from other authorities as set forth by the Finance Act (Christensen, 1983). One exception concerns appointments to permanent secretary which are scrutinized by a special Cabinet committee, the decision of which is confirmed at a full Cabinet meeting. Formally, however, the decision lies with the individual minister.

Public officials are divided into two groups: civil servants who are employed on the basis of a civil service law (*tjenestemænd*) and public employees who are employed on the basis of collective agreements with unions (*overenskomstansatte*). Top civil servants are *tjenestemænd*. Previously they were always employed on a lifetime basis, but now a few are employed for a limited number of years. Thus, for practical purposes, the differences between the two groups have been diminishing and we shall not elaborate on these differences here. What makes Denmark remarkable is that most top civil servants—including the permanent secretaries—are members of personnel organizations which are more or less trade unions in character (Nielsen and Hoff, 1991). The organizations involved are AC, the Danish Confederation of Professional Associations, and different associations such as DJØF, organizing lawyers, economists, political and social scientists for example. The offices of top civil servants have—for almost two centuries—been almost exclusively filled by those with a university education. In our study approximately only 5 per cent of top civil servants in 1996 were without an academic education (see Table 10.3) versus a 12 per cent figure in 1977 (Christensen, 1984: 283).

Nonetheless, the classification of job positions 'is negotiated between the Ministry of Finance and the central organisation to which the union organising the individual servant or all servants belongs' (Christensen, 1994: 79). The most senior grouping of all public employees—including permanent secretaries—has its own Commission handling questions such as classification and reclassification. It is even possible to negotiate both on an individual and collective basis. This may happen if an individual civil

servant is able to convince DJØF that it should move AC to open negotiations about his or her classification (Christensen, 1994: 79).

Since 1919 positions in the civil service have been openly advertised
in newspapers and relevant journals so that everyone could apply
(Gammeltoft-Hansen *et al.* 1994: 142). There are, however, some rare exceptions to this general principle. Commentators have always complained
when competition has not been open (Andersen, 1943: 191). The personnel
organizations have similarly tried to apply pressure to the ministers when
they did not declare the office open to free competition. For example, in
October 1996 a director for aviation was simply appointed without any
application procedure and no prior experience with aviation. The minister
was heavily criticized for this by the unions, the media, and the opposition.
The example shows that while rules in Denmark may be bent, the norm of
open competition prevails.

Throughout the twentieth century—and specifically up until the late
1970s and early 1980s—recruitment and promotions for top positions were
based mainly on a mix of seniority, or length of service, and qualifications
on the basis of merit, that is to say on the basis of the qualifications and
experience related to the specific post (Betænkning, 1976). This system
produced an extremely loyal, disciplined bureaucracy, certainly among the
most uncorrupted in the world (Bogason, 1991; Christensen, 1983: 59–60).
Denmark maintains a reputation for extremely low levels of corruption. In
fact in 1997, Transparency International in Berlin asked business people to
rank fifty-two countries, and they judged Denmark as the world's most uncorrupted country. Other Scandinavian countries and New Zealand also
came among the top ten, the UK ranked fourteenth and Nigeria was
placed as most corrupt country.

However, this system of promotion has several disadvantages
(Betænkning, 1976). First of all, qualifications (especially leadership qualifications) have played too small a role in promotions because merit criteria
have often caused dissatisfaction among civil servants and their organizations when they violate the principle of seniority—i.e. when they result in
the promotion of officials over the heads of others who have been in the
service for longer. Secondly, civil servants have resisted proposed organizational reforms aimed at securing inter-ministerial mobility. This resistance
arises because as civil servants were employed above all by a particular
ministry, they could not bring their seniority and merit qualifications to
another ministry (Smith, 1977). In essence, personnel could wind up losing
their seniority 'investment' if they left. It has been suspected that this system not only caused inflexibility as well as unwanted bureaucratic growth,
but it also created too fragmented and sectorised a national civil service
(Betænkning, 1976).

In 1975 an agreement signed by both the Minister of Finance and the relevant trade unions redefined the terms of appointment for new top civil servants. The agreement meant that those employed in a ministry could be moved to other posts, whether within the department, the agencies of the ministry, or other ministries. This provision covered permanent secretaries, head of divisions, and assistant secretaries. Furthermore, in many ministries there were rotation systems set up for the junior civil servants. This was a radical change in the direction of increasing inter-ministerial mobility (also see Table 10.2).

Formal aspects of the recruitment system have just been described. But how does the system itself actually function? First, the minister and the permanent secretary—unless the vacant office happens to be that of permanent secretary—conduct informal interviews with the applicants. Subsequently the minister then consults the permanent secretary and reaches a decision. This decision must be confirmed by the government's Committee on Appointments. It is difficult to assess the degree to which any particular minister actually determines who is appointed, since this ability to choose usually varies according to the minister's status within the Cabinet.

The current arrangements for promotion replace the old system which involved consultation with committees for each ministry on which its employees were represented. Acting in the interests of the employees, these committees contributed to strengthening the tendency for automatic appointments based on length of service. These same committees were abandoned without much resistance. Since the 1980s private consultants have in some cases examined the applicants to see if they had appropriate qualifications for leadership. While it is not generally known how often this has been done, at least in one case (the Ministry of Education) the use of private consultants had to be abandoned since they were found to be of little help. The quality of the tests employed by these consultants remains a topic of some controversy.

Do ministers make appointments on the basis of the party-political affiliation of the official? Rumours about such cases have circulated in newspapers and television from time to time. And although there is no systematic knowledge, the general impression among Danish political scientists is that such cases do exist, but are rare. Many of our small government parties simply cannot find the necessary talent from within their declining ranks to fill positions in the civil service. Furthermore, some ministers prefer civil servants who are *not* members of their party since party members are more difficult to get rid of if unwanted. In addition, the Danish party system operates basically as a consensus system with only few fundamental disagreements *between* parties. Some of the deepest

conflicts of Danish politics, such as the EU question, do not follow traditional party lines on a left to right dimension. The most important qualifications (or rather, what the politicians *believe* are such qualifications)
seem to be the capability of applicants to offer ministers political advice as
well as their abilities to form new policies. We appear to have little knowledge of how ministers define advisory and policy-making qualifications.

In sum, while the old criterion of seniority has declined, it is not exactly
clear what has replaced it. We know that, in public debate, it is stipulated
that general leadership qualifications are the answer. Changes in the central
public administration owe more to the new political environment where a
ministry, to a much larger extent, needs to be able to cope with all types of
requests from the outside, e.g. from business organizations, trade unions,
local governments, as well as the EU. Each ministry remains primarily an
element in an organizational network by which it must secure coordination
of political processes.

Today the loyal, political, and neutral bureaucrat is, in the Weberian
sense, rare. Stronger and more proactive leaders, with the ability to form
strategies, seem to be the rule as their role in the formation of the political
agenda has strengthened (Klausen, 1996: 44). However, because political,
economic, and cultural conditions—along with historical traditions—
vary for each ministry and each agency, there is not simply *one* type of top
civil servant but several.

Inter-ministerial Mobility

Mobility between ministries, as well as between the public and the private
sector, is increasing (see Table 10.2). In the period from 1950 to 1970 this
mobility seemed to be rather stable (approximately 28 per cent moved).
The increase is most marked between the years 1990 to 1996 where 44 per
cent of the top civil servants served in two or more ministries.

In the 1980s successful climbers were likely to have served in at least two
or three departments before appointment to a top management position
(Christensen and Ibsen, 1991: 88). In 1994 Christensen concluded that
'successful high-fliers in governmental careers are increasingly bureaucrats
. . . who have worked as principals and bureau chiefs [i.e. assistant secret-
aries] exclusively at the departmental level' (Christensen, 1994: 83). Our
figures confirm the tendencies found by Christensen and Ibsen. In 1996, 55
per cent had a career in one ministry only. Compare this figure with the 65
per cent who had a one-ministry career in 1950. The change has mainly
been restricted to increased interdepartmental mobility.

TABLE 10.2. *Mobility Among Top Civil Servants* (%)

	1935	1950	1960	1970	1977	1990	1996
One ministry	77.8	65.2	58.4	66.0	63.5	66.2	55.0
Two ministries	15.6	16.1	16.8	20.0	18.0	23.4	33.6
Three or more ministries	4.4	11.6	11.2	4.7	3.7	7.6	10.7
Another background	—	0.9	5.6	5.3	9.0	—	—
Missing	2.2	6.3	8.0	4.0	6.0	2.8	0.7
N	45	112	125	150	167	145	140

Another tendency is that an increasing number of top civil servants continue their careers *outside* the department. Traditionally a ministerial career was for life. However, a growing number of top civil servants now leave the ministries to become top executives in either the private sector or the growing 'grey' sector of semi-public agencies. Here they can be paid in accordance with supply–demand principles of the private job market, which in many cases means much higher pay. Others are simply transferred to sinecure posts. Civil servants normally retire between the ages of 67 and 70. Between 1967 and 1976 only five retired early to take up positions outside the ministry, between 1977 and 1986 sixteen did and between 1987 and 1996 this figure rose to nineteen (data derived from *Kraks blå bog* and *Hof- og Statskalenderen*).

One could ask whether this tendency will influence the traditionally strong loyalties of Danish top civil servants? Are they in some cases exploiting their top positions to form personal networks and using their knowledge for their own gain? For the moment, these questions cannot be answered as there has been no research and little public debate.

Another consequence of the intensified competition and shorter stays in top positions is the growing frequency of appointments. All other factors being equal, the growing number of opportunities to appoint in itself has increased the individual ministers' possibilities for selecting personnel of their own choice.

The growing inter-ministerial mobility, together with the more flexible career patterns, means that an appointment as a top civil servant cannot be assumed to be the incumbents' final office. For permanent secretaries especially, this is seldom the case. The average age of top civil servants in 1996 was 51 (see Table 10.3). Fifty years earlier that same figure was 55 (Stjernquist, 1948: 147 and 154). The average age at appointment is 47, while the average seniority in the present job is just four years. Permanent secretaries follow this tendency. Both their average age and their average length of service has decreased. In 1996, for example, the average length of service for permanent secretaries was 3.9 years compared to 7.2 years in 1946 (Stjernquist, 1948: 159).

Pay

Rewards for top civil servants in Denmark and other Nordic countries are low in comparison with other European countries (Hood and Lambert, 1994: 27). Following a reform in 1969, all collective agreements have to be negotiated between the Minister of Finance and a committee representing all civil servants' organizations. Different job positions were placed in a system of wage grades. Individual salaries could nonetheless vary to a limited extent through the effect of negotiated 'add-ons', either for particular groups or, in some cases, for individuals. However, 'add-ons' were not based upon individual performance.

Up until 1975, salaries tended to increase in real terms each year. Over the next fifteen years, however, salaries declined—between 1975 and 1991 higher civil servants suffered a 30 per cent loss in real terms. Top civil servants have come to be viewed as victims of a restrictive and egalitarian income policy which stresses solidarity between higher and lower income groups (Christensen, 1994). In 1985, funds were set aside to introduce more flexibility into public-sector pay, initially on a small scale. The system has since expanded. Top civil servants have been advancing the doctrine of comparability with executives in private business by working for a further decentralization of the pay system. Some of the top civil servants have used individual strategies in order to improve their payment and, to some extent, succeeded (according to Christensen, 1994: 79–81).

The tendency over recent years has been to accommodate a more decentralized, individualistic stipulation of wages for top civil servants, based upon the performance of the individual. Today, a permanent secretary's base salary is between 538,000 and 680,000 Danish kroner. Add to this figure pension and different bonus plans, e.g. top management bonuses, individual bonuses, top leader pools, etc., and in total some of the most highly paid permanent secretaries can earn more than one million Danish kroner annually (Mortensen, 1997: 49). Heads of division and directors earn approximately half a million a year depending on personal bonuses.

Recently, another bonus of 75,000 Danish kroner a year has been added for the few top civil servants who are employed on limited contracts. Some directors also receive such bonuses. Exact information about the pay of each top civil servant is difficult to determine due to today's more decentralized system.

One must be careful not to jump to hasty conclusions regarding the social status of top civil servants based solely upon their pay (which is still modest in comparison with that of top executives in the private sector and of top civil servants in many other countries including those in the EU). In a country such as Denmark, where egalitarian norms are the rule, there can be no one-to-one relationship between pay and social status.

Party Membership and the Senior Civil Service

In Denmark the minister is the only politically appointed person in a ministry. In principle, all others are considered career civil servants. Since 1901 two features have characterized the Danish top civil servant. First, although civil servants are free to seek election to Parliament, it is not customary for those in high office to do so. They seldom pursue other types of political careers, including ministerial careers. In our 1996 sample, only two officials stated they had (or have had) a political post as an elected party member. Nine others indicated they had been active in their trade unions. A political career does not necessarily improve the opportunities for a civil servant. For example, a period as minister would—quite unlike the French and other cases—mean loss of seniority, loss of merits, and thus loss of career chances.

Secondly, civil servants have insisted upon a 'non-political' status and generally have attempted to prevent political appointments from creeping in. They have considered their personal political convictions as a private matter. Therefore, it has been impossible systematically to research this question. Yet the general impression is that for many decades the majority of civil servants were mainly conservative at heart (though there were few manifestations of this). During the second half of the century civil servants have become more evenly distributed throughout the leading parties. But available evidence suggests that many of the top civil servants—most likely a considerable majority—are not members of a political party at all.

Occasionally there are allegations that a particular director or a permanent secretary was appointed on the basis of political merits, but this is the exception rather than the rule. In recent years, there seems to have been a growing number of appointments with political connotations, mainly in regard to ministers' private secretaries and the growing number of employees assisting ministers with the handling of the media. This, in turn, is commonly perceived by the media as an attack on the good, old, non-political Danish system of appointments. With the exception of these posts, it is doubtful whether there has been an increase in the rate of political appointments since 1980.

Status in the Civil Service of High Status Ministries

In 1992 the pay for a number of highly prestigious secretaries was transferred to a new super-grade referred to as grade 42. They were the permanent secretaries of the PM's Office, the Ministry of Finance, and the Director
General of the Ministry of Foreign Affairs (Christensen, 1994: 81). The
upgrading of these three top positions indicated that these ministries (at
least at that time) were the three most prestigious ministries.

In the late 1990s the government formed an informal coordination
group consisting of the ministers and permanent secretaries of the PM's
Office, the Ministry of Finance, the Ministry of Economic Affairs, the
Ministry of Foreign Affairs, and the Ministry of Environment and Energy
(all ministries with a small number of senior women officials, it should be
noted). This informal grouping serves at least two functions: to coordinate
between the two parties in government and to develop cross-departmental
initiatives.

Traditionally, the Ministry of Foreign Affairs and the Ministry of
Justice have considered themselves as the most important ministries. Thus,
only the very best law graduates have been able to enter these ministries—
especially the Ministry of Justice (Hartlev, 1996). For different reasons
these two ministries have lost status. The Ministry of Justice has been
marred by the so-called Tamil case where a former Minister of Justice was
found guilty of illegal administration while his civil servants, and most
prominently his permanent secretary, did little to stop it (Christensen,
1996*b*: 265; Henrichsen, 1995). For its part, the Ministry of Foreign Affairs
lost status due to an increased internationalization of the central public
administration which has weakened its role. A growing number of ministries have become directly involved in contacts with other central administrations as well as the EU. Furthermore, since January 1993 the current
Prime Minister Poul Nyrup Rasmussen, together with his civil servants,
has become heavily involved in international affairs. The media has often
covered stories about the declining influence of the Ministry of Foreign
Affairs.

The Ministry of Finance and the Prime Minister's Office have, on the
other hand, strengthened their positions. The Ministry of Finance acquired
its status as a 'superministry' in 1924. Since then the Ministry's control over
other ministries' spending decisions has intensified. A new budget steering
system was introduced in the late 1980s. Additionally, some public cor-
porations have been established in the 1990s with representatives from the
ministry as board members (Greve, 1995, 1997*b*). Recently a new career

pattern in the Ministry of Finance has emerged. Simultaneously, the personnel has become relatively young and it is becoming usual for officials to spend only a part of their career within the ministry. Officials in the ministry are required to work intensively while they are there, and the ministry can be a springboard to other ministries or to local governments where their careers can continue to mature.

The Prime Minister's Office (PMO) was established in 1914—its development was difficult due to the fiction that the King was the real leader of the government, so it had a very limited role for many years. However, in 1964 it was reorganized in an effort to support the Prime Minister's functions as a leader and coordinator of the government. In 1994 the PMO was reorganized yet again to strengthen this support further. At the same time, Prime Minister Rasmussen personally became more involved in the policies of other ministries. On the one hand, this has strengthened the status and importance of the ministry. On the other, it has tended to plunge the ministry into problems and even 'crisis'. One such crisis resulted from the handling of the Rushdie case in October and November 1996. In connection with a prize ceremony the PM and his civil servants were involved in a number of presentational gaffes which provoked condemnation in the Danish as well as the international media.

For many years the PMO was not a particularly attractive ministry for young graduates (Vahr, 1991: 9), but it has grown in reputation and prestige. Handpicking of personnel has been the preferred mode of recruitment since the late 1970s. A stint in the PMO is now considered an asset for successful high-fliers (Vahr, 1991: 9–10). Most of the civil servants are recruited from line ministries, often for a limited period of two to five years. Today, the Prime Minister's department is still rather small, with only thirty-one civil servants in 1997. But the ministry and its personnel are undergoing change. As with the Ministry of Finance, opportunities to stay within the ministry seem to be diminishing. At the moment it is uncertain whether the ministry will stabilize with a higher status or whether further crises will diminish its role. Nonetheless, it does seem logical that the ministry should play a more important role in the future. For one thing, the growing internationalization of policy-making undermines the traditional coordinating role of the Ministry of Foreign Affairs. For another, no other ministry has the authority to secure coordination in foreign affairs but the PMO, since the Prime Minister ultimately appoints and dismisses other ministers. The alternative, of course, would be a process of 'balkanization' between ministries which would lead to an uncoordinated approach towards participating in EU policy-making. This is not such an unlikely scenario, particularly in a smaller member state of the EU.

Social and Educational Background
Characteristics of Top Officials

The monopoly status of lawyers in the senior civil service was maintained until the 1920s, when economics qualifications started to gain recognition similar to that accorded to a law degree. While in some ministries economists had been performing specialized functions such as analysing statistics for several decades, only in the 1930s did economists begin to appear on a larger scale in the higher reaches of the bureaucracy. After 1940, a growing number of economists occupied posts as permanent secretaries (and there have been economists in these posts ever since). Hence, it is no minor coincidence that, since the 1970s, the approach to decision-making in the public sector has placed more emphasis on economic arguments. Political science has been taught at Danish universities since 1959 and since the 1970s a few top civil servants have had political science degrees.

In sum, the trend has been for economists and political and social scientists continually to increase their share among the ranks of top civil servants. That does not mean, however, that lawyers have been crowded out of top positions (see Table 10.3). Over the sixty years since 1935, the proportion of lawyers among top civil servants has seldom been much less than 40 per cent, with a peak of 54 per cent around 1970. Counting only those with academic qualifications, lawyers have been the most significant group up until 1990. Today, almost 80 per cent of the top civil servants have university degrees in either law, economics, or political science. There has been remarkable change in the balance between these three groupings as the ratio of top civil servants with a law background has declined dramatically relative to the number of economists and political scientists. It has taken a couple of decades for political scientists to climb to the top positions. As late as 1990 only two of 145 top civil servants had studied political

TABLE 10.3. *Educational Composition of Top Civil Servants, 1935–1996 (%)*

	1935	1950	1960	1970	1977	1990	1996
Law	40.0	47.3	51.2	54.0	52.1	52.4	39.3
Economist	6.7	7.1	14.4	16.7	16.2	16.6	28.6
Political scientist	—	—	—	0.7	0.6	1.4	9.3
Other graduates	20.0	17.0	15.2	13.3	14.4	18.6	16.4
Non-graduates	33.3	28.6	19.2	15.3	16.8	11.0	6.4
N	45	112	125	150	167	145	140

science. But in 1996 there were thirteen political scientists, of whom one is a woman.

During the twentieth century, the social background of top civil servants has mirrored the social background of candidates with a higher educational background. However, the social composition of the senior civil service does not mirror that of the entire population. Males from families where the father was university educated, including families where the father held a managerial, professional, or associated professional job, were overrepresented. It has been disputed whether the career patterns in the central administration strengthen this social exclusivity by offering faster promotion to those officials coming from more privileged social strata. In a convincing study, Christoffersen (1987) has shown this was the case (Christensen, 1980: 279; Stjernquist, 1948).

Women at the Top

Since 1921 women in the civil service have been allowed to compete on an equal basis with men. Even prior to that a few women had been exceptionally granted equal employment opportunities to those of men. By the end of the twentieth century it is clear that the Danish public sector is no longer a male sector (Knudsen, 1994). However, this is not so obvious if we look at civil servants in the ministries. Though the female share has tripled from 1965 to 1994, during this time it had only grown to 36 per cent. And the distribution of women is uneven as well. In three ministries, women make up half the staff; in four other ministries, women make up less than one quarter of the senior staff (Nexø Jensen, 1997a: 16).

It is evident that women have not climbed the career ladders as easily as most men (Christoffersen, 1987; Maegaard, 1987). While the first female permanent secretary was appointed in 1953, Denmark has only had four female permanent secretaries since then.[1] Currently, Denmark has none. In 1990 women held only 4 per cent of the top positions—a figure which by 1996 had increased to 11 per cent (see Table 10.1). The increasing representation of women reflects changes in the recruitment of women to higher education rather than active application of a gender preference policy by personnel authorities (Knudsen, 1994).

---

[1] One of these, Karin Kristensen, was permanent secretary only for some months (1993 to 1994) in the Ministry of Housing. Then she moved to the Ministry of Health Care to a more modest position as commissioner. Agnete Vøhtz (1953–65) and Inge Thygesen (1984–97) were the incumbents of the office of permanent secretary in the Ministry of Education. Maria Topp was permanent secretary (1979–87) in the Ministry of Ecclesiastical Affairs.

Interaction and Informal Contacts

Historically, the formal organization of Danish ministries, i.e. the departments, has been quite simple. They were formed as simple hierarchies. The basic building block was an 'office' with an assistant secretary in charge of a small hierarchical unit. In the first half of the twentieth century this represented the smallest independently operating unit, since employees with a lower rank than assistant secretary had no competence to sign letters on behalf of the ministry. The size of the offices varied but, in the 1940s, the average was six to seven principals—all with different titles (such as *ekspeditionssekretær*, *fuldmægtig*, and *sekretær*) mainly reflecting differences in seniority and pay, not differences in function (Betænkning, 1976: 97). Furthermore, there was also clerical support. Formal coordination between the offices was gathered in the hands of the minister and his permanent secretary.

At that time there were few employees outside the hierarchical line. For instance, the minister had but one private secretary. And the private secretaries had a limited range of non-political, technical functions, mainly helping the ministers with logistical problems with the calendar, communication, etc. Most ministers wrote all their speeches, and even many letters, personally. After the Second World War some private secretaries started to write 'official' (mainly representative) speeches, while the ministers themselves wrote their 'political' speeches (Knudsen, 1995: 306). In 1985 there were twenty-three private secretaries and only one press secretary. Ten years later, in 1995, there were forty private secretaries and nine press secretaries (*Mandag Morgen*, 6 Nov. 1995). Now almost all ministries employ press secretaries. Additionally, the number of private secretaries is still growing and, in some cases, the appointments have an obvious political connotation. In reality, Danish ministers now have a small *cabinet* not unlike the *cabinets* of the French tradition. The only difference is that Denmark has not formalized the system. A number of ministries also had some specialists called consultants or commissioners with specific analytical and advisory functions.

There were few formalized inter-ministerial contacts. It is surprising to learn that even informal contacts between permanent secretaries in some cases could be rare until the Second World War. It should be remembered, though, that the pre-war central public administration was both small and—with the exception of one or two ministries—physically concentrated in the same complex of buildings. In addition, nearly all top civil servants educated as lawyers were, at that time, at the same university studying under the same few teachers. Thus, it is very likely that informal contacts were actually quite strong.

There have been a number of changes since the first half of this century. Among the most important is an increase in delegation in each office so that principals are authorized to sign for the ministry in routine matters. At the same time delegation to non-university trained staff has also been attempted for some decades (Smith, 1977). In addition, since the 1980s hierarchies in the civil service seem to have become blurred. Titles which are not so easily placed on a career ladder have became more common. These titles include *kommitteret* (well-known for many years and used for specialized functions, but also as a sinecure for removed permanent secretaries), *konsulent* (consultant), *specialkonsulent* (special consultant), *chefkonsulent* (chief consultant), *departementsråd* (departmental advisor). To some extent this development reflects the need for more flexible wages. However, it also shows that the traditional hierarchical structures of the ministries are beginning to wither. Another change in recent decades has been the development of *ad hoc* groups to solve various problems and form ideas for new policies. Thus, individual ministerial responsibility has tended to diminish. The growth of formalized inter-ministerial contacts, comparatively rare in the first half of this century, can be seen in the increasing importance of inter-ministerial committees.

Political Party Policies towards the Senior Civil Service

Parties have not tended to develop policies towards the civil service for historical and constitutional reasons. However, from 1994 to 1997 a parliamentary committee—dubbed the power committee—debated whether Denmark's power structures should be thoroughly investigated. From this it began to appear that the civil service might be one focus of this investigation. In 1997 a majority in the Parliament asked the Minister of Finance to establish a committee to examine the relations between ministers and civil servants. It remains an open question at the time of this writing whether these initiatives will take effect. But it is interesting to note that in recent years, for the first time in Danish history, political parties have shown an interest in the role of top civil servants.

Conclusions

The Danish central public administration has a history dating back many centuries. One can still trace its traditions, norms, values, and practices over time. And these traditions influencing top civil servants, to some extent, are rooted in a Weberian model of bureaucracy and bureaucrats. At the same time numerous changes are taking place within the environment of the Danish ministries—both on a national and international level—which are affecting the role and performance of the civil servants.

The first change in the role of top civil servants in Denmark is a decrease in the number of managers compared to the total number of employees in the ministries. This trend, together with changes in the political setting, has emphasized the demand for supposed general leadership qualifications and competence in political guidance. Secondly, the educational background of successful candidates for senior positions has changed from an overwhelming dominance of lawyers to a cross-representation of economists and political scientists, as well as other academic backgrounds. Thirdly, the mobility of public employees has increased. Among top civil servants competition seems to have become a top priority. In addition, the career pattern of climbers has changed from an intra- to an inter-ministerial matter. Top civil servants also seem to be in office for a shorter period of time than their predecessors, who were likely to make it a matter of lifetime occupation. Fourthly, we find a tendency towards more women among the top civil servants, although women still seem to have difficulties in reaching the very top positions. And fifthly, in future studies it may become less obvious whom to include among top civil servants, since the hierarchies themselves seem to be blurring as more titles are introduced.

REFERENCES

Andersen, Poul (1943). *Politik og forvaltning* (Copenhagen: Nordisk Administrativt Tidsskrift).

Antonsen, Marianne, and Hanne Foss Hansen (1992). 'Central styring, selvstyring og omverdensstyring: Balance eller konflikt?', *Nordisk Administrativt Tidsskrift*, 73(3): 230–55.

Beck Jørgensen, Torben, and Claus-Arne Hansen (1995). 'Agencification and De-agencification in Danish Central Government: Contradictory Developments—Or is there an Underlying Logic?', *International Review of Administrative Sciences*, 61(4): 549–63.

Betænkning (1976). *Personalebevægelighed i centraladministrationen* (Betænkning, 786; Copenhagen: Statens Information).

Bogason, Peter (1990). 'Danish Local Government: Towards an Effective and Efficient Welfare State', in Joachim Hesse (ed.), *Local Government and Urban Affairs in International Perspective* (Baden-Baden: Nomos Verlag).

—— (1991). 'Denmark', in Tim Knudsen (ed.), *Welfare Administration in Denmark* (Copenhagen: Ministry of Finance).

Christensen, J. G. (1980, 1984). 'Centraladministrationens organisation og politiske placering', *Samfundsvidenskabeligt Forlag,* Copenhagen.

—— (1983). 'Karrieremønstre i dansk centraladministration', in Lennart Lundquist and Krister Ståhlberg, *Bureaukrater i Norden.* (Åbo: Åbo Akademi).

—— (1994). 'Denmark: Institutional Constraint and the Advancement of Individual Self-interests in HPO', in C. Hood and B. G. Peters (eds.), *Rewards at the Top: A Comparative Study of High Public Office* (London: Sage), 70–89.

—— and M. Ibsen (1991). *Bureaukrati og bureaukrater* (Herning: Systime).

Christensen, J. P. (1996*a*). 'Politik, forvaltning og ansvar', *Politica* (Tidsskrift for politisk videnskab), 3.

—— (1996*b*). 'Skandalesager og embedsmandsansvar', *Politica* (Tidsskrift for politisk videnskab), 3.

Christoffersen, Mogens Nygaard (1987). 'Magtens mænd: Om rekrutteringen til magtfulde poster', *Samfundsøkonomen,* 5.

Danmarks Statistik (1997). *Statistiske efterretninger* (Copenhagen: Danmarks Statistik).

Eldrup, Anders (1995). 'Dansk forvaltningspolitik: Set med Finansministeriets øjne', in Per Lægreid and Ove K. Petersen (eds.), *Nordiske forvaltningsreformer, Danmarks Forvaltningshøjskoles Forlag* (Copenhagen).

Gammeltoft-Hansen, Hans, Jon Andersen, Kaj Larsen, and Karsten Loiborg, *Forvaltningsret* (Copenhagen: Jurist- og Økonomforbundets Forlag).

Greve, Carsten (1995). 'Statslige selskaber og Finansministeriets rolle', *Administrativ Debat,* 4.

—— (1997*a*). 'Et politologisk syn på privatisering, selskabsdannelser og udlicitering', in Carsten Greve (ed.), *Privatisering, selskabsdannelser og udlicitering* (Herning: Systime).

—— (1997*b*). *Styring og demokratisk kontrol af statslige aktieselskaber* (Copenhagen: Institut for Statskundskab, Københavns Universitet).

—— (1998). 'Statslige aktieselskaber i et NPM perspektiv', in Kurt Klaudi Kalusen and Krister Ståhlberg (eds.), *New Public Management i Norden: Nye organisationsformer i den decentrale velfærdsstat* (Odense: Odense Universitetsforlag).

Hansen, Hanne Foss (1996). 'The Public Administration System of Denmark', in Paolo Rondo Brovetto (ed.), *European Government: A Guide through Diversity* (Milan: EGEA), 65–85.

Hartlev, Mette (1996). 'Retssikker personalepolitik', in M. Hartlev, Tim Knudsen, and Per Wahlsøe, *Justitsministeriets fremtidige organisering* (Copenhagen: project Offentlig Sektor—Vilkår og Fremtid), 40–64.

Henrichsen, Carsten (1995). 'The Tamil Case: A Perspective', in Hans Gammeltoft-Hansen and Flemming Axmark (eds.), *The Ombudsmand* (Copenhagen: DJØF publishing).

Hood, Christopher, and Sonia Lambert (1994). 'The RHPO Problem', in C. Hood and B. G. Peters (eds.), *Rewards at the Top* (London: Sage).

Jensen, Carsten (1991). 'Omstilling i Danmark og Storbrittanien', *Politica*, 23(2): 185–96.

Jensen, Lotte (1997). *Demokratiforestillinger i den almennyttige boligsektor*. Ph.D. afhandling. Institut for Statskundskab, Copenhagen.

Klausen, Kurt Klaudi (1996). *Offentlig organisation, strategi og ledelse* (Odense: Odense Universitetsforlag).

Knudsen, Tim (1994). 'Kvindernes indtog i det offentlige: Fra den maskuline stat til det feminiserede offentlige', *Nordisk Administrativt Tidsskrift*, 4: 285–94.

——(1995). *Dansk statsbygning* (Copenhagen: Jurist- og økonomforbundets forlag).

Lane, Jan-Erik, and Svante Ersson (1987). *Politics and Society in Western Europe* (London: Forlag).

Maegaard, Benedicte (1987). 'Kvinder i departementerne i de danske ministerier: Samt i andre offentlige organer', *Nordisk Administrativt Tidsskrift*, 3.

Ministry of Finance (1995). *Værktøj til velfærd* (Copenhagen: Ministry of Finance).

Mortensen, Lars (1997): 'Ministre fyrer topchefer når kursen ændres', *Børsens Nyhedsmagasin*, 5: 48–50.

Nexø Jensen, Hanne (1997*a*). 'Feminisering af centraladministrationen?', *Nordisk Administrativt Tidsskrift*, 1.

——(1997*b*). *Offentlige organisationer mellem tradition og fornyelse* (Copenhagen: Forlaget Politiske Studier).

Nielsen, Hans Jørgen, and Jens Hoff (1991). *Offentligt ansatte faglige aktivitet og holdninger: Danmark i et internationalt perspektiv* (Research report, 3; Copenhagen: Institute of Political Studies).

Smith, Bo (1977). 'Reformer af den danske centraladministrations personalepolitik', *Nordisk Administrativt Tidsskrift*, 58(2): 78–94.

Stjernquist, Henry (1948). 'Centraladministrationens embedsmænd', in Ministerialforeningen (ed.), *Centraladministrationen 1848–1948* (Copenhagen: Nyt Nordisk Forlag Arnold Busck).

Sørensen, Eva (1995). *Democracy and Regulation in Institutions of Public Governance* (Copenhagen: Institut for Statskundskab. Licentiatserien 1995/2).

Vahr, Jesper (1991). *The Prime Minister and his Staff: The Case of Denmark* (Aarhus: Institute of Policial Science, University of Aarhus).

11

The Welfare State Managers: Senior Civil Servants in Sweden

JON PIERRE AND PETER EHN

Retrenchment, Institutional Change, and the Senior Civil Servants

Sweden, as most international observers with an expertise in comparative politics will know, has served as the epitome of the welfare state for a large part of the twentieth century. Students of constitutional arrangements will also associate Sweden with a peculiar separation of the policy-making and policy-implementing functions of government. For scholars in comparative public administration Sweden offers an interesting case of a (purportedly) depoliticized *Rechtsstaat* type of bureaucracy implementing such a politically charged project as a comprehensive welfare state. For those with an interest in decentralization of unitary states too, the Swedish case has a lot to offer, with its intriguing combination of a strong state and strong local governments with extensive and growing autonomy in relationship to higher tiers of government (Smith, 1985).

While most of these images of the Swedish government and politics remain true, there have also been a number of important and significant changes fuelled by the budgetary crisis of the state during the past ten to fifteen years. Alongside the functional decentralization of the agencies (Lundquist, 1972), there has been an equally important displacement of control and capabilities from the central state to local governments. The broader causes and consequences of this process are of little importance in the present context. They should nonetheless be noted, because these institutional changes alter the roles of senior civil servants from that of fairly detailed regulation and control functions towards broader, 'quasi-policy-making' tasks. Civil servants' perceptions and attitudes are to an important extent shaped by the institutional arrangements within which they operate. Thus we should expect such attitudes to change as the relationships between ministries, agencies, and local government take on new forms and characteristics.

A broad-brushed account of the recent institutional changes in Sweden could be that of an emerging 'triadization' of the system of government featuring three clusters of autonomous (or semi-autonomous) institutions: ministries, agencies, and local governments. More than anything else, this triadization is driven by economic retrenchment and a search for institutional arrangements which are more conducive to increased efficiency and cost-awareness than the traditional model. Enhanced local autonomy has stripped agencies of much of their legal clout over local authorities. Today, the main role of the agencies in this relationship is more oriented towards monitoring and controlling local authorities than to giving them detailed instructions regarding their role in the implementation of public policy.[1] Similarly, agencies are today enjoying even less guidance from the ministries as the government is convinced that agencies themselves should decide where financial resources can be saved.

An analysis of the senior cadre of civil servants in Sweden cannot ignore this growing institutional separation between ministries, agencies, and local governments. Anton (1980) reported an increasing similarity in values among senior civil servants in the ministries and agencies. However, this pattern reflected an economic, political, and administrative situation which has been significantly altered since then.

Thus, the data on the senior civil servants reported in this chapter portray higher echelon bureaucrats embedded in a public administration operating according to traditions of legality, impartiality, and legal security. These overarching values have recently been challenged on two fronts. One challenge is the increasing emphasis on efficiency and output measures and 'customerization' of public services usually brought together under the heading of New Public Management. The attempt to introduce NPM is part and parcel of a larger project aiming at reducing public expenditure.

The other challenge is related to the tension between *Rechtsstaat* ideals of the civil service on the one hand and the bureaucracy as an administrative vehicle for state-driven social change on the other. Both of these challenges have potential systemic effects. More generally speaking, the three philosophies of a civil service—the *Rechtsstaat* model, the NPM strategy, and seeing the public bureaucracy as an instrument for political and social change—relate to each other in complex ways. For instance, systems of public administration characterized by a strong legal tradition tend to resist NPM measures to a higher degree than other public bureaucracies (Peters, 1996).

---

[1] Today, the state exercises control over local government primarily through 'frame legislation'—defining the objectives of public services but leaving much of the organization of the implementation to the local authorities—and a general state grant with few strings attached to it.

In sum, recent changes in the senior civil service have been caused by the budgetary crisis of the state and the emergence of a less interventionist control regime. The heyday of state-driven economic and social change has gone, probably for ever. The main source of uncertainty now concerns the final destination of the rapid changes in many core aspects of Swedish politics and public administration.

The Swedish Civil Service

In 1996, there were 245,000 employees in the state civil service, equal to 6 per cent of the total workforce in the country. However, the number of employees in the state sector of the civil service has been consistently declining since 1980. Between 1980 and 1993 the number of civil servants decreased by 14 per cent (Högström, 1996: 10–11). This reduction was largely the result of three different types of changes. First, a number of public-service sectors were transferred from the state to local authorities, as was the case with primary education in 1988. Secondly, several agencies engaged in commercial activities such as postal services and telecommunications have been converted into for-profit businesses operating under mainly public ownership. Finally, there has been a series of across-the-board cutbacks coupled with even more extensive austerity measures in selected sectors, not least the defence sector.

Ranks of Senior Civil Servants

We include in the senior civil service the two most senior ranks within the ministries and agencies. These ranks are, for the ministries, the state secretaries[2] (*statssekreterare*) and the assistant under-secretaries (*departmentsråd*). Including the state secretaries in a study on senior civil servants might seem a questionable decision. However, despite being political appointees, one of the key roles of state secretaries is the management of the ministry. Moreover, the level immediately below the assistant under-secretary—the first secretary (*departementssekreterare*)—does not qualify as a senior level in the civil service. Thus, in order to be able to include more than one level of senior civil servants, we include data on state secretaries.

At the agency level, we include in our study the director general (*Generaldirektör*) and the section manager (*avdelningschef*). As is the case with

[2] In some jurisdictions, a more appropriate translation would probably be deputy minister. The translations of personnel categories used in this chapter are the official Swedish translation.

the state secretaries, directors general are quite often *de facto* political appointees. A study from the mid-1980s suggests that some 20 per cent of the directors general are appointed on political grounds. However, political appointment versus meritocratic recruitment is not a dichotomous scale. Instead, there is a wide spectrum between these two extremes, with appointing experienced civil servants who are sympathetic to the policies of the government of the day as a middle standpoint.

Having said that, it is clear that the directors general are part of the core of the senior civil service. Their political appointment is not a 'spoils' arrangement, i.e. they are not expected to resign should a new Cabinet be formed following a general election. Also, their image is clearly that of a civil servant, not a political appointee. The institutional division between ministries and agencies—central to the Swedish system of government—dictates that agency staff, including the director general, are appointed more on the basis of merit than of political sympathies. For this reason, politically appointed directors general are likely to exhibit the same degree of partisanship as state secretaries.

The number of employees in senior ranks is presented in Table 11.1. While there is obviously only one director general per agency, most ministries have more than one minister. In addition to the senior minister there are *biträdande minister* or associate ministers and, in addition, each minister can appoint more than one state secretary. The sharp increase in the number of ministerial staff below the state secretary level between 1975 and 1980 is mainly explained by changes in the Cabinet. In 1976, the three non-socialist parties formed a coalition government. As a consequence a number of senior ministerial staff were employed in order to ensure coordination among the coalition partners at the ministerial level. The continued growth in the ministries' staff reflects a long-term expansion of the government's staff even after the coalition governments were replaced by a single-party (Social Democratic) government in 1994.

TABLE 11.1. *Number of Senior Civil Servants in Ministries and Agencies, 1975–1996*

	1975	1980	1985	1990	1996
Ministries					
State secretaries	15	21	25	24	31
Assistant under-secretaries	46	121	136	150	203
Agencies					
General directors	55	59	67	72	88
Section managers	87	98	131	227	201

Source: Swedish Agency for Government Employers.

Obviously, the gradual increase in the number of directors general reflects the increasing number of agencies. The number of directors general in the 1990s may be slightly inflated, since some former directors general took up employment in a ministry but kept their title. Fortunately, however, this should only apply to a very limited number of directors general.

Systems of Recruitment and Promotion

The senior ranks of the civil service is at the very nexus between the meritocratic norms of the *Rechtsstaat* on the one hand and the need to safeguard some degree of political responsiveness on the other. Each political system displays its own balance between meritocracy and politicization of the bureaucracy. In Sweden, given the slightly peculiar system of government in these respects, the issue of creating such responsiveness is arguably less salient compared to other, more traditionally organized governments.

During the post-war period there have been three different models of organizing the government's tasks and responsibilities in its capacity as employer. Up until the 1980s, civil servants were employees of the state and not of any particular authority. This meant that civil servants could easily be transferred from one ministry to another or from ministries to agencies. From the mid-1980s until 1997, along with the decentralization within government, each authority (ministry, agency, or regional administration) was legally defined as employer. The change was primarily motivated by a greater need for flexibility in salaries, since some agencies were competing with private-sector employers for the same expertise (Ehn and Sundström, 1997). From 1997, finally, all ministries were technically merged into one governmental staff (*regeringskansliet*). On this occasion, one of the main drivers of reform was the low mobility among the civil servants. However, each individual agency remains an employer in its own right. Thus, the current system of recruitment and promotion is one of the most decentralized among the OECD countries. Today, recruitment and promotion matters are completely pushed down to the level of the individual authority. This is also true for state public administration at the regional level.[3]

Generally speaking, the Swedish civil service is a meritocratic system. Recruitment and promotion are based almost exclusively on factors such as tenure and expertise. The number of political appointees remains fairly low by almost any international comparison, if not as low as in previous years; Wallin (1997: 341) estimates the number of politically appointed

[3] This extensive decentralization has been described in PUMA reports as a step towards a 'total fragmentation' of the civil service.

employees within ministries at 150. Thus, the state secretaries are clearly politically appointed. In addition to the deputy ministers, ministries normally employ political advisers (*sakkunniga*), a large number of whom are appointed on political merit. Such experts have also played an important inter-ministerial, coordinating role during coalition governments. Finally, the information secretary of the ministry is sometimes but not always appointed on the basis of political criteria.

At the level of the agency, the director general position is frequently—but far from always—a political appointment. The appointment of directors general for agencies is sometimes seen as one of the few levers which the ministries have to ensure some degree of political responsiveness among the agencies. Apart from the head of the agency, there are essentially no political appointees at this organizational level. However, it is important to note the difference between, on the one hand, political appointments in positions which have a clear and generally accepted political character, such as state secretaries and information secretaries, and the appointment of people who are sympathetic to the government of the day—and where these sympathies are an important factor in the selection of the appointee —on the other. We will look at these issues later in this chapter.

Party Membership among Senior Civil Servants

Survey studies on senior civil servants include items on party membership. Unfortunately, however, the questionnaires only asked if the respondent was a member of a political party but did not ask which party. By combining data on party membership with self-placement on a left–right scale we can generate a fairly clear picture of the political sympathies of the senior civil servants. Tables 11.2 and 11.3 present those data.

Table 11.2 suggests that there has been a clear increase in political affiliation among senior civil servants.[4] This pattern is most noticeable within the senior ministerial staff but is evident also among the top civil servants within the agencies. This development becomes all the more intriguing when we place it in the larger context of Swedish politics. The 1971 data reflect the political awareness and commitment among senior civil servants embedded in a political system which at that time had been governed by the same political party for almost forty years. Thus we would have expected a fairly high degree of political involvement among senior civil servants at this time—an involvement which had evolved over an ex-

---

[4] Among the Swedish electorate as a whole, slightly less than 10% were members of a political party in 1990.

TABLE 11.2. *Party Membership Among Senior Civil Servants,*
1971 and 1990 (%)

	1971	1990
State secretaries	46	100
Directors general	30	49
Assistant under-secretary	22	36
Other senior civil servants in authorities	21	18
Senior civil servants in commercially oriented agencies[a]	17	13

Source: The 1971 data are from Mellbourn, 1979: 102. The 1990 data are from the ELSA project (Ehn, 1993).

[a] Agencies which managed service areas such as telecommunications and railways before they were converted into companies.

TABLE 11.3. *The Ideological Orientation of Senior Civil Servants: Party*
Members Divided According to Self-Placement on a Left–Right Scale, 1990 (%)

	Clearly leftist	Centre	Clearly rightist
Directors general	88	22	20
Assistant under-secretary	50	23	20
Other senior civil servants in authorities	42	23	9
Senior civil servants in commercially oriented agencies	0	9	13

Source: ELSA project data.

Note: The base for the percentage is the number of persons within each of the different categories who have been placed in the respective ideological category.

tended period, partly as a result of socialization into the organizational culture of the public administration, and partly as a subtle factor in the recruitment of senior civil servants.

In 1990 the political picture was different. The Social Democrats returned to office in 1982 after six years of non-socialist government. However, if the political agenda of the 1960s and early 1970s was centred around issues and programmes expanding the scope of government and redistribution, the situation in 1990 highlighted a situation where cutbacks in public expenditures were the order of the day.

In order to take the discussion about the politicization of the senior echelons of the public bureaucracy further we will need data on the ideo-logical orientation of this politicization. Table 11.3 provides data on that issue. This shows that the politicization of the senior civil service means pre-dominantly an ideological orientation towards the political left. If we were to include the state secretaries, with their 100 per cent party membership, this image becomes even clearer since the state secretaries were political appointees of the Social Democratic government.

Turning to the directors general, Tables 11.2 and 11.3 could be interpreted as showing that the recruitment to these posts has been increasingly guided by political considerations. A closer look at the directors general reveals, however, that politicization is a more complex process than these data might suggest. Drawing on additional data from the surveys and other sources of information such as *Who's Who?*, we can identify 23 per cent of the directors general in 1971 as political appointees. These directors general have a Social Democratic background and have been appointed by a Social Democratic government.

In 1990, the picture is more complicated: 31 per cent of the directors general were appointed primarily on political grounds, something which would indicate a slight increase in political recruitment to this level of the senior civil service. However, this development should not be confused with an increase in the number of Social Democratic political appointees; only some 26 per cent of the directors general are Social Democrats. Part of the explanation for this pattern is that between our two points of observation—1971 and 1990—Sweden had non-socialist governments during two different time periods (1976–9 and 1979–82). In the early 1980s, a Royal Commission found that 20 per cent of the directors general had been politically recruited (SOU, 1985: 40 and 277).

The discussion on the politicization among the senior civil servants at the level of the agencies is more complicated than the increasing percentage of party membership might indicate. The number of clear and unambiguous political appointments has increased only moderately. The growing number of party members is not just an indication of increasing political recruitment to these posts. A contending explanation might be that there has been a more general change in attitudes towards political involvement among the senior civil servants. The traditional role of the civil servant was associated with political impartiality and detachment, and standing above the political sphere of government. Today a new generation of state employees, embracing a different view on public employment, have reached the senior levels of the civil service. For these civil servants, impartiality and loyalty to the government of the day are not inconsistent with personal political involvement.

Inter-ministerial Mobility of Civil Servants

As already mentioned, the organizational model which was employed between the mid-1980s and mid-1990s was abolished primarily because it

TABLE 11.4. *Staff Mobility at the Ministerial Level of the Civil Service* (%)

Level of civil service	1986	1988	1994
Senior	10.5	8.7	8.3
Junior	16.8	10.6	9.6
Assistants	16.2	18.3	6.0

Source: Riksdagens Revisorer, 1996: Appendix 4, p. 58.

was believed to be an institutional obstacle to inter-ministerial mobility and flexibility. The low staff mobility within and among the ministries has for a long time been perceived as a significant problem. Furthermore, in spite of the institutional changes implemented during the past ten to fifteen years, mobility has not increased but rather decreased as can be seen in Table 11.4.

Mobility has decreased overall but most markedly at the lower levels of civil servants. The problematic labour market situation in the 1990s is one of the likely explanations for the low mobility; the ministerial staff—as well as the civil service *tout court*—currently hires very few people and mobility to the private sector can be assumed to be quite limited. Very few civil servants have moved from the state bureaucracy to regional and local governments.

One important consequence of this high degree of stability is that younger people find it difficult to get into the senior civil service, which in turn exacerbates problems of poor representativeness among the civil servants (see below). Some 25 per cent of the ministerial staff have had the same position for more than fifteen years, and 50 per cent of the ministerial staff are 55 years of age or older, of whom most have spent more than twenty years within the same ministry. Moreover, since there is a slightly higher degree of mobility at the agency level, the rigidity of the ministerial staff is also widely believed to exacerbate problems for the ministries in controlling and guiding the agencies (Riksdagens Revisorer, 1996: App. 4, pp. 58–9).

Another long-term consequence of low staff mobility is that there is no influx of new and fresh ideas, particularly from the private sector. There is a growing risk that the civil service will become increasingly isolated from the society it is governing and that the bureaucracy's perception of political and social problems will be inadequate and outdated. Finally, the inflexibility of the civil service raises questions about how easily the bureaucracy responds to the rapid internationalization of the state (Jacobsson, 1997). The international integration of the civil service poses a set of new challenges which largely fall outside the routine, due process conduct of business in the bureaucracy and therefore require different types of skills than those previously required for civil service employment.

Status in the Civil Service

We have no data measuring the prestige or status of different ministries and agencies. An informed assessment suggests that, similar to most other countries, the Ministry of Finance enjoys more prestige than other ministries. In the case of Sweden this is a consequence of the cutback programmes implemented during the past ten to fifteen years which effectively made the Ministry of Finance the centrepiece of the government. The Ministry of Foreign Affairs and the Ministry of Justice could probably also be said to enjoy a slightly higher status than most other ministries but these operate to some extent in different subcultures than other ministries.

Social and Educational Background Characteristics of Top Officials

We do not know very much about the social and educational background of senior civil servants. However, a couple of studies have shed some light on these issues. A study conducted by a recent Royal Commission on the degree of representativeness in the civil service suggests that women, younger people, and immigrants are underrepresented. Furthermore, the degree to which a wide variety of social groups are represented in the civil service is negatively correlated with the hierarchical level, i.e. the bias is more marked at the senior levels of the public bureaucracy (Högström, 1996). Table 11.5 compares the percentage women in the civil service as a whole with the percentage found at senior levels.

With regard to educational background, a survey study in the late 1970s showed that 90 per cent of senior civil servants held a university degree,

TABLE 11.5. *Gender Differences in the Civil Service* (%)

	Total civil service	Senior civil service
Men	59	77
Women	41	23

Source: Högström, 1996, drawing on data provided by Swedish Agency for Government Employers.

Note: The definition of senior civil servants in this table is not perfectly consistent with the one used elsewhere in this chapter.

usually in law (Mellbourn, 1979). More recently, Högström, drawing on aggregate data, found that civil servants have a higher level of education than the average population; 53 per cent of white-collar state employees hold a university degree compared to 30 per cent of all Swedes in employment. As was the case with the gender bias discussed earlier, differences in education levels increase as we move up the level in the civil service; today, 87 per cent of senior civil servants hold a university degree (Högström, 1996).

Informal Contacts across Ministries and between Ministries and Agencies

The relationship between ministries and agencies remains what Petersson (1989) refers to as one of the great mysteries of the Swedish system of government. *Ex officio* contacts between ministries and agencies are very restricted in the Swedish system of government. In particular, discussions on specific issues are not consistent with the legal framework. However, informal contacts between ministries and agencies are all the more frequent and, indeed, essential to the efficiency of the Swedish civil service system. Such contacts are very much in the interests of both parties. For the ministries, such communication can help clarify and explain legislation and hence make the agencies' implementation of the government's policy more consistent with the ideas and objectives of the policy-makers. Similarly, agencies have a substantive interest in maintaining a dialogue with ministerial staff, not least at the pre-policy stages, in order to have an input on the policies which they are later to implement.

The frequency of these types of contacts between ministries and agencies have been studied, first in the 1960s and later in the late 1980s. Together, the two studies suggest that there is a striking stability in the networks between the two types of institutions (Pierre, 1995). Thus in 1968, more than 60 per cent of the informal contacts between ministries and agencies were conducted on a weekly basis, and twenty years later (in 1988) Petersson (1989: 71; authors' translation) found that, among the ministerial staff, 'close to 62 per cent are in contact with at least one agency at least once a week'.

What makes these data so intriguing is not that they describe established networks between different types of institutions in a system of government but that according to the overarching philosophy of the constitutional arrangement such contacts should not be very frequent at all. Evidently, not all contacts between ministries and agencies are inconsistent with the Constitution but even so the strength and stability of the existing networks between the two types of institutions are noteworthy. The growing emphasis on output rather than input control have made informal contacts and networks even more important than before. Ministries have tried to compensate for their reduced formal-legal control over agencies by a greater reliance on informal channels of communication.[5] Indeed, the current model of governing the civil service is explicitly predicated on intensive informal dialogue between ministries and agencies at senior as well as junior levels of the organizations.

The Relationship between National and Subnational Officials and those Working in Agencies

The institutional triadization of the Swedish government mentioned earlier has created new patterns of formal and informal communication between the three sets of institutions. Moreover, the decentralization of the public bureaucracy in the 1970s and 1980s—relocating several agencies from Stockholm to cities throughout the country—triggered a series of problems of coordination in the civil service (Wallin, 1996). In both cases, there has been a growing need to maintain formal and informal communication between authorities at different tiers of government. Informal contacts between institutions at different levels of government have become much more frequent over the past couple of decades (Petersson, 1989).

The significance of these informal contacts cannot be exaggerated. An extensive study on the distribution of political power in Sweden conducted a couple of years ago emphasized that networking is gradually becoming the predominant trend of governance and that a *de facto* 'horizontalization' of the politico-administrative system was gradually replacing the previous, *de jure*, hierarchical order of the system (Petersson, 1989; SOU, 1990: 44). The frequent contacts between the civil service in Stockholm on the one hand and local and regional authorities throughout the country on the other could, by some, perhaps be seen as a continuation of the hierarchical order. However, the main emphasis we wish to place on those networks in the present context is the predominantly informal nature of these contacts. Thus this type of central-local communication is not a case of central government exercising its power over subnational authorities but rather an example of how informal interinstitutional communications are becoming almost as important as *ex officio* patterns of exchange.

---

[5] This is not to suggest that output control by definition has to be less precise than input control or formal-legal control over the agencies. In Sweden as in most countries where this development has taken place, output control can be highly detailed and specific.

Political Parties' Policies towards the Civil Service

The politics of public administration has been a salient issue in Swedish politics at least for the past fifteen years—this period would cover the campaign of 'renewing the public sector' (Gustafsson, 1987)—and has included almost all aspects of the public bureaucracy. While the senior civil service *strictu sensu* has not been the object of any far-reaching proposals, there are two aspects which have been frequently discussed and debated which have a particularly strong influence on the roles and status of senior civil servants.

The first is how the relationship between policy-makers and the civil service should be organized. Although this is an issue which almost by definition is politically charged, the debate has not been accompanied by any major conflict between the Social Democrats and the bourgeois parties. All major parties have experienced some frustration with the limited institutional leverage they have had over the agencies. This was the Social Democrats' experience when they took office in the early 1930s with a reformist agenda, only to find that a 'non-politicized' bureaucracy can be just as slow and inert as a 'politicized' civil service. The non-socialists, entering office in 1976 after forty-four years of Social Democratic rule, encountered not just the constitutional problem of governing the agencies but also the problem of ministerial senior civil servants being more sympathetic to the opposition than to the new government. One of the state secretaries in the first non-socialist government describes the situation thus (Levin, 1983: 91; authors' translation): 'When Jan-Erik Wikström [newly appointed Liberal minister of education] and I walked into the Department of Education we were met by a forest of red [the common Social Democratic badge at the time]. Six of eight tenured senior civil servants were active Social Democrats . . . In several sections of the Department the Social Democratic dominance was overwhelming.' However, in spite of these frustrating experiences, no party has strongly advocated a reassessment of the current organization of government—neither within the ministries nor between ministries and agencies. There has been a debate from time to time whether ministries' leverage over the agencies should be strengthened (see Pierre, 1995), but no significant measures have been implemented to this effect.

The second issue of importance to the senior civil service refers to the organization of the decision-making process in the agencies. Traditionally, peak decision-making in the Swedish agencies was organized in accordance with the Weberian model of a public bureaucracy, i.e. decisions were made by the collective of senior-level employees. Beginning on a larger scale in the 1960s, however, these boards were replaced with so-called 'laymen boards' (*lekmannastyrelser*) composed mainly of representatives of interest groups, other agencies, members of the Riksdag, local elected officials, etc. This model of interest representation blends well with the overall corporatist nature of Swedish politics and policy-making. Even so, the system has been questioned on the grounds that it was a less professional and efficient model of organizational decision-making and that this stage of the policy process should be protected from parochial political pressures. The laymen boards were also believed to further complicate the government's control of the agencies (SOU, 1985: 40).

The laymen boards are intriguing not least because they are bureaucratic decision-makers who are neither meritocrats nor political appointees but representatives of organized interests and other governmental bodies. Again, since the Swedish system of government seems to rely to a great extent on informal networks to make the slightly idiosyncratic system of divided policy-making and policy-implementing functions work, laymen boards are excellent means of integrating agencies with key actors and interests in the politico-administrative milieu within which they operate.

Although much of the initial enthusiasm for these boards seems to have worn off there are no indications of any firm political desire in any political party to have the system abolished (SOU, 1985: 40). There is, however, a tendency among the agencies to abolish the laymen boards and replace them with boards composed of senior-level employees of the agency. There has been much frustration with the laymen boards, partly because of the low degree of professionalism in the system. From the point of view of the agencies, the system has its advantages as well as disadvantages. Some have suggested that the model of interest representation has been reversed, i.e. instead of the laymen representing organized interests they have become representatives for the agency *vis-à-vis* the ministries and the public. Another problem is that a large number of these 'laymen'—which in constitutional terms are subordinate to the Cabinet—are members of Parliament for whom scrutinizing the decisions and actions of the Cabinet is a high priority.

Social Status of Senior Civil Service

Finally, looking at the overall social status of senior civil servants, there seems to be a consensus among all studies on this problem that higher level social strata are overrepresented at the expense of lower strata. The reader will not be surprised to hear that this pattern, too, correlates with seniority in the civil service (Högström, 1996; Mellbourn, 1979).

Civil servants have for a very long period of time enjoyed a tremendous prestige. This applies not just to the senior levels of the civil service but to middle and lower levels of white-collar employees as well, such as teachers, judges, section managers, and so on. However, the inherent prestige and status associated with public employment has been declining over several decades. A reform of the legal framework of the civil service in 1965, and the relaxation of the legal accountability of civil servants which followed it, probably undercut the notion that civil servants epitomized the state and suggested that they were bureaucrats not too different from private-sector white-collar employees.

The individualistic political culture heralded during the 1980s and early 1990s further challenged the idea that serving the common good is a noble and respectable cause. This would imply that the status of the civil service is declining. However, it could also well be that there is cyclical effect here and that in just a few years being an employee of the state may yet again have become a prestigious occupation.

Conclusions

This brief account of Swedish senior civil servants suggests that this group of civil servants probably shares many of the features which we usually associate with the traditional, Weberian civil service. Senior civil servants could be described as part of the upper-middle class in Sweden, or what is other national contexts is referred to as a political class. Certainly, the representativeness of the public bureaucracy is a complex issue (March and Olsen, 1995; Peters, 1988, 1995) and the material presented here probably lends itself to more than one explanation. Clearly, there are huge differences on most socio-economic variables between civil servants and the population. That in itself does not warrant the conclusion that there is an alarmingly low degree of representativeness among the senior civil servants. The few indicators available on the political and ideological views held by the senior civil servants suggest that here we find a high degree of similarity between the bureaucrats and the population. Indeed, there are no significant differences with regard to socio-economic status between public and private sector senior white-collar employees.

The discussion about socio-economic similarities and differences between the administrative élite and the population relates indirectly to the discussion about the institutional arrangements of the state. A lack of congruence between élite and citizen could be ameliorated by a tight political control over the bureaucratic élite. However, the Swedish system carefully separates policy-making from the day-to-day functions of the civil service, hence there is no institutionalized political accountability of the civil service as a whole. In these respects—and despite having served one and the same party for more than forty years—Swedish public administration has proven surprisingly resilient both towards a higher degree of politicization and also towards the recent fascination with New Public Management in many countries. True, several reforms such as internal markets and customer choice in several sectors have been introduced but on the whole NPM Swedish-style still seems to be more hype than action.

The values and norms of senior civil servants clearly reflect the system of which they are part. The apparent reluctance to embark on the NPM project—which has its supporters among some agencies but not among the large majority of the civil servants—could be attributed in part to the relative insularity of the senior civil service. This explanation is sustained by the very modest political control exercised over the agencies. Interestingly, the sometimes profound reassessment of many core welfare state programmes which has taken place as a result of the problematic economic situation has not been accompanied by any attempts by the ministries to tighten their control over the agencies. Cutbacks are conducted with a firm reliance on the expertise within the agencies.

Finally, the low staff mobility in the civil service—primarily at the senior level—remains a significant problem. This feature indirectly exacerbates other problems such as how to open up the civil service for internationalization and ensure some degree of representativeness of the civil service.

REFERENCES

Anton, T. H. (1980). *Administered Politics: Elite Political Culture in Sweden* (Boston: Martinus Nijhoff).

Ehn, P. (1993). 'Svenska Högre Statsjänstemän 1971–1990: En Altitydstudie', paper delivered at the Swedish Political Science Association, Gothenburg, Oct.

—— and G. Sundström (1997). 'Samspelet mellan regeringen och statsförvaltningen' [The Cooperation between the Government and the Civil Service], *Det Svåra Samspelet* [The Complicated Cooperation], SOU 1997(15): 73–210, Report from a Royal Commission.

Gustafsson, L. (1987). 'Renewal of the Public Sector in Sweden', *Public Administration*, 65: 179–92.

Högström, P. (1996). 'Studie av representativitet i statsförvaltningen' [A Study on the Representativity of the State Public Administration] Mimeo. (Stockholm: Commission on the Politics of Public Administration, Ministry of Finance).

Jacobsson, B. (1997). *Europa och Staten* [Europe and the State], SOU 1997(30), Report from a Royal Commission.

Levin, B. (1983). 'En Skog av Röda Nålar: Om politiseringen av Departement och Förvaltning' [A Forest of Red Neals: On the Politicization of Departments and Agencies], in B. Rydén (ed.), *Makt och Vanmakt* [Power and Powerlessness] (Stockholm: SNS Förlag), 91–100.

Lundquist, L. (1972). *Means and Goals of Political Decentralisation* (Lund: Studentlitteratur).

March, J. G., and J. P. Olsen (1995). *Democratic Governance* (New York: The Free Press).

Mellbourn, A. (1979). *Byråkratins Ansikten: Rolluppfattningar hos svenska högre statstjänstemän* [The Faces of the Bureaucracy: Role Perceptions among Swedish Senior Civil Servants] (Stockholm: Liber Förlag).

Peters, B. G. (1988). *Comparing Public Bureaucracies* (Tuscaloosa, Ala.: University of Alabama Press).

—— (1995). *The Politics of Bureaucracy*, 4th edn. (New York: Longman).

—— (1996). *The Future of Governing* (Lawrence, Kan.: University of Kansas Press).

Petersson, O. (1989). *Maktens Nätverk* [The Networks of Power] (Stockholm: Carlssons).

Pierre, J. (1995). 'Governing the Welfare State: Public Administration, the State, and Society in Sweden', in J. Pierre (ed.), *Bureaucracy in the Modern State: An Introduction to Comparative Public Administration* (Cheltenham: Edward Elgar), 140–60.

Riksdagens Revisorer (1996). *Statlig Personalpolitik* (Stockholm: 1995/96: RR7), App. 4.

Smith, B. C. (1985). *Decentralisation: The Territorial Dimension of the State* (London: George Allen & Unwin).

SOU (1985). *Regeringen, Myndigheterna och Myndigheternas Ledning* [The Government, the Agencies, and the Management of the Agencies], Report from a Royal Commission, SOU 1985(40).

—— (1990). *Demokrati och Makt i Sverige* [Democracy and Power in Sweden]. Report from a Royal Commission, SOU 1990(44).

Wallin, G. (1996). 'Intern Dialog och Externt Kontaktutbyte' [Internal Dialogue and External Networks] Mimeo. (Stockholm: Department of Political Science, University of Stockholm).

—— (1997). 'En Politiserad Förvaltning?' [A Politicized Public Administration?], in *Brobyggare: En vänbok till Nils Andre'n* [Festschrift for Nils Andre'n] (Stockholm: Nere'nius & Santerus), 339–52.

Conclusion:
Senior Officials in Western Europe

EDWARD C. PAGE AND VINCENT WRIGHT

There are quite clearly highly diverse trends in the development of bur-eaucracy in Western Europe both in terms of the pace of change and its character. In some countries patterns of change appear to be quite distinct and this emerges quite clearly in the country studies in this book. In Germany changes in the role of the civil service have resulted from the role of parties, Parliament, and changes in the practice of federalism, and this has produced limitations on the political discretion of civil servants that has also itself produced a greater sensitivity to their political environment —'political craft' among civil servants becomes helpful to career prospects. Greater inter-ministerial mobility is one of the major trends noted in Denmark and the Netherlands. In Greece and Spain the transition to democracy brought changes in personnel in the senior bureaucracy as well as attempts to restructure the bureaucratic system, although these appear to have had limited effects. In Italy, an 'ossified' bureaucracy has managed to resist any attempts to reform it to make it an effective tool for developing and delivering the policies of a modern welfare state. In Sweden perhaps the most important change has been towards a guiding role over agencies. In Britain the changes have been the most marked, incorporating a New Public Management approach and involving a greater sensitivity to politics analogous to that noted in Germany. In other countries changes in the bureaucracy have been less marked. In Belgium the federalization of the country in 1993 reduced the size and importance of the federal bureau-cracy, but appear to have enabled it to resist pressures for the type of new public management reforms which have characterized state bureaucracies. In Austria attempts to change to the party-dominated system of appoint-ment and promotion have had only small effects on the character of the service.

Change does not appear to have followed any one expected pattern. Particularly noteworthy is the lack of any consistent impact of universal socio-economic trends. The feminization of the workforce in the post-war era has brought more women into the civil service, but they still remain grossly underrepresented in the ranks of the senior bureaucracy. Even where women are best represented in the higher reaches of the civil service as, for example, in Sweden, there is little to suggest that this has caused any fundamental shift in the culture or character of the senior civil service. The expansion of education might be expected to have changed the social composition of the top civil service, but where we have been able to assess changes over time, as in the Netherlands, the impact appears to have been very small; the senior civil service has been for a long time, and remains, a middle-class preserve. The higher reaches of the bureaucracy are now only marginally less likely to come from middle-class backgrounds than they were in the immediate post-war years.

The impact of *political* changes, even the most spectacular, such as the overthrow of dictatorship (Greece and Spain) or the collapse of a party system (Italy), do not seem to produce movements within the administrative system of a similar magnitude. In fact, in some countries much smaller scale events appear to produce changes much larger than those produced by apparently more dramatic political transformations: the election of a party which discovered a reforming zeal (Britain) or the subtly increasing role of Parliament in policy-making (Germany) seem to have had a greater impact on bureaucracies than the collapse of a party system in other countries. Moreover, structural changes do not appear to follow any clear and consistent pattern. While one can point to increasing inter-ministerial mobility in some countries, such as the Netherlands, this is not a striking feature of contemporary bureaucracies.

At first glance this diversity and the failure of change to conform to expectations might lead one to three sorts of conclusions. One is suggest that strong and persisting diversity in bureaucratic systems and in their patterns of development contradicts arguments about the 'convergence' of political and administrative systems. Such an argument, however, would attribute a greater importance and coherence to 'convergence' arguments than they deserve, and simply to point to differences could just make one appear to be at a loss as to what to make of cross-national variation. A second would be to invoke the spirit (if not the letter) of the works of Max Weber (1972) and C. Nothcote Parkinson (1958) and point to the relative imperviousness of bureaucracies to change even under the most extreme circumstances. A similar argument might invoke the argument put forward by Armstrong (1973) in his *European Administrative Elite* that bureaucracies are capable of adapting to changed social and economic circumstances to maintain their status and political power. However, while such arguments which emphasize the resistance to change or the ability to maintain power in the face of change outside might be easier to sustain in some countries than in others, they lack an understanding of how the role of bureaucracy is changing in modern societies. A third conclusion would involve the 'North/South' distinction which is part of popular culture, European administrative folklore, and some academic studies; that northern states such as Germany, Sweden, Denmark, and the United Kingdom have changed a great deal while southern bureaucracies have proved much less open to substantial reform. Such an approach suggests a degree of similarity within the North and the South that simply does not exist—the Netherlands, Belgium, Germany, and Denmark are four northern countries with radically different patterns of bureaucracy and rather different experiences of reform. Moreover, it fails to account for what precisely it is about the North or South, apart from geography, that leads to such different experiences.

Bureaucracies and Change

If we wish to understand change, and the impact of the array of factors that we believed on a priori grounds might have an effect on it, we have to understand the different starting-points of the countries in our study. Each country has a unique set of experiences of state and nation building, as well as of the role that bureaucracy occupied within these processes, and consequently bureaucratic forms and structures tend to reflect unique national experiences—experiences of dictatorship, revolution, and empire have all left their imprint on many of the bureaucracies of Western Europe. However, we may point to fundamental differences in bureaucracies if we consider how the broad principles which underpin them reflect different answers to two fundamental questions of bureaucracy: efficiency and control. These two questions result from the central character of bureaucracy in the modern state. As Hegel (1972), Tocqueville (1969), and Weber (1972) among others have emphasized, the modern state is inconceivable without an extensive and powerful bureaucracy. For Max Weber an extensive bureaucracy was part of the process of the 'rationalization' of the world; for Tocqueville it was an inevitable consequence of democracy. For both Weber and Tocqueville the question of control over the bureaucracy was a critical question. For the former it was how we could prevent creating an 'iron cage of bondage' in which the progress of rationality made human choice progressively limited; for Tocqueville it was something similar—how to avoid being cared for by a benevolent group which takes away human choice by seeking to provide for us in ways that we did not know we wanted.

For these theorists the issue of control was a relatively abstract and philosophical question set against the long march of rationality and democracy through human existence. However, there are much more short-term questions of control that politicians face in Western Europe; how to ensure that the bureaucracy does what democratically elected politicians require? In particular, this means not only how they ensure that it does not consciously sabotage policy initiatives of a legitimized government, a relatively rare phenomenon in West European democracies. More importantly, it raises the question of how to ensure that the expertise and authority available in the bureaucracy is placed fully at the disposal of a democratically elected government. This question was especially important in the transition from dictatorship to democracy in Germany and Austria after 1945 and in Spain and Greece in the 1970s; to make the bureaucracy serve the new state at least some purging of the old guard was necessary, even though in all cases it was far from complete. However, it is not only a matter of importance in such cases of *regime* change: it is also important during changes of *government*. While the precise mechanisms used to strengthen control differ between our countries—and this will be one crucial feature of the way in which we classify and understand change developed below—we can note that during most government transitions governments seek to shape to a greater or lesser extent the relationship between politicians and bureaucrats in favour of the politicians.

The second question is that of efficiency: is the civil service good at doing its job? Of course, the answer to this question depends upon the precise nature of 'its job'. Part of the job is running things. Although this depends upon which country we are talking about, in general this involves running health, education, welfare, and law and order services, regulating the economy, and so on. Another part of the job is to shape policy. Here efficiency would be related to the character of the expertise and experience that may be expected to be brought to the policy process. Both of these dimensions of 'efficiency' are, of course, highly subjective, and it is impossible devise clear and coherent measures of the term. Even if one could come up with measures derived from, say, popular or élite evaluations of bureaucrats, it might be hard to attribute strengths or deficiencies to bureaucrats. While the organizational and policy entrepreneurship skills of bureaucrats in France and Germany appear to be more highly prized than in Belgium, Greece, or Italy, this might well be because of the character of the political systems and the framework of law, statutes, and organizations within which they operate.

So we have two central questions for the role of the bureaucracy, its political controllability and efficiency, but we have no way of evaluating performance on these measures in a clear and simple manner. We can, however, point to differences in *broad underlying principles*, reflecting how different countries have traditionally understood and dealt with these two central problems. These underlying principles, we believe, allow us to make important distinctions between different forms of bureaucracies and allow us to explore the causes and character of changes in the senior ranks of post-war bureaucracies.

Political Control

How can one ensure that bureaucracies are responsive to the governing party or parties? The first broad way is to ensure the *neutrality* of the civil service. By ensuring that officials are 'neutral' executors of government policy, whatever the political hue of the government, officials would then conform to Max Weber's ideal type as their neutrality means they will work for one government just as effectively and loyally as they would for another. To use his more extreme formulation, neutral officials will 'carry on working normally for the regime that comes to power after a violent revolution, for the enemy government of occupation just as it did for the legitimate governments they replace' (Weber, 1972: 128). This is not only valid for the implementation of policy and delivering existing services, but also in the process of policy advice. The traditional civil servant's argument in Britain had been that civil servants have no power of their own since 'power stems from the people and flows through Parliament to the minister responsible to Parliament' (Young and Sloman, 1981: 20). The argument that political neutrality is impossible need not detain us here: the central point about this underlying principle is that a tolerable degree of political control is offered by the professionalism of bureaucrats who recognize that whatever their reservations about a particular policy, once these reservations have been expressed and been overruled, they must get on with the job of advising how best to develop and implement it.

Two countries stand out as representing this approach to political control: Denmark and the United Kingdom. While in Denmark responsibility for appointing senior officials is a responsibility of the minister, no spoils system has developed in which political appointees are brought in to run the departments. The resistance to this appears to come both from within the bureaucracy itself (where the political affiliation of senior officials is a private matter and not a matter of public debate) and from government politicians themselves who value the non-partisan character of their senior officials. In the United Kingdom non-partisanship has been a fundamental feature of the culture into which recruits have been socialized. We would also include the Netherlands in this category. While Raadschelders and van den Meer show that the picture is by no means clear, with some evidence pointing to party-political factors shaping chances of senior appointment, they conclude that it would be mistaken to see this as a means of political control of the kind found in Germany: 'in practice top civil servants normally do not act in a (party) political way'.

A different approach to political control is offered by those countries for whom appointment to the 'commanding heights' of the bureaucracy is the dominant principle of political control. Such an approach characterizes France, Sweden, and Germany, where senior appointments within the national or federal bureaucracy are subject to direct partisan influence. Furthermore, in such systems the 'commanding heights' approach is not used to recruit to top posts officials with little experience in the senior civil service. As Pierre and Ehn point out in Sweden and Rouban in France, the distinction between 'political' and 'merit' appointments is not clear cut and it is usual for civil servants (if one excludes the 'political' state secretaries in Sweden and Germany) to dominate even among these political appointees.

A third approach is offered by those countries in which party affiliation has traditionally formed the basis for recruitment and promotion within the upper reaches of the civil service. Here the difference between such systems and the 'commanding heights' approach is partly one of degree; there are more appointments made, and lower down, involving political influence. There is also a difference in the goals of politicization, rewarding political support as well as securing political control within the government machine. In such systems appointments are part of the spoils of electoral success as well as a means of seeking to impose political control. This was marked in Austria with the implicit adoption of the *Proporz* system, according to which posts in the federal bureaucracy were allocated according to party strength. The same may be said of Belgium: in their chapter Brans and Hondgehem outline the elaborate arrangements in Belgium for seeking to ensure that officials at senior and lower levels in the bureaucracy reflect the strength of government political parties in Parliament. In Greece party politicization is a fundamental component of the whole of the promotion process within the civil service. We might also include Spain as reflecting this particular approach to political control, although since political appointments are predominantly (not exclusively) in what Molina terms the 'politico-administrative circle', it fits less squarely within this group.

Italy matches none of these three models of political control. While patronage and clientelism are rightly associated with the operations of the entire public sector in Italy, higher *administrative* positions in Italy are reached primarily through age and length of service. Despite the possibility of making direct appointments to senior posts, above all directors general, this has been used only to a limited extent and has met successful resistance from what Cassese terms 'the ossified world of the senior civil service'.

Partly as a result, 'the senior civil service is not integrated into the political class or into the economic management structures of the country'.

Performance

While we have yet to show the significance of the different forms of political control, let us outline the principles underlying the even more difficult concept of performance. There are broadly two basic principles by which the performance of senior civil services may be judged. The first is by some form of analogy with the behaviour of organizations within a market. Of course, there is no single market definition of effective performance, but here we are referring to a bundle of possible ideas that include the ability to react to the environment, to innovate, to provide a good or service cheaply, and so on. The crucial point here is not which particular performance criterion is used, but that the comparison is based upon the understanding that the state can have its performance evaluated in the same way, on the same criteria, as any other organization, private or voluntary. Such a comparison contrasts with a conception of performance which is assessed on the basis of an understanding that the state pursues distinctive public purposes, and therefore cannot be directly compared with private or voluntary organizations. Otto Hintze (1964), the staunchly monarchist historian/sociologist writing at the end of the First World War, argued that the state had always had distinctive purposes and could not be analysed or understood in the same way as a *Betrieb* (business), yet the state had started to lose the kind of majesty that Hegel had claimed for it ('God's passage through the world') and state administration was indeed becoming a *Betrieb*. By invoking these two different conceptions of performance we are invoking the same sort of distinction: is the performance of the state to be assessed as a distinctive organization or is it to be evaluated using the same criteria as other organizations?

This distinction is, we believe, crucial for understanding reform and change in the higher civil service. The choice of comparison affects how any perceived shortcomings are assessed and what proposals might be explored to remedy them. Now, of course, choices of the relevant comparison will differ from group to group or person to person within any political system. We can, however, point to two broad conceptions of the senior bureaucracy: one a *public authority conception*, which sees bureaucracy as part of a distinctive state service which can and should enjoy rights, duties, and privileges which are distinct from those prevailing in the non-state sector; the second is a *service provision* conception. Since this term touches on an area where many countries have introduced reforms

over the past few years it is important that we do not mistake present current conditions for longer term traditional conceptions of bureaucracy. So
how can we define these two broad conceptions?

It must be recognized that in referring to two separate conceptions we
are talking essentially of a matter of degree. Civil services in all systems
considered here have at least some features which reflect public authority
conceptions (in matters such as pay and conditions of work and freedom
to engage in overt party-political activity), and the competence of officials
is judged in terms of practical results even in countries which we will describe below as reflecting a 'public authority' tradition. In Belgium, for
example, the incompetence of the Interior and Justice ministries in handling
a series of child abduction and murder cases was a major political issue in
the mid-1990s. Yet we can point to several features of political systems
which seem to suggest that the dominant conception of the civil service is
of a group of state servants who can be compared only to a limited extent
with private or non-state bodies.

One indicator of this is a separate judicial system for administrative
matters. While this is outside the scope of the chapters in this book, we may
point to the existence of a higher administrative court as an indicator of
the distinctiveness of administrative organization within a society. As
Chapman (1959: 182) writes, 'the way the question of controlling public
administration is approached reflects both a philosophy of the state and a
national social psychology'. A second indicator is the importance of
seniority in promotions within the career civil service. As the same author
points out, the reliance on seniority is a means of avoiding an 'appreciation
of respective merit' and 'underlying this approach . . . is a whole philosophy
of administration: that the state needs from its civil servants the greatest
possible guarantees of "character suitability" and these guarantees are best
given by placing the greatest reliance on the official's general record over a
long period of time' (Chapman, 1959: 167). A third indicator of a public
authority conception of a civil service is the preponderance of lawyers
within the senior ranks. Such a preponderance may be associated with the
notion that the qualifications for public service are distinctive from those
of non-state organizations. If we look at all three measures we might distinguish (Table 12.1) between countries on the basis of the relative strength
of a public authority conception. We would include Austria, Belgium,
Greece, and Italy as having a strong public authority conception on the
strength of all three indicators. We would include Britain as the only example with none of the three indicators of a public authority conception,
and might also include Denmark and the Netherlands with only one such
indicator as low on a public authority conception. France, with a relatively
low importance attached to seniority, but otherwise containing two other

TABLE 12.1. *Indicators of Public Authority Conceptions of the Civil Service*

Country	Court	Relative importance of seniority	Lawyers
Austria	Verwaltungsgerichthof	High	High
Belgium	Conseil d'État	High	High
Britain	—	Low	Low
Denmark	—	Low	High
France	Conseil d'État	Low	High
Germany	Bundesverwaltungsgericht	Low	High
Greece	Dioiketiko Efeteio	High	High
Italy	Consiglio di Stato	High	High
Netherlands	Centrale Raad van Beroep	Low	Low
Spain	—	High	High
Sweden	Kammarätt	Low	High

indicators, might nevertheless be ascribed to the public authority conception of the role of the civil service, not least because the corporative structure gives a legally defined responsibility for the corps in shaping promotion and career prospects, reinforcing the role of the bureaucracy as separate from the civil society it governs. For similar reasons we might include Spain with the high public authority nations. The most surprising inclusion with high public authority nations (on the basis that it has two of the three indicators set out above) is Sweden where the importance of lawyers in the civil service along with the separate high court for administrative affairs suggests that this distinction between public authority and service provision conceptions is not simply a conventional North–South distinction.

Managerial Changes

The development of New Public Management reforms can, to some degree, be understood as an application of the logic of the *Betrieb* to the (in many countries) erstwhile Hegelian magical state. The impact of these reforms touched many countries and been widespread across a broad range of public-sector organizations. Most European nations have to some degree embraced New Public Management changes—the intensity of the embrace differs, as does the degree to which public administration has been fundamentally altered. The intensity and impact of New Public Management is notoriously difficult to assess cross-nationally, in the sense of describing which countries have been more substantially altered by it than others (Wright, 1994).

However, there is some evidence that how far such reforms are likely to shape the *senior* levels of the bureaucracy is likely to be affected by the strength of a public authority conception of the state, since in the high public authority nations, above all Austria, Belgium, Greece, and Italy, as well as France and Sweden, whatever the impact of New Public Management elsewhere in the state sector, the impact at the senior level of the national administration appears more limited. As Wright (1994: 122) noted, one important factor shaping the spread of new public management is a 'legitimising discourse' for making the state more like a business. This discourse 'has taken a negative form (anti-big government, anti-remote and profligate bureaucrats, anti-state) or has been more positive in tone: privatising and marketising in the name of individual choice'. Such a discourse takes root with greater difficulty where the notion is more widely accepted that the state as a form of organization cannot be equated with a business—where it retains its Hegelian magic—that is to say where there is a public authority conception of bureaucracy. Moreover, such a vision of the state bureaucracy as distinctive from a business—standing above civil society—appears to be easier to maintain in relation to the senior levels of the state bureaucracy than in relation to the service delivery agencies of modern states.

Changes in Political Control

The purpose of these two distinctions, based on patterns of political control and the strength of public authority conceptions of the civil service, is not simply to produce a typology, but to help understand patterns of change in civil services. If we take our first distinguishing characteristic, the form of political control, it is possible to detect two trends on the basis of this distinction; first, a trend towards a 'commanding heights' approach to political control and, second, a possible trend within the 'commanding heights' approach to a more pervasive form of 'politicization' from below. Let us outline each of these.

The trend towards a commanding heights approach to politicization may be seen in the pressures in the two countries (Britain and Denmark) which have in principle a 'neutral' civil service towards some greater political control of the top posts and, in those countries with extensive 'party book' politicization there are pressures to limit the extent of political appointment to the most senior posts (Belgium, Austria, Greece, Spain). In Britain, while any politicization of the Thatcher/Major years was not overtly a party-political one, it was one based upon getting the right characters ('can do' candidates) in the top jobs, indicating an increased concern with influencing the character of the commanding heights of the bureaucracy. But possibly a stronger pressure towards a commanding heights approach comes through the increasing use of internal and external advisers that Locke and Dargie point to in Britain. Similar developments are found in Denmark, where Jensen and Knudsen point to ministerial assistants as a growing exception to the norm of neutrality. While developments in these countries do not point to a radical transformation of the norm of neutrality, they do suggest the possibility that ministers might prefer to rely upon their own choice of adviser and thus evolve a *de facto* if not *de jure* politicized layer at the highest level within a ministry.

In Belgium, Austria, and Greece extensive party-political patronage throughout the bureaucracy poses a similar problem, paradoxically, to that of systems characterized by political neutrality. To hold a party card may be less a sign of commitment to a political cause and more a sign of the seriousness of one's career aspirations—'in terms of predicting loyalty . . . the party book is not worth the paper it is written on' (Liegl and Müller: p. 116). Thus, the problem becomes one of establishing trust and support among the senior levels of the bureaucracy that goes beyond simply belonging to the same party. Belgium and Austria both introduced apparently unsuccessful reforms in the 1980s which sought to limit patronage to the more senior appointments. In the absence of reliable support, Austrian ministers have sought to build up personal loyalties among top officials, whilst in Greece 'special secretariats' have developed to assist ministers in policy development. In Belgium the *cabinet ministériel* (or private office of a minister) has long been a vehicle for ministers to bypass a distrusted bureaucracy and to surround themselves with advice and assistance in running their departments. While it would be mistaken to speak of a clear or rapid movement towards a 'commanding heights' approach to political control, not least because extensive party-political patronage is entrenched in the administrative systems of these countries, both the reform attempts of the 1980s in Belgium and Austria and the use in all three countries of alternative means of ensuring that the commanding heights of the bureaucracy are controlled by those in whom a minister has some trust, suggests movement in the direction of a commanding heights approach to political control.

In Spain, the effect of patronage has, to some degree, been used to transform the system closer to a commanding heights model. Spain and Italy show some remarkable similarities: the corporate composition of the civil service created a civil service which was exceptionally powerful in governing its own affairs and, despite the importance of clientelism and patronage within the political system generally, was effectively isolated from any direct political control through political parties. In both Spain and Italy the corporate structure was both a block to reform and a source of power for senior bureaucrats. In Italy the 'ossified world of the senior civil service' managed to resist the attempts by political parties to attempt to gain control of key posts. In Spain, by contrast, party-political patronage has been used to change if not the principle and importance of the corporate structure, the responsiveness of the commanding heights of this structure to the governing parties and 'neither the PSOE nor the PP have difficulties in filling [senior] posts from highly qualified civil servants who are politically close to them when they are in office'. In Greece, 'governments have been much more successful in penetrating the higher civil service than modernizing it', while in Spain governments were partially capable of modernizing it in the sense of making it more receptive to political élites. Both penetration and modernization appear to have eluded Italian political élites.

In those countries with a commanding heights approach, the notion that the very top appointments are filled by political appointments, normally from among senior civil servants, means that civil servants must seek to establish political contacts if they have ambitions to rise to these positions. It has long been a characteristic of the French bureaucracy that a high-flying career involves 'posts in prestigious ministries, political friendships . . . participation in a ministerial *cabinet*, professional networks that facilitate vertical and horizontal professional mobility'. The trends in the other commanding heights countries, Sweden and Germany, show some tendencies towards the emergence of a distinctive political career path for civil servants aspiring to reach senior positions similar to that which has existed in France for decades at least. This is most clearly seen in Germany where senior officials are developing 'political craft' as a means of career development. In Sweden, Pierre and Ehn point to the growing importance of party-political membership which, although they caution against a simple equation of this growth with a growing 'politicization', is again consistent with the notion that civil servants in commanding heights systems are developing *curricula vitae* which pay attention to their political as well as their professional characteristics.

Conclusions: A Matter of Trust?

There is a common underlying theme in the development of relationships between bureaucratic and political élites which applies to most of our countries—a *deinstitutionalization or personalization of political trust*. Common to both party-card administrative systems and systems based upon the norm of civil service neutrality is an assumption that political loyalty comes with membership of the institution—the political party in the one case, the civil service in the other. There is a common trend among systems which stress the norm of civil service neutrality to seek to appoint, either as civil servants or advisers, people in whom one has trust. This trend appears stronger in Britain and Denmark and is less easily detected in the Netherlands. Trust does not have to be defined strictly in party-political terms, in Britain to be 'one of us' in Thatcher's civil service was a personality trait and a state of mind rather than a question of voting intention or party membership. The central point is that increasing political influence in senior appointments suggests the possibility that membership of a 'neutral' civil service is decreasing as a guide to trust among political élites. In the same way, a civil servant's membership of a political party may no longer serve as a guide to trust in countries where political appointments have traditionally been important, whether because of extensive patronage or because of a commanding heights approach. Instead, officials have to develop closer personal ties with political masters by acquiring political craft and contacts. In Austria, for example, while the pattern of party politicization appears to have remained unchanged in the post-war period, this apparent continuity masks a change in the character of politicization, as ministers come increasingly to rely on developing personal loyalties among officials rather than simply on party membership

Trust and confidence are also at the heart of changes in those countries which have experienced substantial managerial reforms. The common routes of producing good top civil service officials and the methods that have evolved within civil services for managing the business of government and administration no longer generate the quality of manager or the quality of management in which politicians have confidence. Loss of confidence in traditional recruitment and organizational arrangements seems to have had its greatest effect where the bureaucracy itself had weaker status as organizations representing a public authority separate from civil society. In part this might be because in such systems the shortcomings of traditional bureaucratic structures are more easily targeted than in systems in which bureaucracy still retains some of its Hegelian magic (contrast, for example, Britain and France), in part it might be because this Hegelian magic provides the bureaucracy with a range of political powers which allow it to resist major reforms of internal structures (see, for example, Italy and Spain).

If we wish to understand the question of change in bureaucracy in this way, we might point to a decreasing confidence in traditional patterns of bureaucracy as the single most important feature of change which has produced reactions which differ in each of our states. For example, in Italy and Greece, it appears to have produced an isolation and a stalemate between political and administrative élites. In Britain and Denmark it has generated new management structures and greater reliance on political management within the senior bureaucracy. In Spain it has produced extensive party politicization of the bureaucracy, and in Sweden and Germany it has served subtly to change the way in which bureaucrats in formerly career jobs manage their careers with a view to increasing the confidence that their political masters may have in them.

Understood as a question of trust, change in bureaucracy is linked to much wider political changes that have been identified outside the literature on bureaucracy. Most obviously, the changing role of political parties in the establishment of trust between political leaders and bureaucrats reflects a much broader trend in the character of political parties; from parties of mass integration with defined ideologies and constituencies to the broader catch-all, or possibly even cartel party based upon a broad-gauge centrist ideology and open to influence from a larger array of societal interests. Under such party systems party membership is not a guide to political trust within the bureaucracy. Moreover, party government based upon catch-all ideology serves to weaken the support that individual ministers might expect from the government seen as a collectivity and makes it more likely that they will want to use their ministries to build up networks of trust and support. Change in bureaucracy may also be linked to broader discussions of declining trust in political institutions— if citizens are less likely to trust political institutions and politicians, they are also likely to be unimpressed by the Hegelian hocus-pocus of a traditional civil service, as are the politicians they elect.

REFERENCES

Armstrong, J. (1973). *The European Administrative Elite* (Princeton: Princeton University Press).

Chapman, B. (1959). *The Profession of Government* (London: Allen and Unwin).

Hegel, G. W. F. (1972). *Grundlinien der Philosophie des Rechts* (Frankfurt-on-Main: Ullstein).

Hintze, O. (1964). 'Der Staat als Betrieb und die Verfassungsreform' (1918), in *Soziologie und Geschichte: Gesammelte Abhandlungen zur Soziologie, Politik und Theorie der Geschichte* (Göttingen: Vandenhoeck and Ruprecht).

Parkinson, C. N. (1958). *Parkinson's Law* (London: Murray).

Tocqueville, A. D. (1969). *Democracy in America* (New York: Anchor Books).

Weber, M. (1972). *Wirtschaft und Gesellschaft*, 5th edn. (Tübingen: JCB Mohr).

Wright, V. (1994). 'Reshaping the State: The Implications for Public Administration', *West European Politics*, 17(3): 102–37.

Young, H., and A. Sloman (1982). 'No, Minister' (London: British Broadcasting Corporation).

INDEX